Mapping Intermediality in Performance

Mapping Intermediality in Performance

Edited by
Sarah Bay-Cheng, Chiel Kattenbelt,
Andy Lavender, and Robin Nelson

Amsterdam University Press

MediaMatters is a new series published by Amsterdam University Press on current debates about media technology and practices. International scholars critically analyze and theorize the materiality and performativity, as well as spatial practices of screen media in contributions that engage with today's digital media culture. For more information about the series, please visit: www.aup.nl

Acknowledgements

The editors wish to acknowledge financial and other support from: the Digital Humanities Initiative at Buffalo and the University at Buffalo (SUNY); Central School of Speech & Drama, University of London; Manchester Metropolitan University and Utrecht University. We should like also to thank those photographers who have freely given permission to reproduce their images. We should like to thank Jeroen Sondervan, the series editor, for commissioning this volume and Chantal Nicolaes and the production team at AUP for realising the publication so efficiently. We also thank Emmy Kattenbelt for her work on constructing the index and Miguel Escobar for designing the diagrams of the nodes. Last but not least we thank the contributors for their willingness to engage in many dialogues and to adjust their writings to the purposes of the book in what, for us, has been a gratifying, because genuinely interactive, process.

Cover illustration: Participant in an immersive performance by CREW, © Eric joris
Cover design: Suzan de Beijer, Weesp
Lay out: JAPES, Amsterdam

ISBN   978 90 8964 255 4
e-ISBN   978 90 4851 314 7
NUR   670

Contents

How to Approach This Book

This volume in the *MediaMatters* series aims provisionally to map territory which is under development, the territory of intermediality in performance in digital culture, which, in Deleuzian terms, is being de- and re-territorialised (1987). The project has developed organically as a network of situated concerns and engagements and thus is more an exercise in mapping, a journey charting a network of selected ideas and practices, than an attempt at exhaustive coverage, let alone fixity. This approach presented the editors with three immediate problems: how to present a network map of interconnected nodes in book form, how to indicate possible lines of flight connecting terms within and beyond the scope of the book, and how to clarify concepts without isolating them inappropriately from a dynamic process of interrelatedness and deferral.

Positionality in a network mapping exercise is problematic for, as Castells has remarked, "a network has no center, just nodes" (2004, 3). The idea of a network, without fixed bearings and entailing recursive loops, which might be entered and exited at any point marks our sense that each aspect of digital culture is best understood in relation to another, which leads to yet another and so on. In Castells's view, "nodes may be of varying relevance for the network. ... However, all nodes of a network are necessary for the network's performance. ... The network is the unit, not the node" (2004, 3). The structure of the book is thus conceived as a global network of multiply inter-connected ideas and practices, and readers are invited to approach the volume accordingly. To assist access following the introduction, **prospective mapping**, and a **network of terms**, we have marked five **portals**, gateways into the network which afford a range of situated perspectives. These are: **performativity and corporeal literacy; time and space; digital culture and posthumanism; networking; and pedagogic praxis.** Finally, a **retrospection** affords a review of the book through the lens of the historical avant-garde. Readers might enter the book through any of the portals which offer access to **nodes: modes of experience, dimensions, actuality-virtuality,** or **interrelations.** Each node is illustrated by a cluster of **terms** and related **instances.** In *Network Culture*, Terranova suggests that "to think of something like a 'network culture' at all ... is to try to think simultaneously the singular and the multiple, the common and the unique" (2004, 1). The structure of the book accordingly invites a dialogic engagement with key concepts and key questions with specific reference to theatre and performance practices after the intermedial turn (→ PROSPECTIVE MAPPING).

A system of arrows points the reader to links across the network. The **network map** (→) affords a structural mapping of terms, and sub-sections extracted from it group proximal terms around nodes. The key accents of some established terms are changing in contemporary usage and all function in discursive exchange with each other. Transparency (→ TERM), for example, in the European avant-garde theatre tradition denotes making the process visible, whilst in the Anglo-American context of media theory, it typically means the opposite, concealing the process. However, simply to suggest that the key terms of debate are so slippery that no definitions at all can be offered would be unhelpful in a book aiming to assist understanding. But to offer apparently clear and tight definitions of terms would also be misleading. Thus, though provisional definitions are offered, they are unsettled by drawing attention to their origins and histories, or by acknowledging the various accents of their past and current usages. Each term is set against related terms, as noted, and leads into analyses of illustrative instances. This aims to clarify and offer insights, whilst avoiding fixity. We draw attention to the fact that reading a book entails a mode of interactive engagement, but we offer short overviews at each portal to bring out key links as they follow lines of flight between portal, nodal terms and instances. You are encouraged to forge your own pathways but the portals are landmarks and the nodes afford waymarks. You may head directly to any of the portals or you may choose to follow a traditional linear trajectory. The prospective mapping sketches the key concepts and questions that will be encountered. But before you jump to your preferred point of entry, an additional word about the nodes and instances.

Any example of intermedial theatre or performance is likely to be multi-tracked in its principle of composition and likely to evoke a range of intermingled – and possibly conflicting – perceptions and feelings. Thus, although the instances grouped around nodes aim to foreground specific aspects, they are not exclusively concerned with that specific cluster of terms, and inevitably have links across other clusters. These are indicated by the system of arrows. Some instances for discussion are well known, indeed, some have global visibility, whilst others represent the less widely distributed work of practitioner members of the group. Given that contemporary theatre practices and digital culture are considered processual on every level, this book aims to afford insights into the processes of making theatre and performance as well as experiencing it. Thus, alongside external **experiencer** (→ TERM) analyses of established practices, insider insights are also available in the range of instances, and some accounts are offered from 'both-and' positions. The number of perspectives entails a range of voices. Some practitioner-researchers, for example, speak in the first person about how they have grappled with the impacts of media technologies in the production of a piece. In the UK particularly, but increasingly worldwide, 'practice as research' has afforded a means of insight into the processes of artworks and new, less traditionally 'academic', discourses have been developed to convey their relational insights.

The **pedagogic praxis portal** gives access to fresh thinking about modes of study and fresh approaches to acting where new circumstances require new technologies. The concluding **retrospection** may paradoxically offer a good starting point for some since, by tracing the development of pre-digital and the proto-digital arts and media from the 20th into the 21st century, it contextualises the book's claims for a distinctive intermedial moment in digital culture.

This volume comprises contributions from members of the Intermediality in Theatre and Performance research group of the International Federation for Theatre Research (IFTR), and its genesis lies in the collaborative work of that group over a number of years. Thus, whilst editorial consideration has been given to ensuring that significant developments in the field are represented, the terms and instances in the book to some extent reflect the selective and eclectic interests of individual thinkers and practitioners immersed in the domain as they have emerged in a group research context.[1] Most of the contributors are located in Theatre and Performance Studies with an inclination towards media theory and practice rather than based squarely in Media or Intermedia Studies. Our research is thus oriented towards performance in ways that are characteristic of digital culture.

Introduction: Prospective Mapping and Network of Terms

Prospective Mapping

Robin Nelson

This volume is a successor to Chapple and Kattenbelt (eds.), *Intermediality in Theatre and Performance* (2006) in that it has grown, as noted, out of the IFTR group's work. Two aspects follow from this context, which might now helpfully be framed in Elleström's recently constructed "Model for Understanding Intermedial Relations" (2010, 11).[2] The first is an emphasis on the principles of composition of live theatre as a "strongly multimodal media" (Elleström 2010, 38) phenomenon with, in Kattenbelt's formulation, a distinctive capacity to be a hypermedium which "stages" other mediums (see 2006, 37).[3] The second is an established acknowledgement that the relations between different media in a multitracked text are ultimately a matter of perception and interpretation, namely Boenisch's sense that intermediality is an "effect of performance ... created in the perception of observers" (2006, 113) because the relational aspect between thing and sign is a matter of experiencing. Ellerström nevertheless contends that, "it is crucial to discriminate theoretically between the material and the perception of the material if one wants to understand how media can be related to each other" (2010, 13). In sustaining a concern with both principles of textual composition and distinctive experiences that new modes of theatre and performance might generate, this volume acknowledges the usefulness of the theoretical distinction between them whilst recognising their praxical proximity.

Building then upon the earlier volume and subsequent publications by IFTR group members, this book affords a tighter focus than the last publication on digital culture and the implications for theatre of what has been called the 'intermedial turn' (see below). A primary concern is with the impact of the "technical media" (Elleström 2010, 12 ff.) of digital technologies, not only as they are used in live theatre, but in how they have challenged the very conception of theatre. In Elleström's terms, the 'contextually qualified' medium of theatre, that is to say, theatre as traditionally understood in a socio-historic context as a live phenomenon in the here and now, may be in the process of being re-qualified contextually as it accommodates an integrated production, recording and storage medium with its digital disposition to interactivity. For as Elleström remarks:

> The defining features of a technical medium are its capacity to realize specific material interfaces and the perceiver's capacity to interact with these interfaces and with other users of the medium (2010, 30).

The material modality – one of four in Elleström's model on all of which theatre operates (see 2010, 24) – does not determine the medium but may be disposed towards some principles of composition rather than others.[4] The capacity of digital technologies multi-modally to integrate sound, visuals, words and temporal dynamics (in respect of the ease of digital editing in both real time and during recording) have, perhaps radically, extended the multimodality of theatre. Moreover, they have invoked the possibility of transformations from the physical to the virtual in additional dimensions of space and time. Peter Brooks's (1986) seminal conception of a physical body knowingly observed in an actual but empty space is troubled by new circumstances.

The domain of theatre has been unsettled by the challenge of digital technologies but also by its expansion into – some would say its appropriation by – the notion of 'performance'. Over the past 30 years, the study of the performing arts has embraced not only a broad spectrum of practices which were formerly categorised under other art disciplines but also a wide range of social activities under the banner of 'performance' that were previously considered aspects of everyday life. Furthermore, disciplines beyond Theatre or Performance Studies have mobilised the concept of 'performance' as a heuristic tool to account for a broad variety of social interactions (see McKenzie 2001; Auslander 2003; McAuley 2007). As McAuley has summarised it:

> [p]erformance, as conceptualised in performance studies can range from the most highly elaborated artistic activity to minimalist examples of expressive behaviour, for organised social events such as a sporting contest or war veterans' parade to the informal gathering of young people hanging out on a street corner, from ceremonial occasions to daily interactions (2007, 1).

McAuley makes an explicit connection with theatre but notes that "performance requires people (or animals or even things) who perform and people who witness the performance" (2007, 1). A book that attempts a mapping of intermediality in performance is thus confronted by a dynamic and rapidly expanding territory and a minefield of contested terms. Not only have former boundaries been transgressed, but there is a danger that all categories might collapse unhelpfully into each other, rendering obsolete the notion of 'intermediality' as a bridge between mediums (broadly understood to include other arts practices and other disciplines). Elleström formulated his multimodal model in an attempt to address this problem. Adopting a 'both-and' approach, as favoured in this book, he remarks:

> [i]f all media were fundamentally different, it would be hard to find any inter-relations at all; if they were fundamentally similar, it would be hard to find something that is not already interrelated. Media, however, are both different and similar, and intermediality must be understood as a bridge between medial differences that is founded on medial similarities (2010, 12).

This book does not aim to historicise the term intermediality, nor offer a history of intermediality similar to that which has already been included in other publications (Rajewsky 2002; Schröter 2006), but the **retrospection** will invite a re-positioning of claims for the distinctiveness of intermediality in digital culture by pointing out the pre- and proto-digital in modernism and the critical avant-garde. It is helpful, however, briefly to review the current state of affairs. In a recently published *International Encyclopedia of Communication* (Donsbach 2009), Klaus Bruhn Jensen offers a clear and up-to-date, though multi-level, definition of intermediality. Although the proposition of this collection is that intermediality may now best be understood in relation to performance, and specifically through a dialogic engagement with instances of practice, Jensen affords a relatively neutral and broad account of meanings of the term, which serves to assist an understanding of the "intermedial turn":

> Intermediality refers to the interconnectedness of modern media of communication. As means of expression and exchange, the different media depend on and refer to each other, both explicitly and implicitly; they interact as elements of particular communicative strategies; and they are constituents of a wider cultural environment (cited in Donsbach 2008).

Throughout the history of the arts and media, different disciplines or arts have worked together in a range of combinations. Greek theatre and the Jacobean masque, for example, brought together different combinations of words, visuals, sounds and movement. Some recent approaches to intermediality continue to consider the distinctiveness of art forms and how they might relate to each other or be transposed one to the other. Indeed, transmediality, as a sub-set of intermediality research, addresses the translation or transposition involved, for example, in the musical version of a novel or the poetic rendering of a painting (Wolf 2002, Simanowski 2006, Kattenbelt 2008). But the IFTR research group's current focus on intermediality is rather on 'modern media', their inherent (technological) inter-connectedness and their self-conscious interplay, as marked in Jensen's account. Taking all discourse to be 'mediated', we are interested in the 'mediatised' in the sense of technologically (digitally) wrought, as it functions in performance.

The group's first research activities primarily addressed the impact of new media on live theatre events in what might be called multi-media theatre (Kattenbelt, 2008), but this interest has been extended by new circumstances as they have arisen in a dynamic culture. Jensen's definition again affords clarification:

> Three conceptions of intermediality may be identified in communication research, deriving from three notions of what is a medium. First, and most concretely, intermediality is the combination and adaptation of separate material vehicles of representation and reproduction, sometimes called multimedia, as exemplified by sound-and-slide shows or by the audio and video channels of television. Second, the term denotes communication through several sensory modalities at once, for instance, music and moving images. Third, intermediality concerns the interrelations between media as institutions in society, as addressed in technological and economic terms such as convergence and conglomeration (cited in Donsbach 2008).

Mapping Intermediality in Performance is concerned with all three of the definition levels noted above. On level one, it is concerned, for example, with how a live actor speaking in a performance space, which also projects a live feed image of her on to an on-stage screen (a projection screen or television monitor) engages two means of representation and reproduction, which require negotiations by both the actors and the spectators. On level two, it is concerned with the complexities of work of such practitioners as Robert Lepage (→INSTANCE: *THE ANDERSEN PROJECT*) which may utilise multi-screen video projection (both pre-recorded and live feed), a strong sound score, dynamic machinery that re-configures stage space and various other technological devices as well as live performers, affording a rich and complex sense experience.

Although we are only generally concerned with the economic infrastructure which has brought about new circumstances, on level three we address the capacity for convergence of digital technologies. The process of encoding in 0:1s of all digital media affords convergence between visual, verbal, sonic and gestural encoding and decoding. One advantage, particularly relevant to the perspective of theatre and performance of this aspect of digital culture is the capacity to manipulate data in real time in a way which was not possible with earlier analogue technologies such as film. Thus, whilst the impact of the projection of moving images on pre-recorded film in live theatre events was utilised by predecessors such as Meyerhold and Piscator, the capacity for live feeds and manipulation of imagery in real time greatly extends the possibilities of contemporary theatre practices. In general terms, events do not need to be fixed in advance, but can be more processual in the moment with new practical and aesthetic implications. Work that deploys and manipulates multiple media 'live' requires a response via "several sensory modalities at once" and they may even demand modulations of the entire human sensorium. This observation leads us to Jensen's summary observation:

> As a term and an explicit theoretical concept, intermediality has perhaps been most widely used in reference to multiple modalities of experience, as examined in aesthetic and other humanistic traditions of communication research (cited in Donsbach 2008).

In this volume, we are explicitly pursuing the idea that there may be something distinctive about the ways in which mediums work together in digital culture to challenge established modalities of experience. To this end, questions need to be formulated in new ways and fresh conceptual frameworks need to be adopted and adapted to new circumstances (→ PORTAL: PEDAGOGIC PRAXIS).

For example, one proposition repeatedly made in *Intermediality in Theatre and Performance* was that intermedial work in some sense inhabits a space 'in-between' media. In subsequent group discussions, this notion of the 'in-between' was considered unsatisfactory because it seemed insufficiently precise, depending on a sort of negative definition (neither this nor that but something in the middle). Accordingly, we now seek to mark the concrete effects of being definitively multiple and interrelational. We have come to see that detailed attention needs to be paid to the range of 'inters' in 'interrelationships', differentiating them in their various functions and effects as Ellestrom's nuanced model facilitates in detail. Although not entirely abandoning the various conceptions of the 'in-between', we have come to think that the compound 'both-and' better characterises contemporary performance culture.[5] The manifestations of digital culture – the media forms, operational modes of devices, and cultural habits of consumers and users – not only inherently entail a relationship with an 'Other', but are structured according to a necessary interrelation with any number of 'Also-Others'. In the first instance, this may appear to resemble 'in-between-ness', the oscillation between identifiable points of reference. But this very aspect of digital culture – where devices, events and activities are formed out of relationships, necessary interdependencies, and mutually co-relating entities – provides a structuring principle that helps to explain the paradigmatic character of the digital.

Intermedial theatre may be both physically based and on-screen; experiences may be both actual and virtual; spaces may be both public and private; bodies may be both present and absent. Taylor and Harris address "the digital's ... materiality and immateriality. These are not contradictory qualities but rather essential, mutually constituting elements" (2005, 18). The term "glocal" was coined to describe the phenomenon of being both global and local (see Malecki and Moriset 2008, 221). Latham and Sassen note that both "[v]ariability and specificity are crucial dimensions" of digital formations (2005, 6). Moreover, mediums come together in various ways. In some instances, they collide and create a frisson in the process; in other instances, one medium is imbricated within another so that they are almost dissolved into each other but the form of one remains just visible in the solution of the other. Amy Petersen Jensen argues for hybridity (of the viewer as subject; of media in and for performance) as constitutive of coherence across discrete entities:

> It is possible then that the mind and body of the theatre spectator is one such site – a hybrid subject ... in which the form and content of two mediums, theatre and media, compete and collaborate to form unique receptive interactions with individual texts and their performances. Here, in this hybrid space, the participatory spectator prefigures a new type of performance that develops out of the interaction between two mediums (Jensen 2007, 122-3).

Müller remarks that "the terms 'hybrid', 'hybridity' and 'hybridization' seem to have become almost as fashionable as 'multi or intermediality'" but notes "a rather blurred or unspecific way of handling this term[inology] within the framework of intermedial research" (in Elleström 2010, 245). Indeed, in another context, Becquer and Gatti (2005) have pointed out that 'hybridity' sometimes implies a hierarchical relation privileging an originary term, rather than the combination of media on a basis of equivalence. In their view, 'syncretism' can be usefully differentiated since it avoids reduction to a hierarchical opposition when mediums come together. 'Syncretism', they propose, denotes "a heterogeneous front of distinct [elements] in altered relations to each other" (2005, 447). Thus, with a range of 'inters' in play, this volume aims to present through examples of praxis some of the specificities in the various interrelationships in textual composition and in the modalities of experience generated through performance events in a digital age. As noted, principles of composition are closely related to new perceptions, and our interest is in how – singularly and collectively – intermedial performances may have elicited a new cultural way of seeing, feeling and being in the contemporary world.

The extension of Berger's seminal phrase "ways of seeing" (1972) to embrace feeling and being in the world serves to emphasise a drift away from an eye-mind relation to theatre. A highly illuminated phenomenon (since the advent of the earlier technologies of gas and electric light), the staged performance in Western culture was historically presented in a darkened auditorium where the stage event is typically observed from a significant distance. The spatial relations emerged in their physical arrangement in theatre buildings as developed during the period from the Renaissance to the late nineteenth century. The spectatorial relations inviting the eye to observe and feed the mind likewise arose from the enactment of the Renaissance perspective. In part, we remain interested in performances staged in building-based theatres with such an established spatial organisation but which also embrace new media technologies. It is in this context that Kattenbelt's notion of theatre as a hypermedium that stages other mediums, remains particularly important. But digital culture has generated a widespread interactive engagement and playfulness in environments which require a fundamental reconfiguration of temporal and spatial relationships, since they do not adhere entirely to Kattenbelt's defining characteristic of theatre as "the social meeting between performer and spectator in the live presence of the here and now" (2006, 33).

Müller has argued that "the variety of aspects of the concept of 'intermediality' makes it very difficult or almost impossible to present some sort of general overview" (in Elleström 2010, 237) but, under these circumstances, Rajewsky (2005, 44) rightly points out that everybody who uses the term needs to define how they are using it. This book uses the concept "with respect to those co-relations between different media that result in a redefinition of the media that are influencing each other, which in turn leads to a fresh perception" (Kattenbelt 2008, 24). Kattenbelt has been persuasive in arguing that theatre is distinctive, among the arts and media, in its capacity to stage other media in a process of theatricalisation, which incorporates them under the conditions of their established media specificity without transforming them (as in transmediality), and without abandoning its own specificity of liveness in the here and now. But in the re-territorialised domain of "intermediality in performance" Kattenbelt's formulation is troubled, for example, by a phenomenon such as virtual theatre, which involves co-presence in time but in virtual, rather than, actual space. Similarly, it is further questioned – though not necessarily undermined – by the fact that 'performance' understood as an extended set of practices in both actual (but not theatre-specific) and virtual spaces (social networking sites, for example) may not be 'theatre'.

If, as Kattenbelt has posited, theatre as a hypermedium is disposed more towards "diversity, discrepancy and hypermediacy ... than to the idea of unity, harmony and transparency" (2008, 24) because, in the process of theatricalisation, "the other media become 'signs of signs' as opposed to 'signs of objects'" (2006, 37), a key question is whether this remains the case in the expanded domain of performance. This volume sets a number of aspects in play rather than offering, at this stage, an overarching meta-theory. It may be, however, as Kattenbelt proposes, that "at the level of the medium, theatre is a physical hypermedium, whereas at the level of the sign system, the Internet is a virtual hypermedium" (2008, 22).

While, historically, theatre audiences observed a constructed world in actual space, immersive environments, actual and virtual, allow us both to see space and move into and through it. In respect of virtual environments, however, the space is not already there, as it is in theatre buildings and actual site-specific environments, but is created in the process of our moving through, and playing within, it. If actual, site-specific environments were created to disrupt established eye-mind relations and the aesthetic of contemplation from a distance, virtual environments have the potential more fundamentally to modulate our sensorium.

Contemporary theatre practice may well be less concerned with offering meanings than pleasures and experiences, the frisson of momentary dislocation of normative bearings and the opening up of new perceptual modes extending the range of human experience, and perhaps even projecting us into the posthuman (see below and → PORTAL: POSTHUMANISM).

We recognise, then, that in digital culture virtual potentialities to a considerable extent displace representations of reality. However, we do not want to fall back on an unsustainable technological determinism. In aiming to characterise a historical moment, we acknowledge continuities as well as ruptures. Indeed, the performance of self-reflexivity is an aspect of the book's procedure with a specific, in-built retrospection (→ RETROSPECTION). We see digital technologies and their potentialities as functioning in a force field of influences, working reciprocally – we might say intermedially – upon each other. As Hans-Thies Lehman (2006 [1999]) has famously formulated it, theatre had already begun to move from a 'dramatic' into a 'postdramatic' phase prior to the full emergence in the 1980s and 1990s of digital culture. Some of the changes have undoubtedly been accelerated by digital technologies but there are other factors involved. The socio-economic shift from modernity to postmodernity prefigured the intensities of digital culture in its disposition towards time-space compression. Postmodernity's attendant temporal mode of 'short-termism' is accompanied by a semiotic liberation and discursive playfulness in the artefacts of postmodernism, summarised by David Harvey as "an aesthetic that celebrates difference, ephemerality, spectacle, fashion and the commodification of cultural forms" (1989, 156).

In a broader study of digital culture than the scope of this book affords (though see → PORTAL: DIGITAL CULTURE), digital technologies would need to be located in the broader context of cultural change. But this volume's focus is, as noted, on theatre and performance practices that have arisen in digital circumstances. It seeks to illuminate them and the phenomenological and conceptual challenges they pose. In one respect, then, there is an implicit, if loose, periodisation of technological influence in the approach. Just as Benjamin sought to address the impact on works of art of "the age of mechanical reproduction", we seek to identify the digital culture's impact on theatre and performance after the intermedial turn. However, just as Benjamin's attitude to the demise of auratic art has been variously interpreted as optimistic or marking a sense of loss, we are aware that different assumptions are made in the continental European and the Anglo-American traditions about the impact and effects of intermedial practices. The former, perhaps in the wake of Brecht's radical separation of the elements (→ TERM: SEPARATION), tends to hold that they inherently involve a critical distance and awareness of the mediums coming together, whilst the latter interrogates the impact of the interrelationships, noting that a combination of mediums can work simply to enhance a traditional dramatic illusion. Indeed, in this context, Kattenbelt has usefully offered a lineage of developments of interruption techniques in theatre through Kandinsky, Brecht and others in opposition to the Wagnerian *Gesamtkunstwerk*'s striving for perfect illusion and Bolter and Grusin's much more recent sense of a gravitation towards "immediacy" (see 2006, 28- 35).

One major impact which has led us to modify our primary understanding of theatre and performance is the way in which everyday life itself has, as noted, been widely re-conceived as performative. On the one hand, the vastly extended digital technologies of surveillance have fostered a culture in which people have a sense of being observed almost everywhere, all the time. Global satellite mapping, for example, has been criticised because of the coverage and details it now provides, almost intruding into individuals' private homes and lives. Perhaps, more positively in the playful spaces of the Internet, individuals can also construct a broad range of virtual identities, experiencing what it is like to be other than their primary identity, just as theatre actors have done for centuries. These types of liberations are not, of course, entirely digital since there are many ways in which behaviour is increasingly staged in the actual as well as virtual worlds. Performative theories, which also challenge the idea of an essential and immutable core identity, have arisen independently of virtual environments (see Butler 1993). In everyday life, it is not uncommon for people to describe their shift into various performance modes in different aspects of their lives, and discussing their behaviour ("I was like…") as if they were recounting a performance of one aspect of their identities. Nevertheless, the almost instant access to large audiences in virtual rather than actual, geographical communities of social networking sites such as YouTube have really encouraged people to perform and distribute digitally whatever sense of themselves they inhabit. Thus, some examples of contemporary performance practices not traditionally recognised as theatre are included in this volume along with those recognisably theatre practices, which have embraced new technologies.

Fast communications across time and space by means of digital technologies has created the appearance that the world is smaller and that time moves faster in a manner inconceivable just half a century ago. Indeed, as with space, established conceptions of time are dislocated. Cubitt has delineated what he describes as the ontology of digital culture in terms of fleeting time, ephemerality and erasure. He suggests that digital culture:

> provides us with a compulsory opportunity to erase and start again. It renders every document ephemeral. Where erasure is a constant option, accidental erasure, like unconscious forgetting, is a constant generator of random cultural mutation. The fixed form of textuality is lost in the possibility of erasing (2000).

Recalling Phelan's much-cited conception of performance as ephemeral, namely that which "becomes itself through disappearance" (1993, 146), there would appear to be an ontological resonance between live theatre and digital media.

Above all, satellites and fibre optics have facilitated rapid two-way communications such that it really is possible for performers located on other continents and in other time zones to dance together in real time. Indeed, instant interactivity has become the name of almost every game, whether it means literally playing a video game, sending a video capture in real time to a friend on your mobile phone for it to be down-loaded and manipulated before it is almost instantly returned, or just pushing the red button on your handset to view the ballpark from a different angle. The capacity of digital connectivity is so broad that a mind-set that expects all devices to be interactive has quickly emerged in our culture.

Accordingly, it is almost impossible to separate the cultural impact of digital circumstances from the "combination and adaptation of separate material vehicles of representation and reproduction", which constitute Jensen's (2008) first definition of intermediality. There are major questions, which can only be touched upon in this book, for example, whether the increased visibility of ordinary people in performance situations, as indicated above, marks the development of a truer democracy than has previously been realised. There are questions regarding the politics of a new aesthetics of disjunctions which address issues of whether it can achieve a radical distribution of wealth and power or whether the politics of aesthetics that Rancière advocates (→ PORTAL: PEDAGOGIC PRAXIS) is a more subtle and contemporary response to issues where more institutionalised politics has failed. It may be that the extension of sense perceptions and the new, deterritorialised communities indicated above have potentialities which have not yet been fully realised. Alternatively, it may be that a virtually democratised world will fail to find a counterpart in a fully democratic actual world. Steve Dixon (with Barry Smith), in the encyclopaedic *Digital Performance* (2007), argues that digital artists are taking up the progressive manifestos of the Futurists, but these types of utopian vision have a habit of being dashed. As Lanfranco Aceti has remarked, the mobile phone images of the June 2009 uprisings in Iran distributed across the Internet to inform the world and enlist support for a resistance movement have regrettably turned into surveillance footage which has led to increased arrests and repression.[6] The jury on digital culture remains out.

It may, of course, turn out that we are on the cusp of a paradigm shift into a new age where former paradigms are displaced. Posthumanism, in some respects, goes beyond Turing's sense of humans augmented by technologies from the basic blind man's stick to the computer-driven prosthesis of Stelarc to a formulation which sees 'Man' being displaced from the centre stage of history (→ PORTAL: POSTHUMANISM). In its more apocalyptic version, this sense of the posthuman suggests a collapse of differences between humans and (digital) machines.[7] Among theorists, Donna Haraway (1991) remains optimistic about the liberational possibilities of these new circumstances; amongst performance artists, Stelarc is perhaps the practitioner most committed to Cyborg culture, arguing that the body is obsolete.[8]

In the theatre, paralleling the displacement from centre stage of 'Man as the measure of all things', the actor's agency and centrality are further diminished by her demotion from the apex of the hierarchy of stage signs. The performer today is just one of many signifiers in a complex, multi-layered event. In intermedial theatre, 'embodied man' as represented by the actor in Brook's empty space has been displaced by microphones, cameras, TV monitors, laptop PCs, projection screens, motion sensors and related technologies. But such digital paraphernalia do not necessarily entail the abandonment of a human paradigm and many practices continue to explore the human condition in the Enlightenment tradition. However, in the assumptions made about interactivity, impact and effect, an uneasy slippage between paradigms is evident with the frequent assumption (posited by poststucturalists) of the experiencer (→ TERM) as a conflicted, non-self-identical subject who may end up perpetually performing her various identities in an endless process. The digital doubling of bodies, virtual bodies, robots and cyborgs have entered the intermedial stage, if not to displace humans, then most assuredly to engage with them and question some of their most fundamental assumptions. An intermedial stage, both literally and metaphorically, is what concerns this book.

Network of Terms

Sarah Bay-Cheng

The *Oxford English Dictionary* in part defines *map* as "A diagram or collection of data showing the spatial distribution of something or the relative positions of its components". It was these relative positions or points that Michel de Certeau problematised when he argued that the map transforms the activity of passers-by (or their performances) "into points that draw a totalizing and reversible line on the map. They allow us to grasp only a relic set of the nowhen of a surface of projection" (de Certeau 1984, 97). There are myriad affinities between de Certeau's view of the totalising map and the dynamic social, technological, and performative relations of contemporary intermedial performance. For example, is the "nowhen" of a surface projection not akin to the ubiquitous screen of mediated performances?

While de Certeau regrets the loss of life's activities to the totalising features of the map, theatre and performance historians, scholars, and critics conversely attempt to reassemble the ephemerality of performance through what he calls the "relic set", that is, the incomplete documentation, artifacts, and records left behind after a performance. Whereas de Certeau rejects the map in favour of the more embodied *tour*, seemingly always in the present tense, this book engages the metaphor of the map as both an attempt to describe and to theorise contemporary intermediality theatre and to facilitate the reader's own tour of this field. Keeping in mind the totalising danger of the map (and other spatial metaphors such as *field* and *area*), the network of terms offers a constellation of descriptive and discursive points designed not only to outline the specific dimensions of this field, but also to demonstrate the dynamic relations among them. We do not intend this map to be a totalising one, with fixed points and lines, but as an ever-shifting terrain that responds to the changes in terms, practices, and reception of contemporary intermedial performance. In this sense, we are indebted to, and yet deviate from, Raymond Williams's influential *Keywords: A Vocabulary of Culture and Society* (1977, 1983). This network of terms does not follow Williams's expansive list of terms, but it does retain something of his impulse to "cluster" terms such as his original collection from his *Culture and Society* (1958), "culture / art / industry / culture / democracy / class". At the same time, we submit that for all of its usefulness, the fluidity of contemporary performance dynamics requires new approaches to words and terms without reifying a particular word or meaning.

Terms here reflect multiple points of entry into the discourse of intermediality, theatre, technology, and performance. Some adopt cultural theory as an entry point; others the phenomenological perspectives of the performance event itself. In each section of the book, our aim is for these terms to suggest a few key points of inquiry to orient the reader, but these are by no means the only relevant terms. Indeed, the reader will note immediately that, in every definition, there are many more possible terms that could present themselves. Such is the expansive nature of definitions; one can never hope to identify every relevant description. To negotiate any field, however, requires a few landmarks often with some arbitrary lines drawn among them. This drawing of tentative lines perhaps best describes the act of mapping nodes and clusters of closely cognate terms that are presented throughout this book. The selection of terms emerges from the rest of the authors' contributions and, as such, they reflect the diversity of perspectives and disciplines that inform the terms, portals and instances. We hope that this discursive map will not eclipse the performances or activities that lay behind them, but will instead open up new conceptual territories and domains for exploration and the unexplored spaces between fixed points.

Portal: Performativity and Corporeal Literacy

'Performativity' and 'corporeal literacy' are the guiding concepts of this portal affording a perspective through dynamic embodiment on intermediality in performance and posing two specific questions. The first question, addressed by Kattenbelt, concerns how intermediality in performance can be understood as a mode of performativity. Kattenbelt proposes that intermediality in performance is very much about *staging* media and, in consequence, changes the interrelations between their materiality (or ontology), mediality (or functionality) and modes of perception (with respect to medium-specific conventions). These changes are characterised in terms of a refunctioning of the media involved and a resensibilisation of perception. The 'staging' process is contextualised within the performative turn in culture and society, which might in part be constructed as a response of the arts to an all-embracing theatricalisation, particularly insofar as the performative turn is understood also as a process of increasing mediatisation.

The second question, addressed by Maaike Bleeker, concerns how the performance of perception might be understood in terms of its corporeal dimensions. Bleeker points out that all technological systems (of communication) "engage with the bodies of their users" and require a specific literacy. The performance of perception in contemporary digital culture is highly characterised by corporeal aspects, wherein body/machine interfaces assume haptic modalities of embodied interactions. On the one hand, Bleeker associates intermediality in theatre and performance with interventions in synaesthetic processes of perception, which "bring to conscious awareness the facilitations, affordances, restrictions, and demands played out on the body". On the other hand, she foregrounds a process of "playing with different modes of perceiving or even undermining these". Accordingly, this portal is primarily related to the "modes of experience" node.

We have chosen several terms in order to highlight key aspects of the intermedial experience in performance and digital culture. The term experiencer emphasises "the body as medium of perception" and, correspondingly, a "haptic dimension of space". The term embodiment is specifically related to (digital) technology and foregrounds how the embodied experience of the self is "extended, hybridised and delimited through technology". The term intimacy, when it is specifically related to intermediality, is based on the assumption that the experience of closeness is "generated through the *performance* of shared frames and dynamics". The term presence refers to "proximity in time and space" but the notion of proximity is complicated by the use of digital technologies since the physical and the virtual are imbricated within each other in such a way that the experience of presence is no longer determined by "an absolute ontological condition". The term immersion evokes a similar complexity: the paradoxical experience of being submerged in an environment, which we know is not actual but which nevertheless feels 'real'. This frisson of perceptual instability explains the excitement of the experience of being inside such an immersive environment.

An indexicality of the embodied experience is common to all of the terms, emphasising that intermediality in performance is, indeed, very much a matter of redefining our senses and resensibilising our perception through bodily encounters with (digital) technologies. The result is an extended, hybridised or delimited experience, as illustrated by the five instances. Koski discusses how 'regular' notions of presence, embodiment and emotion may become 'awkward' if we analyse them from a performer's 'insider' perspective, her relationship with a Second Life avatar playing out in front of an audience live in the here and now. Turco discusses two experiences of VJing in club culture as a textual interplay between video, music and dancing bodies, in which the relationships between spectators, performers and representations are redefined. From a practitioner's perspective, Fewster recounts how the use of digital video technologies in live theatre performance can create a kinetic interplay between live and virtual presences, which entails a dislocation of the actual-virtual bearings of the performers and audience members alike.

Intermediality in Performance and as a Mode of Performativity
Chiel Kattenbelt

Introduction

This section offers a way into understanding intermediality both in performance and as a mode of performativity. It draws on some of the established conceptions of 'performance', 'performativity' and the 'performative turn' but refines them with the aim of distinguishing both continuities and differences. The discussion is concerned with both aesthetics in respect of the interrelations of the elements in intermedial texts, and their impact, in terms broadly involving a resensibilisation of the perception of experiencers (→ TERM: EXPERIENCER). My claim ultimately is that the performative turn instigated in the early 20th century by the arrival of mass media was intensified by the rapid evolution and proliferation of digital technologies over the past two decades or so. The performative dimension emergent in early 20th-century culture, has risen to dominance under circumstances involving intermedial relations in digital culture. In discussing aesthetic utterances and textual forms along with the aesthetic and quotidian orientations of experiencers, I propose that signification (semiotics) and experience (phenomenology) are imbricated within each other in the contemporary 'performative culture', not separable in a historical sequence, as suggested by Fischer-Lichte (see below).

'Performativity' and 'performance' are terms used with different accents of meaning, in various different disciplines such as aesthetics, action theory, literary and cultural theory, linguistic philosophy, gender theory, anthropology and ethnography. The same goes for the term 'intermediality'. Accordingly, we can no longer use these concepts in academic debates without indicating which accent we are emphasising. Since an overview of the different accents and interpretations of these concepts has already been given in several books and articles (e.g. Carlson 1996; Früchtl and Zimmermann 2001; Mersch 2002, Kertscher and Mersch 2003; Rajewsky 2005; Loxley 2007), and with respect to performativity and performance, there are even anthologies of 'classic texts', which unpack these concepts (Auslander 2003). I will simply outline the key concepts of performativity, performance and intermediality in such a way as to characterise the phenomena they denote. I propose using the concepts as heuristic instruments for the purpose of searching for underlying structures of, and relationships between, phenomena. My aim is to emphasise the performativity of intermediality by arguing that intermediality is very much about the staging (in the sense of conscious self-presentation to another) of media, for which theatre as a hypermedium provides pre-eminently a stage (see Kattenbelt 2006).

The Basic Features of Performativity

Performative Utterance or Act

A performative utterance, whether it be in word, image (gesture) and/or sound, is an act that constitutes what it presents. It brings into existence what – at least in the first instance – it refers to. A performative utterance is an event, an occurrence of which the practical relevance is primarily related to its taking place in the here and now, in its need to be carried out and presented and, in consequence, in its need to be perceived in this very moment. A performative utterance is an intentional act (cf. Seel 2001, 49), which is not just performed in the (literal) sense of being executed, but something that is being staged. The act of staging implies, on the one hand, a performer, the one who presents herself and by doing so constitutes her self, her (gender) identity (Butler 1990; 1993) and, on the other hand, a spectator (the one who supports the role of the performer by taking up the position of being a member of the audience. Staging oneself in front of an audience brings us to the concept of a performative situation, or performance.

Performative Situation or Performance

In his article "Semiotics of Theatrical Performance" (1977), Umberto Eco introduces the concept "performative situation" or "performance". This concept (without defining it explicitly) refers to a situation in which objects, bodies, actions and events are shown by – and, as a result, function as –intentional signs (Eco 1977, 117) in the perspective of (a) possible world(s) or situation(s). The basic characteristic of objects, bodies, actions and events that are shown or framed in a performative situation is, according to Eco, "ostension". He describes this concept as "one of the various ways of signifying, consisting in de-realizing a given object in order to make it stand for an entire class" (Eco 1977, 110). "De-realizing" in this context indicates that the performed objects, bodies, actions and events are disposed of their contingency. In other words, performative signs are – as Petr Bogatyrev (1971 [1938]) noted – "signs of signs" rather than "signs of objects".

Eco implicitly uses the concepts of performative situation and performance as synonyms. The term "theatrical performance" for him seems to refer to a specific performative situation, although he leaves the question of the specificity of the theatrical performance unanswered. He may even have intended to define every performance as (a form of) theatre but – if this is indeed the case – the term "theatrical performance" would be a pleonasm. It would also imply that theatrical signs are exclusively constituted by being framed within a performative situation.

If, however, we wish to define theatre within the domain of the arts or at least within the domain of the aesthetic (as I propose), we may consider a theatre or theatrical performance as a performative situation perceived and experienced from an aesthetic orientation. This means that theatre is not constituted by the performativity of the situation as such, but by the aesthetic orientation of the perceiver. Because of the specific interest by which her orientation is primarily guided, she is pre-eminently an experiencer who also reflects herself as being a subject of experience. This brings us to the concept of performative orientation, of which, as we will see, the aesthetic orientation is a specific form.

The Performative Orientation

Jürgen Habermas uses the concept of "performative orientation" in different ways: on the one hand, with regard to the (ethno)methodology of the participating observations of social scientists (Habermas 1985/1, 167 and further) and, on the other hand, with regard to a specific orientation of the communicating participants who meet each other as social actors inhabiting the same lifeworld (Habermas 1988, 67). I will confine myself to the latter use of the concept. The performative orientation of social actors implies two complementary perspectives: that of a reflexively committed observer and that of a directly involved participant. The communicating participants meet each other in duality, as both 'I' and 'you'. These two perspectives are geared for one another – they keep each other in balance, as it were – with respect to their attempts to achieve a mutual understanding of a situation.

The Performativity of the Aesthetic Orientation

The aesthetic orientation as theorised by Martin Seel (1985) could be considered as a specific form of the performative orientation of social actors striving for a shared understanding of their (life)world. The aesthetic orientation is primarily characterised by an interest in the presentation of experience qualities which make it possible to perceive and experience – within a specific conduct of life – the actuality and internal constitution of one's own experience (Seel 1985, 127 and 247). An aesthetic orientation concerns an emotionally intensified, affective perception and a reflexive orientation toward one's own subjectivity within the context of a presupposed communality in the life experiences of contemporaries who belong to the same, that is to say intersubjectively shared, lifeworld. Because it is in some way framed, or staged, an object that is perceived from an aesthetic orientation occurs relative independently of the external world in which it exists. Paradoxically, it incorporates its own context. Analysis primarily involves demonstrating an internal logic. This relative independence is also characteristic of the position of the perceiver/observer who liberates her own subjectivity from the conventions which constitute and regulate thinking and acting in everyday life, and, in consequence, also liberates it from the constraints of appropriateness (Habermas 1985/1, 230-231). Thus, more space is created for imagination and spontaneity and consequently there is a need for creative reflection of one's own experience (Habermas 1972, 192). This, however, does not mean, that the aesthetic experience takes place in isolation, completely disconnected from the lifeworld. On the contrary, an orientation towards one's own subjectivity, particularly towards oneself as an experiencing subject and subject of experience, creates the possibility of perceiving and experiencing oneself both within the aesthetic framework and in relation to the lifeworld. As Seel (following Martin Heidegger) formulates it, the aesthetic experience provides the subject with insight in the timebound presence of being-in-the-world in its situative conditions of existence (Seel 1985, 209).

The Performativity of the Aesthetic Utterance or Presentation

An aesthetic utterance is an articulation of needs and desires which requires constitutive apprehension in the act of experience. This idea is based on the phenomenological assumption that expression, perception and experience are inextricably linked to one another. Aesthetic articulations are presentations rather than representations. They are characterised by the event that they perform in the production as well as by the perception of them.[9]

As noted, a presentation articulates an experience by expressing its qualities in such a way that they can be perceived and experienced within an internal context of reference. Qualities of experience are related, however, to that which is significant for those engaged in the encounter. In the mode of their referential density and significance, qualities of experience are only communicable via aesthetic objects and understandable from an aesthetic orientation. What aesthetic objects present is, according to Seel (1985, 159), primarily determined by their presentational quality of expression ("*präsentische Ausdrucksqualität*"). The term "*Ausdrucksqualität*" refers specifically to the expressivity of the materiality (→ TERM: MATERIALITY) or phenomenality of the work of art as an object of perception (artefact), implying that the affect of the work of art lies in the experiencer. In semiotic terms, we might say that the concept "*Ausdruckqualität*" primarily relates to the affective experience (cf. Charles S. Peirce: *Collected Papers*, vol. 5, 475) that the work of art creates. Every material is characterised by its specific expressivity and – to a large extent – by the specific procedures or techniques by which it is, or might be, processed.

Self-reference and Self-reflexivity

Two basic features of the performance and the performative orientation, namely *self-reference* and *self-reflexivity*, remain to be addressed. Because of its constituting (i.e., world making) and staging aspect, a performance by definition refers to, and reflects on, itself and on the event in which the performance occurs. Audiences are aware, even during the most naturalistic of presentations, that they are witnessing a staged 'reality', not actuality itself. Self-reference and self-reflexivity are not only characteristics of the performance itself, however, but also of the perceiver who assumes the position of the spectator, of the audience. The performative orientation and, even more so, the aesthetic orientation are very much self-referential and self-reflexive. The aesthetic orientation facilitates a liberating con-

frontation with one's own experience, which is made perceivable through engagement with the aesthetic object. According to Seel, this implies a requirement
to reflect on the possibilities of freedom under the circumstances and conditions
of a historical presence. The aesthetic experience transcends the projections of
daily life precisely to afford a confrontation with its constraints and to open up
possibilities for change. This specific orientation provides the aesthetic perception with its excessive potential (Seel 1985, 329). Aesthetic action (in production
as well as perception) may be considered a form of exploration and reflection,
which reinforces the communicative competence of socialised individuals. This
also implies an assumption that aesthetic action has a therapeutic as well as edu-
cative function, although without being instrumentalised to therapy or education,
since this would be to take the aesthetic beyond its inherent disposition. The
latter is also the case insofar as aesthetic action is instrumentalised for political
or economical purposes and for that reason becomes propaganda or advertisement.

The Performative Turn in the Arts and Culture

In *Ästhetik des Performativen* (2004), Erika Fischer-Lichte discusses the "performative turn" (*Performativierungsschub*) in the arts. She characterises this turn as a shift
in which two relationships are newly determined: the relationship between subject and object and the relationship between the material and corporal nature
(*Material- und Körperhaftigkeit*) of the elements and their sign character (*Zeichenhaf-
tigkeit*) (Fischer-Lichte 2004, 19). The performative turn is a delimitation (*Entgren-
zung*) of the arts because it occurs in performance and as performances (*Aufführun-
gen*), as events, which do not exist on their own, that is to say, independent of
their producers and perceivers. On the contrary, they only exist in the creative
activity of the artist and in the experience of the observer, listener or spectator
(Fischer-Lichte 2004, 29). In other words, the dichotomies noted here (subject/
object, signifier/signified, etc.) more or less lose their "polarity" and "sharpness
of distinction" (Fischer-Lichte 2004, 33).

With her concept of the performative turn in music, the visual arts, literature
and theatre in particular, Fischer-Lichte focuses on the postwar avant-garde.[10] But
it may be that art is by definition performative. I consider the performative turn in
the contemporary arts literally as a *radicalisation* of the performative aspects of art
in order to reinforce the materiality or expressive qualities of the aesthetic utterance, to emphasise the aesthetic situation as a staging and world-making event
taking place in the presence of the here and now, and to intensify the aesthetic
experience as an embodied experience. According to Fischer-Lichte, the performative turn in the arts cannot be understood from a hermeneutic or semiotic
aesthetics, since, for these approaches, a clear distinction between subject and
object (between the artist and his work) and between signifier and signified is
fundamental (Fischer-Lichte 2004, 19). Instead, according to Fischer-Lichte, we

need a phenomenological aesthetics, which is not primarily focused on the aesthetic object in terms of its meaning and interpretation by a process of encoding and decoding, but on the aesthetic perception as it occurs in a corpor(e)al experience. Unlike Fischer-Lichte, I would not consider semiotics and phenomenology – and 'by consequence' meaning and experience – in opposition to each other, in particular not if we use the concepts of "semiotics" and "phenomenology", in accordance with the "pragmaticist" philosophy of Peirce, in which modes of being (the ontological) and modes of experience (the logical) are inextricably linked with each other. From this approach, meaning is not located in an object that supposedly exists on its own, but in the human experience in which we try to reveal the world that we inhabit.

The concept of the "performative turn" could also be used in a broader sense referring to the increasing significance of performance in our contemporary culture and society. The idea has been formulated in a variety of different terms, such as the "society of the spectacle" (Debord 2001 [1967]) and incorporated almost everywhere into "performative society" (Kershaw 1999 and 2003), the "spectacularisation of culture" (Eco 1985) and the "experience economy" (Pine and Gilmore 1999). In *Perform or Else* (2001), Jon McKenzie focuses primarily on the instrumental aspects of contemporary performance by discussing the specific "challenges" related to specific understandings ("paradigms") of performance in terms of intended achievements. The paradigm of Performance Studies is the "cultural performance", which is characterised by its "challenge of efficacy", that is to say, its potential to change people and societies (McKenzie 2001, 30). The paradigm of Performance Management is the "organizational performance", which is characterised by its "challenge of efficiency" which, reductively, means minimising inputs and maximising outputs (McKenzie 2001, 56). The paradigm of scientists and engineers is the "technological performance", which is characterised by its "challenge of effectiveness" of a given task, or, in other words, of a specific application or set of applications in a particular context (McKenzie 2001, 97).

The performative turn in contemporary culture and society is in particular due to the all embracing mediatisation of culture and society as it occurred in the emergence and fast growth of mass media such as film and television in the course of the 20th century and then in the proliferation of the rapid evolution of digital information and communication technologies over the past three decades. In a mediatised culture and society, the mass media – in particular television – have become a substantial part of reality itself, more than just representing reality through a mediating function. In other words, our mediatised culture and society have turned into a *hyperreality* of simulations and simulacra, which means that the signs have become more real than the objects to which they refer (Eco 1985) or, to put it differently, that reality has been replaced by its *representations* (Gilles Deleuze and Félix Guattari 1972 and Jean Baudrillard 1985 and 1986). We might agree with

MAPPING INTERMEDIALITY IN PERFORMANCE

Theodor Adorno that "the more complete the world as representation, the more inscrutable the representation as ideology" (Adorno 1963 [1952-53], 71). This all means that the expression "all the world is a stage" is no longer just a metaphor, but a characteristic feature of our mediatised culture and society.

The Performativity of Intermediality

In my last contribution to theoretical and aesthetic discourses on intermediality (Kattenbelt 2008), I proposed using the concept with respect to those co- or inter-relations between media that result in a redefinition of the media, which by impacting upon each other, provoke in turn a resensibilised perception. This means that pre-existing medium-specific conventions have been altered, allowing for the exploration of new dimensions of perception and experience. Viewed this way, intermediality is more closely connected to the idea of hypermediacy (diversity, discrepancy) than immediacy (unity, harmony, and media transparency) of Bolter and Grusin (1999). Intermediality thus conceived assumes interrelations in terms of mutual affects. In order to situate intermediality in an aesthetic tradition, I referred to Wassily Kandinsky's *Bühnenkomposition* (as opposed to Richard Wagner's *Gesamtkunstwerk*), to Sergei Eisenstein's "montage of attractions" and to Bertolt Brecht's "radical separation of the elements". Following Hans-Thies Lehmann's description of a "postdramatic" contemporary theatre, I referred to stage directors such as Robert Wilson, Alain Platel, Gerardjan Rijnders, and Jan Lauwers. These practitioners have used techniques of fragmentation, juxtaposition, repetition, duplication, speeding up, and slowing down in order to emphasise and intensify the experience of the continuity of the performance itself. They do not sacrifice the experience of the presentation that takes place in the actual continuum of the present for the sake of an illusion of continuity (namely the continuity of the (re)presented action). More specifically, with respect to the use of digital video and audio technologies in their theatre performances, I referred to Guy Cassiers, Carina Molier and Hotel Modern in order to articulate the redefinition of media and the resensibilisation of perception in terms of separating the inwardness of experience and the outwardness of action, spatialising time and temporalising space; confronting the reality of illusion (the live) with the illusion of reality (the mediatised), and extending the lyrical and epical modes of presentation. By the latter, I mean that the actuality of the action (re)presented in the performance is dominated by the expression of the intensity of experience or the articulation of the reflexivity of thought.

In my specific understanding of intermediality, this concept is quite closely related to the performative turn in the arts. Indeed, I propose a broadening of the historical range of this turn by taking the avant-garde of the early 20th century (as distinct from the postwar avant-garde from the 1950s onwards) as a starting point insofar as a playful staging of signs (and media) is a specific feature of it (cf. Klemens Gruber's retrospection at the end of this book). I argue that it is from this tendency that the modern and post-modern arts derive a pre-eminently performative (even theatrical) and self-critical aspect (Kattenbelt 2008, 21).

Some Concluding Remarks

I acknowledge that I conceive intermediality mainly in a tradition of modernist aesthetics in which I locate the foundations of the claim for the inherent critical potential of its aesthetic orientation. I recognise, however, that, in the context of contemporary (postmodern) Western culture and society, such a claim may no longer be considered self-evident. This is particularly the case in view of the fact that many developments in contemporary culture and society are complex and contradictory. We may notice, for instance, on the one hand, a disposition to homogeneity in the globalisation of our world, but, on the other hand, its cultural, social and political fragmentation (cf. Klein and Sting 2005, 8-9; (→ TERM: GLOCALISATION). In assuming that aesthetic communication entails an experiential exploration of the significance and range of a presupposed communality in the intersubjectively shared experience of our lifeworld, I must take into consideration that it may no longer be clear who the presumed 'we', those who supposedly share a lifeworld, actually are. The shared lifeworld of many people (particularly inhabitants of larger cities) can no longer be defined independent of the multi- or intercultural society in which they live. It may also be that many people belong to several quite separate communities, some of which may be separated by significant geographical or virtual distances. Their sense of belonging to a community is thus no longer restricted to meeting each other physically or sharing a physical environment in which they may have common interests. Furthermore, as noted, identity with respect to individuals is today less and less associated with the idea of singularity and individuality in the literal sense of the word (indivisibility). A parallel world of bits and bytes has emerged adjacent to the world of atoms (Negroponto 1995) with new possibilities and opportunities of constructing one's identity and presenting or staging oneself in front of others, albeit under different conditions. However, people continue at least partly to inhabit a shared lifeworld, however fluid their identities and fragmented their social affiliations have become. Until a wholesale migration into the virtuality of replicants occurs, humans will continue to live a significant part of their lives in the world, however complex and fragmented their social network. It is another instance of the 'both-and' mode of experience foregrounded in this book.

Insofar as the aesthetic orientation creates opportunities for change, as I have proposed, we may observe that belief in the construction of a society has been replaced by the belief in the self-construction of the individual. However, agency continues to be constrained by structure in a world governed by the mechanisms of a free market, mainly in the service of a consumer-oriented conditioning strategy that underpins the very ideology of the capacity for the (re)construction of the individual. Thus, individualisation turns out to be a paradoxical process. The ultimate consequence of identity being a matter of personal choice is that it does not matter anymore who you are, since you might be just as well be someone else – or at least someone different.[11] This apparent subjective agency is offset, however, by the fact that people are increasingly objectified by definitional profiles (age, ethnicity, sexual orientation, education, income, interests, etc.). According to Lev Manovich, "individual customization" (rather than "mass standardization") is the logic of the postindustrial society and more particularly the logic of digital media, the technologies of which have outpaced alternatives (Manovich 2001, 29-30). Owing to their programmability and variability, the devices and objects of these media are easily personalised in accordance with one's personal preferences. But the choices are both free and constrained: customisation involves individuals not so much choosing freely but applying standard ready-made suggestions for consumption.

We can no longer deal with a world of bits and bytes in terms of being opposed to reality but, although it poses significant challenges and opportunities, the virtual has not entirely displaced the actual. Indeed, I would continue to argue that the experience of life without being initially oriented towards, and ultimately rooted in, the physical world would entail a certain rootlessness.[12] Life still derives its intensity and depth from its transitoriness. And these aspects of life are nowhere more directly expressed than in live theatrical performances, especially where one's presence is an essential aspect of what would otherwise be a disorienting virtual experience.[13] I thus consider theatre to be the paradigm of the performativity of the arts in general and I consider the performative turn in the other arts to be a radicalisation of their performativity, and, in this sense, a kind of return to the theatre. This paradigm may be experienced as a counter-movement in which the arts refer to, and reflect upon, themselves in order to take up a critical position in the larger context of the performative turn in a culture in which mediatisation represents a strong exponent. Indeed, I ultimately consider intermediality mainly in terms of staging the arts for the sake of self-reference and self-reflexivity.

Corporeal Literacy: New Modes of Embodied Interaction in Digital Culture

Maaike Bleeker

This section affords a perspective on intermedial theatre practices through the lens of corporeal literacy. It proposes that theatre practices create situations in which communication happens through several sensory modalities at once. The perspective brings out the performative character of processes of perception and cognition, focusing particularly on the corporeal dimension of these practices. Accordingly, it draws attention to how perception is performed and also to how theatre performance involves complex processes of selection and combination of sensory input.

The Performance of Perception

Perception, as Alva Noë points out, "is not a process in the brain but a kind of skilful activity on the part of the animal as a whole" (Noë 2004, 2). By means of our perceptual systems, we probe our surroundings as animals. Perceiving therefore is a mode of acting. It is not something that happens to us but something we do. It is something we learn to do. Exploring their surroundings through several perceptual systems (Gibson 1966) simultaneously, children learn to perceive through sight and hearing as well as through smelling, touch, proprioception and kinesthesis. From this active engagement, an experience of these surroundings emerges as both visible, audible, and tangible, and all at the same time.

The theatre presents a staged version of the performance of perception that may illuminate how this performance is marked by culture. The multi-media address presented particularly by intermedial theatre is constructed in such a way as to play into (and sometimes also to play with) culturally specific modes of perceiving. Famously (or infamously) the conventional theatre set-up, putting the audience in the dark in front of a brightly lit stage confirms modes of perceiving of the so-called disembodied I/eye, the (supposedly) passive observer of a world existing independently from her perceptual engagement with it. The aesthetic logic of the dramatic theatre (characterised by Lehmann (1999) as logocentric and teleological) supports a sense of the world that exists as a perceptual unity independent of our perception of it. A similar sense of unity characterises the synaesthetic ideal of the Wagnerian *Gesamtkunstwerk*. Yet the intermedial character of the theatre may also be used to undermine seemingly self-evident modes of perceiving and to draw attention to the performativity of perception: how perception actually produces what appears as the object of our perception. The transition described by Lehmann as the development from dramatic to postdramatic theatre manifests itself in performances in which the different sensory modalities of theatre, no longer united by the dramatic frame, challenge established modalities of audience and spectatorship and turn the theatre into an experimental set-up for exploring and playing with the performance of perception.

Lehmann points specifically to the connection between the development from dramatic to postdramatic theatre and the rise of media culture. The transformation of the aesthetic logic of the theatre, he argues, may (at least partly) be understood as a response to the mediatisation of society. Here corporeal literacy allows for an approach of both the new experiences provided by the theatre and the mediatisation to which this theatre responds from the intersection of our bodies and the technologies with which these bodies engage. The impact of media technologies cannot be understood only in terms of representations or content, those intentional manifest meanings signified to pre-existing self-sufficient subjects. Thus intermedial theatre practices are even more likely to trouble established modes of perception than postdramatic theatre understood more broadly. What particularly remains unexamined is the effect of technology's materiality (→ TERM: MATERIALITY), an effect that transforms its users.

Corporeal Literacy

Corporeal literacy affords a perspective on these new experiences that recognises their novelty while also acknowledging how these new experiences emerge as the result of the performances of bodies cultured to perform perception in some ways rather than others. Furthermore, corporeal literacy is meant to acknowledge the impact of a history of media technologies of various kinds on how our bodies perceive and make sense. Literacy, according to the *Oxford English Dictionary*, is the quality or state of being literate. This condition is mostly associated with language and books, but need not be necessarily. Literacy is also used to describe skills and understanding of other media, as in *visual literacy*, in which literacy denotes the capacity to engage with visual media in an informed manner. Similarly, *media literacy* pertains to a sophisticated understanding of communications media such as film, television and the Internet. Literacy thus understood denotes the capacity to engage in a well-informed manner with modes of communicating information specific to media other than written or printed language. Such expansions of the notion of literacy acknowledge the growing importance of communication through means other than the written or printed word, and promote an expansion of our understanding of literacy to include communication through other means as well. The prefix 'visual' or 'media' describes new objects or aspects of objects or practices of reading that may produce new types of literacy.

Corporeal literacy involves a slightly different approach to rethinking literacy. Unlike the 'visual' in visual literacy or 'media' in media literacy, the 'corporeal' in corporeal literacy does not denote a class of objects or an aspect of the object of reading. Rather, corporeal herein refers to aspects of the cultural condition or "mind-set" (Ong 2002) called literacy. In his seminal *Orality and Literacy*, Ong points out that the technology of writing alters ways of understanding and thinking (including how we think about language) and, ultimately, changes consciousness itself. Important to the constitution of the mind-set of literacy is the way in which writing turns language from an aural transitory phenomenon into a visual spatial one, and how this gives rise to new modes of organizing information as well as to the availability of information over time. No longer depending on oral transmission, language is disconnected from a speaker. Turned into a visually accessible phenomenon, written or printed language mediates in new spatial organisations of processes of thinking and imagining. Literacy, thus understood, more than describing the capacity to read and write, denotes culturally-specific synaesthetic modes of information processing brought about by culturally specific practices of noting down, storing and transmitting information. These practices, therefore, beyond simply providing useful tools, profoundly influence how we think and understand.

Corporeal literacy points to the bodily character of these perceptual, cognitive practices and draws attention to the relationship between bodily practices and modes of thinking commonly associated with the mind. Literacy inscribes these practices in history and culture, linking them to a history of bodies being cultured through interaction with written and printed language. Corporeal literacy thus builds on Ong's insights, while, at the same time, corporeal literacy is meant to argue for a step beyond the rather problematic binary opposition of mind/culture versus body/nature underlying Ong's account. Ong suggests that writing and print caused profound changes to a more primordial oral mind. His prediction that new modes of communication made possible by new media developments will give rise to what he terms a condition of "secondary orality" reinforces the suggestion that literacy is, in the end, to be understood as the condition of being disconnected from orality as a more primordial, embodied state of being. This condition, furthermore, is about to be challenged by communication technologies which, by allowing for embodied interaction, will undo the condition of disembodiment associated with the subject of writing and print culture. Corporeal literacy acknowledges these developments and their importance, not as a return to nature, however, but rather as the next step in a continuous co-evolution of humans and technology. Helpful here is Brian Rotman's assertion:

> The medium of alphabetic writing introduced as silent collateral machinic effects an entire neurological apparatus enabling practices, routines, patterns of movement and gestures, and kinematic, dynamic and perceptual practices as part of the background conditions – in terms of Deleuze and Guattari, the a-signifying dimensions of the medium lying beneath the medium's radar as part of its unconscious – giving rise to the lettered self, a privately enclosed, inward and interiorized mind, structured by the linear protocols and cognitive processing that reading and writing demand (Rotman 2008, xxvi).

Like Ong, Rotman acknowledges the profound impact of the technology of writing and print on how we think and imagine, and like Ong he observes that these technologies gave rise to a new kind of self ("the lettered self") that he describes as a privately enclosed, inward and interiorised mind, structured by the linear protocols and cognitive processing that reading and writing demand. However instead of opposing this lettered self to a more natural, authentic and embodied condition of orality, Rotman – following Clark's assertion that human beings are "naturally born cyborgs" – argues that "the 'human' has from the beginning of the species been a three way hybrid, a bio-cultural-technological amalgam: the 'human mind' – its subjectivities, affects, agency, and forms of consciousness – having been put into form by a succession of physical and cognitive technologies at its disposal" (Rotman 2008, 1). There is no such thing as a natural or original state of mind. From the very beginning, what emerges as 'mind' is the effect of interaction of human bodies with the outside. Subjectivity emerges from this interaction and a variety of technologies, from the very first stone axe to parallel computing, mediate in how this interaction takes shape.

The Alphabetic Body

Rotman introduces the notion of the "alphabetic body" to describe the body cultured by practices of writing and print. The alphabetic body is a literate body which has acquired the skills necessary to read and write, and to engage with written and printed language in a conscious and critical manner. The alphabetic body is the body that does the reading and writing of language. It is also the body that perceives its surroundings, thinks and makes sense in ways that are profoundly impacted by writing and print. Alphabetic writing like all technological systems and apparatuses, operates according to what might be called a corporeal principle. It engages directly and inescapably with the bodies of its users. It makes demands and has corporeal effects. As a necessary condition of its operations it produces a certain specific body. The alphabetic body points to the intimate intertwining of bodily practices of perception and cognition and the technologies of writing and print, and how this intertwining not only impacts the perception of written language but also how we perceive and make sense of other things. This does not mean that these bodily practices necessarily happen at the level of our conscious awareness.

> Communicational media and semiotic apparatuses never coincide with their intended social uses or cultural purposes or their defined instrumentality or the effects sought and attributed to their manifest contents. Always something more is at work, a corporeal effect – a facilitation, an affordance, a restriction, a demand played out on the body – which derives from the uneliminable materiality and physicality of the mediological act itself, and which is necessarily invisible to the user engaged in the act of mediation (Rotman 2008, 6).

New Modes of Embodied Interaction in Digital Culture

Theatre, dance and performance as staged versions of such mediological acts allow for a critical experimentation with the corporeal dimensions of these acts. ("Mediology" is a term introduced by Régis Debray to reframe the study of media in a manner in which not only the content but also the form of media practices is essential to an understanding of media objects.) The intermedial character of theatre and performance make it possible to intervene in synaesthetic processes of perception and to bring to conscious awareness the facilitations, affordances, restrictions, and demands played out on the body. Here one might think of synaesthetic habits such as the ways in which what is perceived as visual or auditory is actually the product of a combination of sensory input, patterns of preference in how perceptual input gets combined, but also the role played by movement and gesture in the performance of perception, a role that tends to get obscured by the alphabet's reductive relation to the corporeal dimension of utterance. Alphabetic writing supports an understanding of the mind or self as disconnected from the body as well as of meaning as separate from embodied materiality. Crucial to this disconnection, according to Rotman, is not only the shift from the aural to the visual observed by Ong but also how the alphabet eliminates the body's inner and outer gestures which extend over speech segments beyond individual words. The alphabet is a means of noting down the sounds produced by the bodily organs of speech. The visual form of the letters used to do so have no relation to the body or to how the sounds of speech are received by those hearing them. As a result, what gets lost is:

> both those visually observable movements that accompany and punctuate speech (which it was never its function to inscribe) and, more to the point, those inside speech, the gestures which constitute the voice itself – the tone, the rhythm, the variation of emphasis, the loudness, the changes of pitch, the mode of attack, discontinuities, repetitions, gaps, elisions, and the never absent play and musicality of utterance that make human song possible. In short, the alphabet omits all the prosody of utterance and with it the multitude of bodily effects of force, significance, emotion, and affect that it conveys (Rotman 2008, 3).

This ignored gestural quality gains new importance now that contemporary body/machine interfaces increasingly include haptic and tactile modalities. Mark Hansen (2006) observes that, with the convergence of physical and virtual spaces informing today's corporate and entertainment environments, researchers and artists have come to recognize that motor activity – not representational verisimilitude – holds the key to fluid and functional crossings between virtual and physical realms. These new developments allow for new modes of embodied interaction between body and machine, highlighting in the process aspects of the performance of perception that remain unnoticed in more conventional means of communicating. Making possible alternative modes of handling information and knowledge, of navigating through information by means of gesture, new information technologies require us to become more corporeally literate in the sense of becoming more consciously aware of corporeal dimensions of the way in which we read and process information.

experiencer intimacy
connectivity   deterritorialisation
intertextuality
interactivity transparency ▪ glocalisation immersion
recursion
displacement
feedback
loop
experience
telematic
hybridity
materiality embodiment virtuality
presence separation

Node: Modes of Experience

Experiencer. In the context of contemporary arts and media, experiencer serves where audience or even "spect-actor" (Boal) prove inadequate. It suggests a more immersive engagement in which the principles of composition of the piece create an environment designed to elicit a broadly visceral, sensual encounter, as distinct from conventional theatrical, concert or art gallery architectures which are constructed to draw primarily upon one of the sense organs – eyes (spectator) or ears (audience). In her interactive virtual reality installation, *Osmose* (1994-1996), for example, Char Davies dubbed her audience "immersants". Though it might not directly involve touch, smell or taste in addition to sight and hearing, work which engages an experiencer draws upon Merleau-Ponty's (1962) insight that the body is a medium for perception of the world, and Deleuze & Guattari's (1980) notion of "haptic space", which denies opposition between the senses. (Robin Nelson)

Embodiment. We *have* a body; we *are* a body. The mere fact that we can use both propositions to articulate the process of embodiment demonstrates a key issue in the field of digital performance. The statement implies that we can easily discern between a body and its embodiment. On a theoretical level, however, these (Platonic) dialectics could easily trick us into believing that there exists a kind of division between material reality as a 'live' condition and the simulation principle of digital technologies. Postmodern perspectives that viewed the world either under the sign of its uncanny double (Freud), as a simulacrum (Baudrillard), or as a hyperreal copy with a complex and problematic relation to the original were popular in both the academic and artistic contexts during the 1980s and the 1990s. Today, such discussions are further complicated by notions of *disembodiment* – a separation of mind and body, closely link to virtuality (→ TERM) and telepresence (→ TERM) – and the rise of studies of embodiment among non-human forms, including robots and avatars (→ PORTAL: POSTHUMANISM).

To understand our digital era as a dialectic between the virtual and the real would slightly miss the point. We no longer find ourselves dealing with the real/virtual, embodied/disembodied dichotomy. To paraphrase Deleuze's "postscript on the societies of control": man is no longer enclosed in communicating spaces. The individual at the beginning of the 21st century is instead perpetually undulatory – in orbit – through a continuous network of embodied states of presence that are increasingly defined according to participation and agency, rather than physical co-present. The implication for digital performance is that the embodied self is extended, hybridised and delimited through technologies. Stelarc, for example, actively performs Marshall McLuhan's famous chiasmic reversal of media as a prosthetic extension of man. Other interactions include motion capture, such as the choreographies of Merce Cunningham, or artificial intelligence, such as the computer-generated head Jeremiah, an embodied avatar developed from surveillance technology (Broadhurst, 2007). (Kurt Vanhoutte)

Intimacy. Across diverse psychological perspectives, intimacy is repeatedly attributed three basic operations: "self-revealing behavior, positive involvement with the other, and shared understandings" (Prager and Roberts 1995, 45). Karen J. Prager further differentiates between "intimate interactions" and "intimate relationships", which "each refer to a different and clearly distinguishable notion of *space* and *time*" (Prager 2004, 19). Taking Prager's categories as a point of departure, it is possible to understand Intermedia as a space where intimate *relationships* – as defined by continuity, consistency, duration, and communicative clarity and confidence – are practically impossible. Conversely, however, in the intermedial space, with its insistence on momentary intensity and complete attention, intimate *interaction* is unavoidable. Within the intermedial space the informed spectator anticipates the heightened self-disclosure of increased visibility, engagement, perhaps even interactivity. Intermedial intimacy is, thus, not generated through the *portrayal* of shared cultural attitudes and beliefs (a relationship that reinforces 'timeless' and 'universal' values), but rather through the *performance* of shared perceptual frames and dynamics (interaction that posits ambiguity and de/reorientation as the constants of contemporary existence). (Bruce Barton)

Presence. In the simplest sense, presence within live performance describes the temporal and spatial proximity between performer and audience, a condition also defined as *co-presence* (Lehmann 2006, 141-142). This definition has been most prominent in the field of phenomenology, which defines presence via the body as in Edmund Husserl's "lived body" [*Leib*], and Maurice Merleau-Ponty's notion of perception "through the body" (1974, 138-139). Stanton Garner applies these concepts to theatre as the "lived bodiliness" of audience and performers in a shared space and time (Garner 1994, 27-28), and Phillip Zarilli points to the *aesthetic body* as a uniquely theatrical presence derived from performers' training (Zarilli 2004).

Digital media complicate such presumptions of live presence. Screen media such as film and television (to which we may now add newer technologies such as dvd, smartphone, and netbook) construct a liveness and media presence beyond physical proximity, as in Philip Auslander's example, the immediacy of live television (Auslander 1999). In this sense, presence is defined not by spatial but by temporal proximity, known as *telepresence*. This, in turn, is distinguished from *virtual presence* – the sense of the self in a simulated environment – by the social exchange between participants, closely akin to telematics (→ TERM). In the context of networking (→ PORTAL: NETWORKING) and social media, presence is increasingly defined by participation, rather than by shared physical or even temporal space. Notions of presence, then, exist increasingly as transitional spaces between the live and the digital more than as an absolute ontological condition. (Russell Fewster)

Immersion. Derived from the Latin *immergere*, meaning to plunge or dip into, immersion in digital culture refers to the sensory experience/perception of being submerged (being present) in an electronically mediated environment. The history of immersive theatre can be traced back to avant-garde experiments like expanded cinema (Youngblood, 1970) and, in performing arts, to Artaud's 'total' theatre and Richard Schechner's environmental theatre. Distinct from the two-dimensional linear perspective of the viewer looking at an image in drawing, painting, and photography, the immersive perspective enables the viewer to see from within the image. Later developments in digital technologies enabled intermedial productions to put the spectator at the centre of the dramatic event as, for example, in Sharir and Gromala's *Dancing with the Virtual Dervish: Virtual Bodies* (1994), which created an advanced sense of fully embodied immersion (cf. Dixon 2007). The experiencer (← TERM), or immersant (Davies, 1994), embodies the narrative environment by controlling both an individual viewing position in relation to the image and the dimensions of the image itself. For this reason, immersion in digital culture is also inherently interactive and performative (← PORTAL: PERFORMATIVITY AND CORPOREAL LITERACY). In the performances of CREW (→ INSTANCE: CREW), omnidirectional video is integrated to create a similar effect. By mingling pre-recorded with real-time filmed images, the user explores a transitional world between different levels of reality. (Kurt Vanhoutte & Nele Wynants)

Instances

Instance: Performing an Avatar: Second Life Onstage

Kaisu Koski

This instance discusses an example of theatre as a hypermedium (← INTRO-DUCTION) in respect of the online, virtual world of Second Life (SL) as an element of an actual onstage performance but, reciprocally, considers the virtual platform of SL as a stage for a live theatre event. It concerns the juxtaposition of the virtual (→ TERM: VIRTUALITY) with the actual and the interrelationship between the performers and their computer-generated characters, the avatars. These themes are discussed through the performance *Aki Anne II*; a second part of an art-research project by Marloeke van der Vlugt. The performance, presented during 2007 in Amsterdam, is inspired by Martin Crimp's text *Attempts on her life* (1997). It appears as a series of monologues spoken from different points of view, aiming to define an elusive character Anne. The character is produced through the collaboration of performers and avatars. The performance is formed according to the structure of Crimp's text, proceeding with 'attempts' at different scenes. The script combines quotations from Crimp, the discussions that have occurred in SL, and material improvised during the rehearsal process.

Transparency (→ TERM) of the means of construction is one of the core principles of the performance: the text appears within a game-like structure influenced by digital gaming, in which the making process is discussed by the performers while they proceed in game levels. The performers' presence (← TERM) provides a self-reflective layer of the performance: the four performers ask each other, for instance, "*have we started yet?*" Furthermore, none of the technology or its function is hidden in any way, indeed the performers' struggle with the interfaces is foregrounded. The stage is fragmented with a central semi-transparent screen, onto which SL is projected, two interactive mats on both sides of the screen, and a row of three computer work stations next to it. The fundament of the performance lies in the interaction between the world onstage and the world onscreen, and the dispersed identities the two-world situation evokes. As a performer in this piece I discuss here, from an insider perspective, the qualities of the performer-avatar relationship, and how the experience of agency is manifested in an actual-virtual performance situation.

Controlling an Avatar through an Interface

The performer-avatar relationship is characterised by the experience of agency: a performer controls the avatar's actions, which, in turn, is a representative of the performer in the virtual world. The performer's command thus always precedes an avatar's action, or, alternatively, a performer's action precedes the avatar's re-action. The ways of commanding differs according to the avatar's activity: in order to trigger a gesture, for instance, the performer needs to press a key once, whereas to enable an avatar's continuous navigation the performer needs to manipulate several keys simultaneously and continuously. In any case, in Aki Anne II the performer controlling an avatar is necessarily connected with an interface, either to a mouse and keyboard or an interactive floor mat. The interfaces here appear as 'mouse holes', physical stations through which the performers access the virtual world. Whereas a keyboard and monitor tie the performer to a space at the table, the floor mat enables an upright position and the controlling can take place using all four limbs. The action-reaction chain is neither immediate nor flawless; the sensitivity of the interactive mat seems arbitrary, and it often takes several attempts before an avatar proceeds without getting stuck or collapsing into virtual objects.

Due to the usage of the interfaces, the stage actions of Aki Anne II are characterised by discontinuity. The performers proceed through distinguished commands, and shift between being on and off the virtual world. When operating as an agent-avatar duo, the performers often create an abstraction of the avatar's action with their bodies. For instance, when setting an avatar to fly, a performer spreads her arms and bends forward behind a transparent screen, remaining in this pose behind a moving landscape of SL. However, while the performer's action is in a technical sense preceding the avatar's reaction, the linearity of the performance relationship can be manipulated. Instead of reacting to a performer's actions, an avatar can, for instance, be introduced as a counter-actor, controlled by (another) performer. Thus, besides commanding the avatar from outside, the direction of the performer-avatar communication can be from 'inside out': the avatar's actions can cause reactions in a performer. In essence, there are thus two main ways to present the relationship: the one-way agent-avatar relationship, where these form a unit, and two-way interaction between a performer and an avatar in which an avatar is seen as a character in its own right.

The performer controlling an avatar is also controlling the view the audience has on the virtual world. In fact, the audience of Aki Anne II witnesses the making of a 3D-sequence in real time. One of the performers functions as a camera operator who frames the imagery in real time, either showing the world through the avatar's eyes or the world and the avatar within it from a third-person perspective. The performer prepares the angle from which the given situation is seen, the size of the image and the camera movement. These rough cuts of real-time images form the core of Aki Anne II, as here-and-now activity that reflects the paralleling

Fig. 1: *Gazes of a performer and audience meet on the central semi-transparent screen*

cinema-like immersion (← TERM: IMMERSION), jerky game play and theatrical intimacy (← TERM: INTIMACY).

Avatar's Performance

Gestures and text are the two main ways by which an avatar communicates. As a starting point an avatar is an empty shell, which can be charged with different gestures. Some of these gestures include vocal expressions, from casual greetings to odd disjoined sentences. These 'emotions' of an avatar appear and disappear unnaturally fast: any expression of anger, empathy or joy arises from a monotonic face in an instant, without build-up. An avatar has its neutral state from which the emotional-physical bursts arise. An avatar's body appears thus as a landscape for sequential drama, which restores its equilibrium when the command has been executed. This neutral state is not, however, inanimate, but it consists rather of subtle ongoing vividness, including blinking eyes and changes in a pose.

The avatar's neutrality is not unrelated to the performers' way of being present. In fact, as in so-called postdramatic theatre (see Lehmann 2006, 135), the actor is rather offering her presence than depicting a character. Often this presence appears as a casual, unemotional state. In *Aki Anne II* one can actually witness a gliding spectrum between a performer being present and absent: by intensively operating an avatar, a performer is also reminiscent of an empty shell. Since all her focus is directed to, and channelled through, the avatar's virtual body, her own body becomes a mechanical and idle object that communicates a little with the audience. On the one hand it could be seen that an avatar here is thus employed as a new surface for a performer's expression. Whereas an actor conventionally aims to merge a character and her everyday self/body in one unit, a performer in *Aki Anne II* employs an avatar as a projection of a character. On the other hand both the performer and the avatar participate in creating a character, the making process of which becomes an integral part. Character, in fact, appears as a *process* and collection of both physical and virtual components, which, in turn, can shift in different roles in relation to each other.

Fig. 2: The stage of Aki Anne II *is layered with semi-transparent screens, interactive mats and computer work stations*

Constructing an Avatar

Aki Anne II depicts the connections between a particular performer and avatar by creating a visual similarity between them: an avatar wears the same colour of clothing as the performer controlling it. The four onstage performers create different relationships with the same character, Anne. These relationships are expressed in the opening scene, where the performers introduce themselves to the audience: "Hi, my name is Silke, I perform Anne's body". Furthermore, this relationship is established by certain rules: Anne never moves unless the performer moves on top of the mat. The performer is influenced eventually by maintaining

MAPPING INTERMEDIALITY IN PERFORMANCE

the avatar's activity: she is out of breath, embodying thereby physical reactions that an avatar can neither experience nor express (← TERM: EMBODIMENT).

The performer who represents Anne's mind creates her voice as well: "Hi, my name is Esther Aki Anne". The performer talks thus both as herself and as her avatar, in first person: "My name is Anne. I was born the 5th of July 2006". In fact, live voice is a strong means by which to create continuity between an avatar and a performer: sound does not require a spectator's visual attention, but enables her to be immersed in a screen world instead. The performer thus projects her voice and emotions onto the avatar while remaining neutral in her own presence. Furthermore, the identification with an avatar is reduced by sharing the control mechanism between two performers: the first performer moves it by using the mat, and the second one controls the rest of the avatar's actions, including the view to SL. In this regard the character of Anne cannot be separated from either of the two performers or from the avatar: all three bodies participate in creating one character.

The third performer does not have an avatar, but she appears as a storyteller/ mother figure of Anne instead. "Hi, my name is Rosa, I'll try to put her story together". She is the only performer truly acting by manipulating her voice radically, and shifting between the characters of storyteller and mother. This creates a situation in which not only the virtual world consists of artificial creatures, but the monologue of Anne's mother is also characterised by artificiality. Her lines build Anne's character by illustrating her background and personality: "The whole of past is there in her face. [...] She now lives, works, sleeps, kills and eats entirely on her own". The performer has no control over the avatar, and operates onstage only. Thematically these positions illustrate a gap between a mother and her teenage daughter: mother talks from 'behind Anne's room door' and can never access her world.

The fourth performer appears as her everyday self, in other words offers her presence as such onstage, and is simulated visually by her avatar. "Hi, my name is Kaisu". This performer-avatar duo offers a counterpart for the storyline by commenting on it from outside, and playing the game in SL against Anne. While the game-level scenes proceed through highly choreographed sequences, reconstructions of actual events that have occurred in SL as well as improvisational encounters, the last scene eventually reveals the winner of the game. The scene takes place in an orgy room, where along with two avatars of Aki Anne II, the other SL inhabitants practice sex simultaneously with each other. The activity in this room thus depicts tragicomically both the search for, and incapability of, intimacy that characterizes Aki Anne II. The scene also introduces a fundamental question in relation to an avatar concerning how far the identification with it goes, and whether the experience can have psycho-physiological consequences for the agent behind a computer. The fourth performer of Aki Anne II, in fact, refuses to employ her avatar in sex acts: she exits the stage and leaves her avatar in the orgy room. The other performers select one spectator, who is invited to step on to the interactive mat to employ the abandoned avatar for sex. Even though the avatar's appearance is modified to match the spectator, the swap brings the avatar forward as a helpless object, which waits neatly on the side of the orgy site until it is appointed to participate. Seen from the other point of view, however, the intercourse here appears as the ultimate initiation into the virtual world: by having sex with other avatars Anne claims her status as a virtual being that belongs fully to SL instead of on a mere game level.

The employment of an avatar as a projection surface for the performer's emotions and imagination functions as an extension of a performer. The experience and expression become separated (→ TERM: SEPERATION): the experience belongs to the domain of performers, and an avatar can only display the expression. However, the borders of a performer shift according to the position in which the avatar appears. An avatar can, for instance, be presented as a counter performer: a character in its own right. While concepts such as presence, embodiment and emotion remain awkward in relation to an avatar, being a character seems to be possible in this context. It is a combination of a permanent name and status in a virtual world, equipped with ever-changing form and possibilities to enrich its performance repertoire.

Whereas in conventional theatre an actor allows the character to be either present or absent through her own body, the character disappearing when the play is over, an avatar as a character remains visible even when the performer stops identifying with it or operating it with an interface. This makes an avatar more vulnerable than a mental concept of a character: only by logging out of the virtual world does a performer make her avatar untouchable for other SL characters. As a result, the performer-avatar relationship swaps between identification with each other and parental caretaking: while a performer identified with her avatar can actually experience physical reactions corresponding to the avatar's situation, as a parent of a 'designer character' a performer needs to protect the avatar. Moreover, while an old-fashioned theatre stage allows actors to work in a relatively protected environment, employing the public sphere of SL as a stage involves similar risks of interference and vandalism as a street theatre performance. The element of risk, whether manifesting in the dependency on the network connection or the presence of other SL inhabitants, seems, however, essential for *Aki Anne II*. The avatar's vulnerability juxtaposed with the arbitrary control the performers possess both alternates the distance between the two worlds and reinforces the emergent quality of the piece.

The relationship between the performer and avatar is not merely a straightforward agent-avatar relationship as in gaming, but the presence of the audience sets the performers in-between the different worlds. When the performer's attention is directed inwards, towards the virtual world, manifested on a screen in central position, SL becomes a membrane through which a performer and a spectator connect. Their gazes meet on a screen, where 'theatre within theatre' rests.

MAPPING INTERMEDIALITY IN PERFORMANCE

The aim in *Aki Anne II* is thus not to pretend that performers are in SL themselves: the controlling position and total visibility onstage remind one of the fact that drama happens elsewhere. This might also mean that life happens elsewhere, since the performers' presence is mostly targeted on controlling the life of avatars. Unlike in puppetry, for instance, the virtual life is strangely real, and goes on after the curtain has dropped. When communicating directly to the audience, the performers acknowledge their fundamental similarity with the audience: their corporeal bodies remain always outsiders from the avatars' eternity. Thus *Aki Anne II* poses questions about possible shifts between human and posthuman (→ PORTAL: POSTHUMANISM) paradigms in a play between actual and virtual modes of performance.

Instance: Intermediality in VJing: Two VJ Sets by Gerald van der Kaap (alias VJ oo-Kaap)

Marina Turco

The Intermedial Effect in Theatre and Performance

This instance explores the intermedial effect within a particular kind of performance, VJing, which generates immersive (← TERM: IMMERSION), synaesthetic spaces and defines clubbing as a liminal, transitional experience through which cultural and social identities are created. Thus the emphasis placed (following Boenisch 2006) is less on the composition of the cultural product itself, the cross-over between two or more media, and more on the moment in the communication process when the transition from one medium into another or a new combination of media causes ambiguity, or uncertainty, in the engagement process. The intermedial effect arises from texts, or cultural forms, which programmatically aim at producing dislocations in the balance between the virtuality (→ TERM: VIRTUALITY) of the sign systems, the stability of representational codes and perception patterns, and the phenomenological, material (→ TERM: MATERIALITY) dimension of the communicative act. It may also emerge when an established text is perceived and interpreted in a new social or historical context. The unstable condition, which begets a feeling of dislocation, can be exploited for various cultural goals. The intermedial effect may contribute to the creation of new aesthetic/ideological paradigms (redefining the boundaries between virtual and real, abstract and figurative), or even beget new psychological and social dynamics.

VJing, the act of mixing video clips live during a dance music party, is an interesting instance of intermedial performance. Club visuals are programmatically intermedial, and intermediality in VJing fulfils a specific social and cultural role. At the textual level, it emerges from the interplay between video, music and dancing bodies, redefining the relationships between spectators, performers and representations; at the contextual level, it corresponds to the interplay between identity and identifications – between every-day social identities and temporary sub-cultural identifications – typical of club culture.

Scriabin's *The Poem of Ecstasy* at Club Now & Wow. Rotterdam, 20 September 2002

(Rotterdam Young Philharmonic conducted by Valery Gergiev – Artistic direction Gerald van der Kaap).

On the ground floor of the huge industrial building, dozens of TV sets are placed against the walls and stacked up into high scaffolds. Two large projection screens hang in the middle of the space, one behind the VJ booth, and the other on the opposite side of the room, behind the podium where the orchestra is about to play. Two sexy girls in baroque outfits swing on the two sides of the VJ booth. Soul music fills the space.

For this unusual project, Van der Kaap created a mix between the traditional theatrical setting of classic music concerts and the more carnivalesque mise-en-scène of a disco party. People who came to listen to the concert walk around, disoriented, looking for the right place from which to watch the performance. The atmosphere is suspended: nobody knows exactly what to expect. From the screens, thunder and lightning announce the beginning of the concert. The public stands all around the podium.

Alexander Scriabin's work is an important source of inspiration for VJs all around the world. The Russian composer designed a system of associations between musical keys and colours, and built a 'colour organ', which could be played like a piano, but instead of emitting sounds, it would project coloured light on a screen. The party at Now & Wow is a tribute to this forerunner of the VJ art. oo-Kaap plays the visuals, loosely following Scriabin's prescriptions on notes-colours correspondences. The screens show pictures of a sheet music and changing geometric forms, fading into each other smoothly. The musicians' image is captured by a video camera and transmitted in real time to the video performer's laptop. By means of mixing software, the VJ adds effects to the pictures, layering it until the musicians are reduced to pink-orange silhouettes. The live footage is interpolated by samples from a black-and-white movie featuring a figure-skating piece. The silhouettes seem to match the skaters' bodies too. The same clips are repeated over and over again. But they are never exactly the same. After less than one hour the performance has ended. The orchestra scatters through the crowd. Dance music starts. Post-colourised samples of old movies are mixed by the VJ at the music beat. The rhythm speeds up gradually. The podium is now occupied by half-nude walk-ons in 18th-century clothes. The elder public gradually leaves, while the dance party takes off, coloured by this unusual, romantic introduction.

Rauw at the Melkweg. Amsterdam, 10 October 2008

The party called *Rauw* (recordings at http://www.youtube.com/user/Brigittolina) takes place in the Max zaal, a rectangular room with a stage for the DJ and the VJ at the bottom end and a balcony all around the walls. Two projection screens (about three by four meters) hang behind the DJ booth. DJ Joost van Bellen opens the evening with an eclectic set (rock, punk and electro tunes). The desktop of Van der Kaap's laptop is projected on the screens. It shows little windows moving around within the frame of an Internet browser. Randomly assembled pictures (people, landscapes, texts) pop up and change place from time to time, like a moving collage. Pink balloons containing words crop up on top of the collage. As the music beat turns faster, vertical lines break up the collage, growing broader until they fill up the whole screen. Within the lines, a yellow arrow streams from the right to the left. The windows and balloons seem to represent the chaotic, colourful human landscape, while the lines and the arrow visualize the passing of time, the rhythm (the beat) and flow (the melody) created by the music.

Fig. 1: VJ oo-Kaap at Rauw. Amsterdam, 13 March 2009, © Dennis Bouman

Later on, the DJ star Arol Elkan shows up on stage. He builds up layers of drums and riffs. Everybody is looking towards the DJ booth. Van der Kaap sends out a moving collage of Elkan's portraits, flyers of his performances and CD covers. Then the vertical lines and the arrow appear again, visualizing the explosion of the full drum kit. A sample from an Andy Warhol's movie *Blow Job* shows a close-up of a guy. On his face, a half-transparent grid with various images represents his thoughts. The basses are low and metallic. VJ oo-Kaap shoots a sequence of words, following one another very quickly. A strobe stop-gap effect is produced by the video bombing and the strobe lights together. The flashing words are on the Factory-guy's face now. The music is obsessive. Overwhelmed by this sensory overload, the dancers let themselves go with the flow. Eventually, they reach a state of ecstasy, merging with the crowd, as if they have become particles of a single body. No other sensual 'stimuli' are needed except the beat and the darkness.

MAPPING INTERMEDIALITY IN PERFORMANCE

Fig. 2: oo-Kaap's VJ set at Rauw. Amsterdam, 13 March 2009, © Dennis Bouman

These two examples provide a glimpse into the diversity of intermedial strategies in VJ performances. The interplay between the several media which play a role in the party, and the different ways in which the participants engage with them, do not follow pre-established rules. The VJ adjusts his performance to the atmosphere, the attitude of the crowd, the music, and the general concept of the party. In choosing specific screen settings and images, he collaborates with the other participants in the creation of an intermedial experience.

Sign Systems and the Intermedial

Video images from movies, the Internet, television, and graphic design trigger different interpretation patterns. Narratives and meanings in a dance party emerge from the interplay between music, video, décor, behaviour, dance and dress styles, between the different sign systems and the kind of engagement that the different media imply. The 'Net collage' at *Rauw*, for instance, is an actual search action on the Internet, a representation of the associative and multidirectional searching paths one can follow on the Web, and a metaphor of the micronarratives and social encounters, which are happening on the dance floor at that very moment. The collage also fits a specific time, the beginning of the party, when the atmosphere is not defined yet, and the music is eclectic and tune-based (not yet track-based).

Later on, the cinematic metaphor replaces the Internet. Film can 'represent' time (it compresses, fast forwards or delays time according to cultural conventions in the function of a narrative), but it can also mediate the perception of time: Warhol's films explore the boundary between objective and perceived duration, through the mediation of film recordings. The Factory-guy sequence at *Rauw* mirrors the trespassing of these boundaries by the clubbers. At this time of the night, clubbers are losing their perception of conventional time. They experience the objective duration, marked by the beat and the crescendos of the music; at the same time, they are entering an interior time zone where the sense of duration is subjective and not quite measurable.

At this point of the night, the video does not represent anylonger, it just shows colours, lights and shapes, reacting to the music beat. The clubbers are no longer spectators but experiencers (← TERM: EXPERIENCER): their entire bodies are turned into perceiving mediums. Synaesthetic processes blur the edges between technological media and the medium-body; synaesthetic relationships between the body senses and the brain produce a feedback loop (→ TERM: FEEDBACK LOOP) of sensations and interpretative patterns.

The Intermediality of Performers and Art Forms

During Scriabin's play, the orchestra is presented on the podium and represented in the video. The video emphasizes the performing activity and the physical presence of the players. At the same time, the body becomes an object to look at, leading the attention away from the real performers. The video image is both a site where the body is experienced, and a medium that represents the body, and abstracts it from its phenomenological reality. The body becomes a symbol that is charged with new denotations and connotations, and generates new associative threads (the players become skaters).

The performers' position and presence, on the other side, redefine the mediality of the video projections. The video functions as a moving décor within which the participants perform their own show (the orchestra plays within an abstract landscape made of colours and geometric forms; the walk-ons within a baroque and sensual décor). The shift across three kinds of hypermedial strategies, generates intermediality:

1. the physical presence of the performers emphasizes, by contrast, the virtuality of the projected images;
2. the materiality of the performers makes the materiality of the video technology relevant (underlining the three-dimensional, sculptural qualities of the screens, projectors, TVs, etc.);
3. the 'virtuality' of the performers' images on the screen, eventually transforms the presence (← TERM: PRESENCE) of the performers (and thus the relevance of their role as producers and participants) into representations of their activity as performers.

Performers and Experiencers

VJing did not arise directly from the visual or performing arts, where the roles of performers and spectators are defined by established cultural conventions or by a programmatic aesthetic statement. VJing arose from a cultural and social imperative of house parties:

> The religious aspects of these 'parties' comprised a leader and followers, and the visual 'presence' of a single DJ alone on a stage could not fulfill that need. The use of multiple screens (...) replaced the lost power of a leader by putting emphasis on a 'total spectacle' (Faulkner 2006, 14).

This co-presence of spectators and performers within the spectacle allows the participants to switch roles and produces interplay between performers and spectators. Even if some performers may play the leading roles – in a dance party it is usually the DJ who has a prominent position and can guide other people's performances in terms of narratives and emotional responses – all participants are allowed to play, with their bodies or through other media. Audience members take clues from each other and collectively decide how to respond to things. A performer can also work from behind the audience or in a projectionist booth, in which case the audience is totally focused on the screen and any clues come from the imagery. The cathexis is not on the screen or even primarily on the DJ. Instead, it is diffuse and mobile forming part of the mating ritual. This dynamic could not be achieved in any more sedentary performance (cf. Spinrad 2005, 107).

VJs are often hidden performers. Their bodies are not so much bearers of signs (movements, dance, expressions), as tools for the production of visual texts, together with a specific technological interface. The video imagery, thus, mediates the feedback between performers and spectators. Nevertheless, the presence of the VJ in the same place as the audience is a necessary precondition for the feedback mechanism to happen. At *Rauw*, the VJ gets clues from the crowd's dancing, and the music in order to choose what kind of images to send out, at what speed. During the ecstatic moment the different performers clearly co-operate in the creation of a coral experience: the VJ reacts to the music and amplifies its effect by using the strobe-light trick. When the emotional peak is reached, the differences between spectators and performers almost disappear. The ecstatic moment, though, is only one of the several modes of engagement in a club party. The clubbers may choose to withdraw from their performances and social activities in order to observe the crowd, watch the video and listen to the music in a more passive way. When DJ Elkan appears on stage, for instance, people freeze for a moment, absorbed into the contemplation of their idol; the VJ underpins this kind of spectatorship by presenting a biographical compilation based on Elkan's appearances in the media.

As emerges from these two examples, the art of the VJ consists in experimenting with as many modes of address as possible, alternating them within a single performance, following or inducing the reactions of the crowd, in order to keep producing the intermedial effect.

Performing Club Culture

Intermediality in VJing is the aesthetic counterpart of another kind of dislocation on a social and psychological level. The processes of identity formation, which are a driving force behind youth cultures, require this ambiguous play between reality and representation. As Ben Malbon argues in his book *Clubbing: Dancing, Ecstasy and Vitality*, in the late 20th century, the fragmentation and erosion of collective social identities led to the instability of individual identities as well. A new relationship arose between identity (a more or less stable and homogeneous entity) and identifications. Identification is the process through which identity is constructed and, at the same time, it is a particular kind of temporary or partial identity that is experienced within a group. During the performance of clubbing, clubbers experience a sensation that both confirms and dislocates identity and identification. For clubbers, it is, as Malbon remarks, a "going beyond of individual identities, an experience of being both within, and yet in some ways outside of oneself at once" (Malbon 1999, 49). It involves a continuous play between performing (being) themselves, as in their daily lives, and playing a part, performing a (social) role, specific for that particular context and moment. Exchanging roles and expressing themselves through different languages, the clubbers experience the tension "between an atomistic sense of identity and a sense of (crowd) identification, between the urge for outward expression and the opportunity for inward reflection, between the music as controlling them (the clubbers) and themselves as in control, between isolation and community" (Malbon 1999, 128).

The sociality of a dance event is built on performances. The role of the intermedial effect within these performances is a crucial one. The aesthetic and semiotic liminality produced by intermediality corresponds to the social and psychological identity-shifting of clubbing. On the edge between the immersive space created by the intense intermedia, a realm of fantasy, fun and freedom, and the material, phenomenological space of the club, the clubbers find a way toward the creation of new identities in a distinctive culture.

Instance: *The Lost Babylon* (Adelaide Fringe Festival 2006)

Russell Fewster

By way of an 'insider' approach to the play between live and on-screen presence (← TERM: PRESENCE), this instance focuses on key moments in rehearsal of my production of award-winning Japanese playwright, Takeshi Kawamura's, *The Lost Babylon* (1999).[14] Contemporary live performance of both scripted plays and devised practices, is increasingly influenced by screen cultures. Theatre now regularly incorporates digital media in the form of projection and television screens. As a consequence, theatrical presence is mediated, in part, by the intervention of the digital into the performance space. Theatre practitioners – directors, actors, set and lighting designers – actively deal with the challenges of negotiating the use of the digital within live performance. Indeed, a new role within theatre is emerging, that of the projection designer, and since the screen image is often brighter, larger and more intense than the human figure on stage, some have expressed concern that mediated imagery threatens to undermine the unique *liveness* of performance.[15]

In practice, then, one faces the challenge of sustaining a balance between the live performer's actual presence and her digital presence. As Keith Gallasch and Virginia Baxter remarked in their 2002 overview of multimedia and new media performance works-in-progress, "it's often about getting the mix right, smoothing out the relationship between the 'visceral and the virtual' not losing live presence to the seductions of the screen" (2002, 22). In the context of a broad debate about liveness and mediatisation, however, each production presents its own challenges and practitioners must find appropriate ways to make their work. This instance thus focuses on the relationship between live and virtual presence as encountered in the rehearsal praxis of my production of *The Lost Babylon*.

Negotiating Theatrical and Digital Presence

For the purposes of framing what emerged in the play of the rehearsal process, I divide the idea of presence into three broad categories:

1. 'Classical presence': actual presence as determined by temporal and physical proximity; the performer and the audience are co-present in the same space and time. This marks both a traditional conception of the performer's presence in the theatre and an important, ongoing distinction between live performance and cinema.[16]

2. Virtual (digital) presence: the possibilities of mediatised projections of performers on a range of screens, sometimes in juxtaposition with actual bodies in the space.

3.   Intermedial presence: the inter-twining of classical presence of the live actor and virtual (digital) presence in a new conception of 'both-and' rather than 'either/or'.

Within live performance the bodies of live performers and projections might each be described as mediums or media with an active play between them. Intermediality proposes that in this play between mediums something new arises: a dynamic interface between the live and the digital. The play between presences may emerge in a newly-combined form or, in another formulation, it may open up a cognitive gap which audiences are invited mentally to negotiate as they perceive the interaction between these two mediums. Working with the actual and the virtual needs careful handling in practice, however, since if the performance is not engaging, audiences may find it alienating, uninvolving and unmoving.[17] A challenge for the practitioner, then, is to find an appropriate balance between live bodies and projections between the visceral and the digital, and to produce something which engages, even if it perplexes, audiences. This is the challenge that I faced when directing the recent stage production of the play *The Lost Babylon*.

The Lost Babylon: Remediating the Cinematic through the Theatrical

The Lost Babylon explores the propensity for real and virtual violence to blur and become indistinguishable in contemporary Japanese society. In the play Kawamura draws on real-life incidents in Japan where violent crimes were committed by young people inspired by the violent media of *manga* (comics) and cinema. To dramatise this theme Kawamura introduces within the play a screenwriter who is writing a screenplay which explores themes of media-inspired violence. As the screenwriter writes, her fictional characters appear live and enact her screenplay. In order to construct this transmission of an animated screenplay, I introduced a live camera that would video-capture, and instantaneously project by live feed, the images of the stage performers playing the film characters. Camera operator, Daniel Lawrence, immediately grasped that: "live video was being used to show the movie being created as the screenwriter wrote the screenplay.... the final product of the movie unfolding on the back of the wall".[18]

While the film characters appeared as video projections, however, they simultaneously appeared live on stage. A 'play' was thus created between the performers' live actual presence and their projected virtual presence. This play, or tension, between the live and the virtual was furthered in two ways by the placement of the camera. Firstly, the camera was hidden offstage resulting in a seemingly direct link between the screenwriter and the projected image. As the screenwriter typed, the characters within her screenplay moved on stage and their video-capture appeared instantly behind them, giving a sense of the creation of a live film. Secondly, the positioning of the camera gave alternative views of the performers (varying perspectives from that of the traditional proscenium arch view), resulting in alternative experiences of space. In short, theatrical space was given a cinematic dimension. The use of film language, close-ups for example, further gave a sense of a cinematic remediating of the live by the digital.

The Amplification of the Live by the Digital: Double Presence

The first appearance of one of the screenwriter's characters (known in the play as the ghost of her murdered sister) was enacted by a Japanese performer (Kaori Endo) walking slowly, in a traditional Noh-derived *Kata*, along the back of the stage while the screenwriter worked on her laptop downstage. The Ghost was simultaneously videoed front on, from the wings of the theatre (upstage right), and the large image of her face was projected on the cyclorama. The Ghost entered in darkness but as the stage lights were brought up her face suddenly appeared on the cyclorama approaching the audience. The affect of the scene, a ghostly presence, was enhanced by the actor's videoed face emerging out of the darkness, appearing on the cyclorama and growing in size as she simultaneously walked across the back of the stage. The video served both to amplify the live actor and enhance the presence of the character. Through the use of live feed video, the Ghost appeared as a double presence, actual and virtual, problematising the audience's perception of space, time and medium specifity.

Performer as Camera

Complementing the differing view offered by the live video of the Ghost was the actual stage presence of the actor playing the Ghost in a swivelling chair she occupied after entering. The chairs and tables used in the play were on castors, enabling them to be moved by the actors as required within scenes while also being relatively easy to strike when necessary. In rehearsal the "dynamic of the swirling chair" created an "additional pan for the still camera", as I noted in my rehearsal diary. While the camera remained in a fixed position the actor could turn the chair in a circle on the spot creating the illusion of a cinematic pan in the projection. This movable property of the chair opened up a wide range of angles for the audience to experience as a confusion of the live actor and her video presence. Within the scenes, the audience was sometimes addressed by the actor on stage and sometimes by the character on the movie screen.

Subsequently, I blocked this scene with a large number of turns of the chair to take advantage of the multiplicity of angles now available (see Figure 1). Will Ginley in reviewing the production wrote: "visual projection abounds allowing alternative views of the space"(2006), while Samela Harris commented that "cameras bring different angles on actors" (2006). Space in a cinematic sense was able to be manipulated by the movement possibilities of the live actor and their use of a flexible set piece. As the camera was static it was the movement of the actor that determined the digital image that appeared projected on the cyclorama. The actors in a sense became the camera as, assisted by the director, they decided what view of themselves would be seen live and what view would be seen digitally.

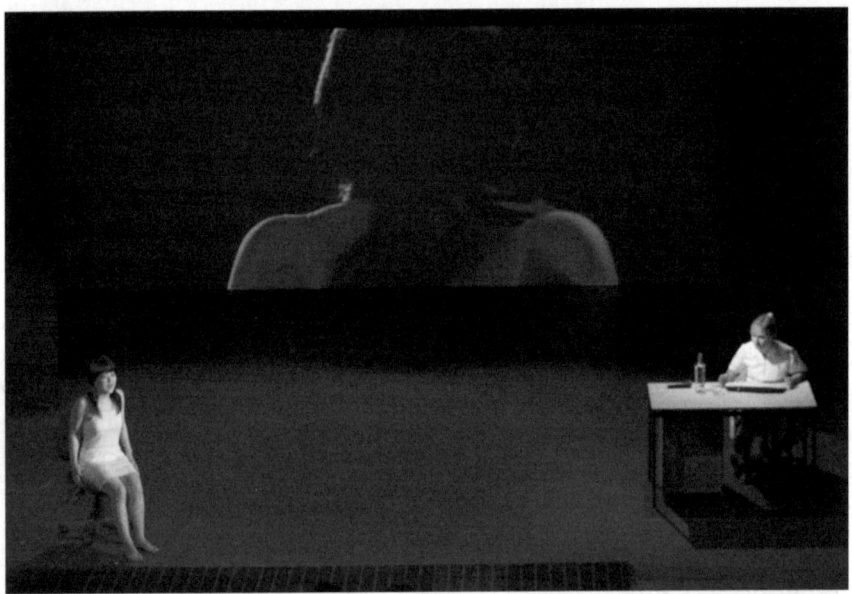

Fig. 1: The Lost Babylon III.1.Kaori Endo (Ghost) while talking to the Screenwriter (Cheryl Bradley), turns her chair downstage away from the camera to draw attention to her live presence, © Nic Mollison

Extending the Play's Resonances

The use of live video also served to reinforce one of the central themes of play, the thin line between virtual and real violence. For example in another scene in the play the screenwriter introduces two new characters, one a schoolboy murderer (based on a real-life figure who had killed some of his classmates as a 'game'[19]) and a psychologist who encourages him to act out his crime, in order to gain a sense of catharsis.[20] Chrissie Page who played the Psychologist similarly discovered that shifting the focus of the camera with the swivelling chair could shift the audience's focus by "manipulating the action on the screen" (2006). Early in this scene the Psychologist says to the Boy:

(Pointing in front of her) Do you see them? There. Moving. Real people. You can go ahead and shoot them (Kawamura 1999, 37).

The stage directions provocatively suggest that the Boy shoot into the audience and the staging of this scene underlined this sense of menace or threat. The Psychologist first swung the chair with the Boy sitting in it to the offstage camera (now hidden in the wings upstage left), so that the initial projected image was of her pointing to the audience, imploring the Boy to shoot them. She then slowly turned the chair towards the audience shifting the audience's focus from the screen to the Boy as he directly confronted the audience. The actor's switch from camera to front-on audience contact reflected the playwright's theme of the virtual reality/reality interface and reinforced the provocative nature of the text (see Figure 2). The audience were first confronted with the projected image of the Psychologist and Boy looking towards them, which changed to the Boy actually pointing his weapon (a full size replica of a military automatic rifle) at them. What had been a digital reality became a live reality, albeit within the context of a staged performance and underlined the playwright's commentary on the transference of screen violence to actual violence.

Fig. 2: The Lost Babylon II.1. As the Screenwriter (Cheryl Bradley) continues to write her screenplay, the Psychologist (Chrissie Page) stays on camera while the Boy (Sean-Michael Kerins) directly and intensely engages the audience, © Nic Mollison

Strategic Effectiveness

In the fast-developing field of intermedial theatre, there has been a range of discoveries made through play, and the refinement of discoveries made on reflection. In exploring the staging of The Lost Babylon, planned strategies were supplemented by serendipity, as noted, in the transmission of a live screenplay. Through the use of video capture and projection, a tension was found between the live presence and the virtual presence of the actors. The liveness of the actor was replicated but from a different angle from the audience's point of view. Any movement by the live actor was immediately seen magnified and from a different perspective projected onto the rear wall. The actor and camera were linked kinetically and a sense of interactivity, or rather reactivity, was conveyed. The video image was determined by the constantly shifting live actor, resulting in a doubling of presence: virtual and live which complemented each other. As the actor Chrissie Page reported:

> People that I spoke to [after the performances] loved the notion of seeing the double image [...] that double reality.

> They found themselves drawn to the screen but back to the stage because they were frightened of missing something.

This 'double image' or 'double reality' impelled the audience regularly to shift their focus, back and forth between the live actor and the video image in an attempt to engage with and to comprehend the constantly shifting play between them. An intermedial presence was arrived at through the interpenetration of live and virtual presences. This kinetic play between the two presences resulted in a need for audience members to negotiate between the biological materiality of the live performer and the technological materiality of the projected performer.

Moreover the video close-up specifically enabled the live performance to stage and frame cinematic representation – one of the play's key references. The actor anchored this representation and emerged as the player of live and digital presence, choosing with the director when to direct the audience to view themselves as live or filmic presence and subsequently switching between these two presences, creating an intermedial presence between the live and the digital. This intermedial presence reinforced the play's commentary on media effects upon society and the potential for the virtual to become real.

Instance: The Work of CREW with Eric Joris

Kurt Vanhoutte and Nele Wynants

Introduction to the CREW Project

This instance reviews the creative and research process of CREW, a performance group and multidisciplinary team of artists and researchers based in Brussels. With Eric Joris, combining a background in film with graphic and product design, as its key figure, the group has been creating theatrical experiments at the melting point of live art and digital media since 1998. Continuing a dialogue with state-of-the-art developments in robotics and computer sciences, CREW triggers the theatrical imagination of design and production, text and sound. The artistic outcome tends to be hybrid; with the technological live art of CREW troubling installed categories of theatricality leading to immersive embodied environments (← TERM: IMMERSION; ← TERM: EMBODIMENT) that challenge common notions of (tele)presence (← TERM: PRESENCE), spectatorship, interactivity (→ TERM: INTERACTIVITY) and narration. CREW explores how these hybridities (→ TERM: HYBRIDITY) can be operated on an artistic, practical and theoretical level. Scientific reflection plays a constitutive role in the creative process. Researchers from different universities develop new technologies for CREW to use on stage. The developers for their part reciprocally find in experimental theatre a laboratory where they can test the progress and feasibility of their interface designs. At the heart of CREW, in other words, there is a constant negotiation between art and science. This twofold origin results in artistic productions fuelled by the same research questions that determine the major motives of media producers and distributors in the entertainment industry: "What happens when digital technology really merges production and reflection within the context of the stage?", and "What kind of experience emerges from these new technological environments?" Though this instance is concerned more with an on-going process than a product, a short account of CRASH, the first public outcome integrating immersive technology in live performance, will serve to indicate the kind of performance produced through the creative-research work.

CRASH, the first immersive performance in 2004-2005, inspired by J.G. Ballard's novel of the same name (first published in 1973) about car-crash sexual fetishism, fixed the spectator on a tilting bed, arousing an almost erotic and unsettling intimacy (← TERM: INTIMACY) vis-à-vis the machine. Before entering the magic circle of immersion, participants had to reside in an anti-chamber where they were instructed to leave the daily world behind together with their coat and bag. Thereupon, an actor wrapped each user with the immersive outfit, headmounted display and earphones. The immersant (← TERM: EXPERIENCER) was able to look around in the imagery, gradually revealing a body that only seemingly (in image space) belonged to her. Manipulation of the surround images, the sound and tactile impulses – the 'actors' touching her body at the same time as the body-image in the display was being touched – intensified the embodiment of the artifactual body. But the schizophrenia of the postmodern condition persisted also in this fetishistic universe and the immersive state resembled that of a body torn apart at the intersection of multiplicity of images and reconstructions produced by the media without any central coordination.[21] In the light of the disembodying effects of technology the lived-body, so to speak, struggled to assert its gravity. The world in which the immersant used to project her complete identity seemed to disappear and the body she thought she knew vanished along with it, to be replaced with a paradoxically lived artifactual body.

Fig. 1: *Manipulating the body-image in EUX,* © Eric Joris

It is worth explaining the working principles of the immersive apparatus in order to get a better understanding of the dramaturgical strategies deployed by CREW, the features of omni-directional video (ODV) and how they build up the theatrical universe with alternative sense perceptions.[22] ODV is a human-machine interface that leads to unprecedented levels of presence and intimacy as well as novel ways of mixing and experiencing different levels of reality. By means of a head-mounted display, the spectator is afforded a surround video environment and becomes a user or an 'immersant'. Equipped with an orientation tracker, the lightweight display shows a sub-image of the panoramic video that corresponds

MAPPING INTERMEDIALITY IN PERFORMANCE

with the user's view direction and desired field of view. The visual and spatial characteristics of this medium are different from virtual reality (→ TERM: VIRTUALITY), where the immersant is enclosed with an artificial environment that is created with software and that is presented as a synthetic world of shapes, volumes and images. By contrast, ODV places the viewer physically inside a video-captured image, thus establishing an environment with very realistic dimensions. Usually the images are taken from the city or the art venue where the show takes place, so that the visitor is familiar with what she sees when the head-mounted display is switched on. In fact, (a) reality is doubled even before the visitor enters the theatre, or even in real time during the performance, and these registered images are being fed back into the video goggles worn by the participants. The virtual space, then, coincides with the embodied space of the self, thus embedding the story world into the physically experienced world of the immersant. The filmed image becomes a space in which the user dwells and that is hard to distinguish from factual reality.[23] It is no surprise that this high-impact medium finds applications in teleconferencing, but also in the military, where ground operations training takes place in encapsulated and controlled environments, and in immersive gaming which seems to erase the boundaries between the virtual and the factual, changing social and even ethical agency.[24]

Challenging Established Binaries: Changing Body-States

But as long as we speak of factual and virtual realities, and claim that the former is replaced by the latter, we are still reasoning within the logic of representation. These dialectics involve the friction between material reality as a 'live' condition as opposed to the simulation principle of digital technologies, where CREW's praxis involves the postmodern refashioning of our mental landscape under the sign of Saturn, the planet of melancholy marked by fear of loss, the experience of history as repetitive catastrophe. The work of art in the age of its digital simulation more often than not engenders Baudrillardean apocalyptic narratives in both the theoretical and the artistic sphere.[25] Eric Joris retains the narrative scenario inherent in the use of technologies that virtualise reality, but to a different effect. Indeed, the premonition of impending doom always lurks below the surfaces of the CREW performances and it is no coincidence that the first theatre production Joris staged in 1998 was an adaptation between panoramic screens of Dante's "Inferno", from The Divine Comedy. In the end, however, reality in the aesthetics of CREW is not so much what is to be mournfully lost as what is to be "regarded as the Nay of all positive structural assertions, but as in some sense the source of them all, and, more than that, as a realm of pure possibility whence novel configurations of ideas and relations may arise" (Turner 1967, 97). Remarkably enough, Turner's account of liminality, a temporary state of transgression in ritual societies and modern communitas, paves the way to understanding the specificity of the immersive high-tech narratives of CREW.

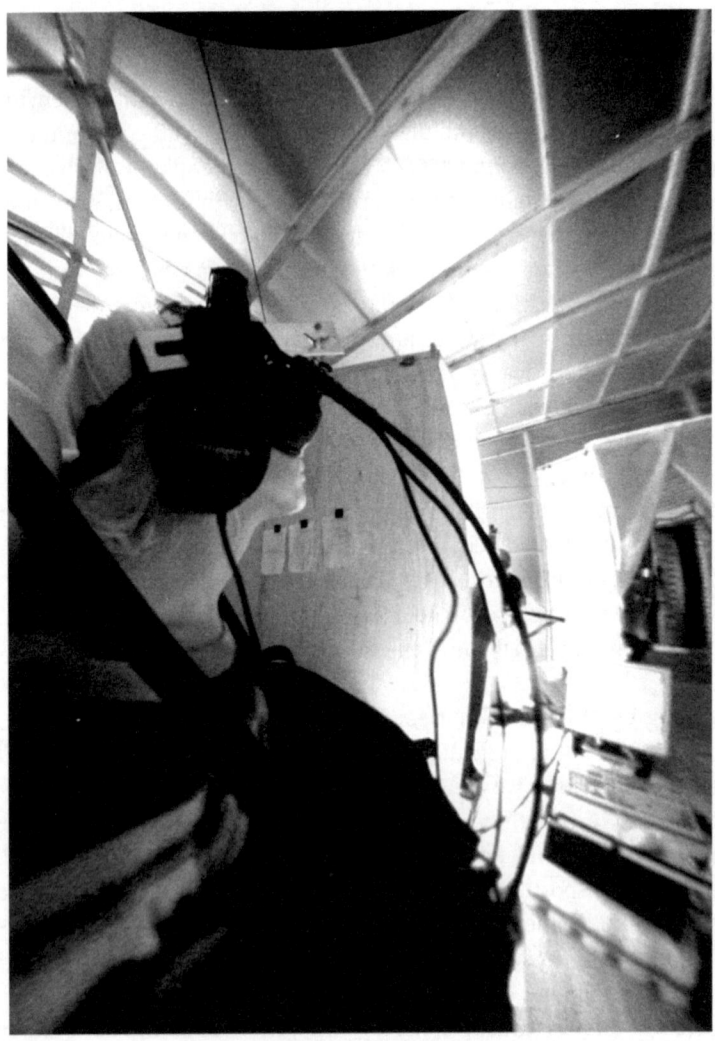

Fig. 2: *Participant in immersive outfit in* CRASH, © Eric Joris

CRASH left many a spectator dazed and confused and a leading theatre critic quite literally brought up an out-of-body experience as a central reference for the effect of the performance.[26] This could be explained with reference to an open-ended form of a *rite de passage* since CRASH fulfilled the conditions for the separation (antichamber) and the liminal midpoint of transition, immersive dislocation, but the reassimilation into the community was somehow left out. Tune in, turn out, drop out.

It is well known that Turner's take on rituals has become very important for the making and theorizing of performance art since the seventies. His early work

MAPPING INTERMEDIALITY IN PERFORMANCE

drew in turn on the anthropologist Arnold Van Gennep, who in 1960 described *rites de passage* such as coming-of-age rituals as having a three-part structure: separation, liminal period, reassimilation (2004). This structure can also be found in the performances of CREW. The person undergoing the immersion is first stripped of the status that she possessed before she entered the magic circle[27], is inducted into the liminal period of transition, and finally is given her new status and reassimilated into the community. Immersants in CREW might be seen as the 'liminars' that Turner accounts for as travellers or passengers – marked out by ambiguity, in time yet timeless, neither here nor there, hazy as they occupy an ontological blind spot rather than an identifiable or fixed position. Put differently, their bodies inhabit the state of liminality that occurs when somebody wakes from dream sleep and in a confusing state of mind is unable to distinguish if a vaguely recalled dream actually occurred.

Undoubtedly, this inquiry might also benefit from a reading that approaches both surrealism and CREW from its other, darker side: as an art given over to the uncanny, to the compulsion to repeat and to articulate trauma (Foster 1993). There is, undoubtedly, more than a hint of surrealism in the work of Eric Joris, who refers to immersion as a "temporarily amoral space". It would, however, take us too far afield to discuss the political urge, if any, in this equation. Liminal states and surrealist dreaming states at any rate share a profound displacement (→ TERM: DISPLACEMENT) of the experiencer (← TERM: EXPERIENCER). In his later writings, Turner coined the term "liminoid" to refer to these experiences that have characteristics of liminality without however involving a resolution of the individual crisis. Liminoid phenomena are to be found in a post-industrial society. They differ from primitive rituals in that they exhibit highly individualised traits insofar as they are a commodity or leisure-time activity, which one selects and pays for – Turner mentions theatre as one of the examples. Liminoid performance is to a considerable degree freer, open-ended and deprived of transcendence, being both in the world and beyond it.

Summary of Outcomes

To return to CREW's performance outcomes, U_raging standstill (2006-2007), EUX (2008), the next performances suitably entitled (in translation) "you" (U) and "them" (EUX), tried to compensate for the unresolved ending through a double closure, one virtual and one factual. The immersant was for the first time technically able to move freely and walk around in the surrounding imagery. Whereas U mainly explored the possibilities for mobility, EUX extended the narrative practice. Here, the immersant first had to live through the several phases of *agnosia*, a disorder characterised by the loss of ability to recognize objects, persons, sounds, shapes, or smells (the inability to recognize your own body and its attendant confusion, the phenomenon of appropriation of virtual parts of the body). In the last act, she unexpectedly runs into her own body dwelling through immersive space, meeting a searching image of herself previously recorded during the performance and now being fed back to her. This *unheimliche* encounter is further brought home through integrating both the inside and outside perspective as the visitor at the end of the performance was given the opportunity to sit back and watch the next initiate come in and walk the immersive path. The novice's point of view was simultaneously being projected on a large video screen, so that the first visitor now could witness, without technology and from a distance, what she had experienced in the flesh a couple of minutes before.[28] Thus the immersant effectively underwent a 'both-and' experience, inside and outside her own ritual. Reaggregation turned into a relay race. Reincorporation into the communitas was replaced by a highly individualised encounter with the *Doppelgänger*.

In March 2009, CREW staged an allegorical microcosm within communitas: *W (Double U)*. This interactive collaborative experiment extended individual experience towards the exchange of visual perception. The fields of view of two users at different geographic locations were swapped by satellite, one being in a theatre in Mons (Belgium), the other strolling in the shadow of the Agbar tower in Barcelona under the auspices of 20203DMedia, a large-scale European media development project.[29] The two participants were equipped with not only a HMD but also a small omni-directional camera mounted on their head, so that video and audio could be conversely transferred. Thus, person A looked through the eyes of person B and vice versa (they can freely look around in each other's environment), guiding and sustaining the other through live audio. The setup of this test-bed was to be technical, but slowly evolved into an intimate *pas-de-deux*, a joint presence in a transitional time and space, where the difference between body image and body self gradually dissolved. The immersive dancers had to telescope an environment in-between embodied and perceived reality in a synthesis of science and art. They (re)constructed the conditions of theatricality in cognitively mapping each other's body as they moved along.

Instance: Rimini Protokoll, *Mnemopark* (2005)

Kara McKechnie

This instance addresses the ways in which the Berlin-based company Rimini Protokoll blends documentary and fiction, authenticity and performance in its multimedia production *Mnemopark*. It particularly focuses on strategies for both mediating and mediatising 'actual' people and places in an intermedial performance setting.

Rimini Protokoll is a collective of three theatre makers, Daniel Wetzel, Helgard Haug and Stefan Kaegi, who have created innovative and theatrical research projects since 2000. Originating from the Department for Applied Theatre Studies at the University of Giessen, Rimini Protokoll collaborates with 'experts of the everyday' ("Experten des Alltags"), such as model rail enthusiasts (*Mnemopark*), crossword specialists from a home for the elderly (*Kreuzworträtsel Boxenstopp*) or long-distance truck drivers (*Cargo Sofia*). These theatricalisations of the everyday variously evoke research projects, verbatim performances, demonstrations and live documentaries. Their dramaturgies are often analogous to the structure of a conversation or an interview. Reality is scripted and overtly mediated for performance. Rimini Protokoll develop new forms of theatricality which don't present reality in an illusionist manner, in a climate where society is more routinely appropriating theatrical means of communication (see Dreysse and Malzacher 2007, 10). The collective is the most high-profile example of a strong trend in German theatre, producing issue-based productions in a new way and exploring new applications of documentary content. These hybrids (→ TERM: HYBRIDITY) between research project and performance express the political through private narrative, and the establishment of character and plot are not foregrounded.

Rimini Protokoll does not work within a 'normal' theatre apparatus – although the company works on commission – and only occasionally with trained actors. There is a hybridity between the roles of director, dramaturg, researcher, adaptor and editor in these "Theaterrecherche" projects, which take impulses from documentary theatre and film practice, modified, mediatised, seemingly without authorial intervention, and therefore seemingly closer to reality. Performing statistics, staging pro- and con- debates about ongoing issues and at the same time looking into the way decisions are made, Rimini Protokoll has contributed significantly to the debate surrounding documentary forms and applications, as well as to new approaches to political theatre. As Stefan Kaegi says in an interview reproduced on the company's website:

> We are interested in the theatricality of everyday life. We don't want to imitate or dramatise reality – we want to lift it onto the stage to see what happens. We

want to make theatre without theatre – a theatre that has nothing to do with the craft of acting skills (Rathmanner 2005). [30]

Mnemopark and Structured Authenticity

Rimini Protokoll triangulate seemingly disparate materials in their research-performance projects. As Kaegi observes:

> We don't begin work in a rehearsal room, but approach a production through documentary methods. We try and find something out, order it and to collate it with other material; that's the way we develop the production (Rathmanner 2005).

In *Mnemopark*, seemingly disparate materials are brought together on stage: the Swiss economy, enthusiasm for model railways and Bollywood films. It sounds like the result of an outlandish bet about what might be crammed into a single performance. As the company explains on its website:

> The world of Mnemopark is based upon an actual railway model – 1:87. What does society look like in its industrially manufactured reduplication? By means of minicameras Mnemopark advances into a model of the alps, into the zones of a mysterious land. Thus a landscape simulation becomes film set. Meadows, forests, and barns are really faked up, though that only leads to a higher degree of their fictive reality.

It is a tribute to Rimini Protokoll's dramaturgical intelligence that this forms a coherent performance, held together by the stories the model rail enthusiasts tell in turn.

Experts of the Everyday

"It's about co-operating with the specialists", explains Helgard Haug, "because we don't expose people but delegate something to them that they are better at doing than we are." As in most of Rimini Protokoll's projects, the participants are not actors but experts who play themselves and construct a role for themselves at the same time. The group finds the tension between the self and the performance of the self to be an ideal basis for their investigations, "because these people didn't pull that serious Giessen face, but were really pleased to be doing what they were good at doing" (Malzacher in Dreysse and Malzacher 2007, 27). The model rail builders prove to be enthusiasts as well as enthusiastic, working on their mini version of Switzerland when the audience enters the space, and then introducing themselves, the model railway set and their craft. Hermann builds two trees during the show, and also passes a case with a snowy landscape around the audience. Heidy remarks later that she and Hermann build in different

MAPPING INTERMEDIALITY IN PERFORMANCE

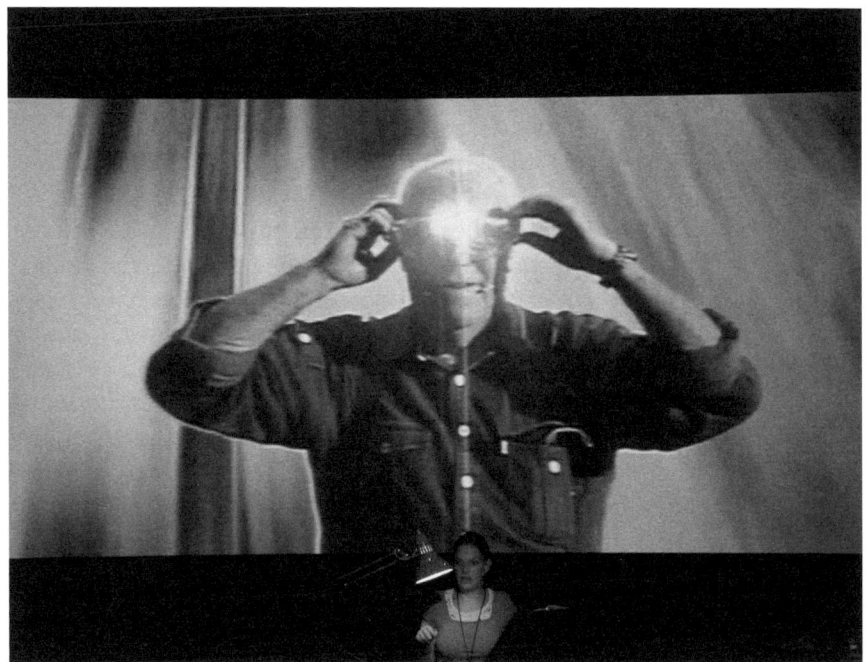

Fig.: Rimini Protokoll *Mnemopark: model rail enthusiast Max goes on a virtual journey to visit his past*, © Lex Vögtli

scales, suggesting a subtext that they do not see eye to eye on other issues, either. The model rail club members have votes about the ways in which new rails are laid; the development of the landscape is the result of a democratic process. They call their construction "Ersatzlandschaft" – an ersatz or replacement landscape – and it becomes clear that this does not just refer to the performance *Mnemopark*. The model rail world provides them with the order, choice and predictability that real life might deny them.

Each of the protagonists has a solo section where they tell the audience about their lives and revisit aspects of it through being inserted into the landscape. For this, they wear glasses that give them the point of view of the lipstick camera attached to the model train. They are themselves filmed live in front of a green screen, which allows them to be superimposed onto another, larger screen, so while Hermann, Heidy, Max and René see the Mnemopark set as if they were inside it, the audience see miniature versions of the four experts travelling through the Swiss landscape on the large screen. Max, reliving the time of his apprenticeship, appears to fly above his native landscape and then falls into models not yet painted. One of the characters suggests that "We have to think about how the future looks", with the response, "We model builders can't do that, model train sets can only deal with reality. They are always built in retrospective".

Heidy returns to the time when she defected from East Germany. These stories are informative and engaging; they personalise the context with which the production is concerned, specifying things we have some knowledge of and introducing us to some we previously had not considered. Amongst many things, for instance, *Mnemopark* presents a viable way to learn about agricultural statistics.

People Seen to Be Behaving (Rather Than Just Behaving)

The skills and stories of experts of the everyday become the object of study in Rimini Protokoll's projects, and this extends to cultural repertoires of behaviour: "what people do in the activity of their doing it" (Richard Schechner, quoted in Shepherd and Wallis 2004, 104). The organisation of such activity for spectating can be termed dramaturgy; but while theatrical dramaturgy is undertaken in the context of an 'artificial' performance, sociological dramaturgy refers to 'real' human behaviour and the impression management that is undertaken in human relationships. The edges between these two forms of dramaturgy become blurred, however, if human behaviour is seen as a performative act (← INTERSECTION: PERFORMATIVITY) , and theatre is seen as a stylised way of linking these behavioural efforts at establishing meaning and embedding them in context. Rimini Protokoll delights in the blurring of sociology and performativity. Verbatim material has similar hybridic qualities and plays a central part in these projects. As Helgard Haug explains: "we talk to people and then establish stories using their own words, which we then put back into their mouths on the stage" (Wetzel 2001).

The performances sometimes have the feel of being a draft version of a piece of documentary verbatim theatre; a draft that deliberately shows the fault lines between what is invented in the moment and what has been agreed previously – and frequently shows the way in which the deceptions of 'authenticity' and 'truth' are set up. According to Daniel Wetzel, "truth is not important – it's much more about the way someone presents themselves or which role they choose to play" (Malzacher in Dreysse and Malzacher 2007, 38).

The *Mnemopark* experts are on stage to perform him/herself. Given the production's success since 2006, with a busy touring schedule, there must be some effort involved in not seeming to be acting after so many performances as oneself. *Mnemopark* works with the following two models:

1. An 'expert' performing themselves in a scripted performance; under instruction not to act.
2. An actor performing a character who is performing him/herself; acting not to be acting, but having to act a double layer: a character, and a character's performance of that character.

In *Mnemopark*, the latter function is taken on by Rahel Hubacher, who is the daughter of a Swiss farmer, but also a trained actor. She narrates a lot of material relating to the Swiss economy and agriculture, explaining, for example, why cows emit more CO_2 than cars and why the mountains of surplus agricultural produce integrated into the model set are personally relevant to her. Hubacher also acts as compère for the interventions and games of the model rail experts. Other Rimini projects have included actors replacing experts and taking on the text created by them, which raises interesting questions about authenticity. Is a text created by a real-life expert robbed of its real-ness if it is taken on by an actor? Does the fact that the text is scripted when it is presented by its 'owner' already provide a purpose, a dramaturgy? Or do we want to believe in unmediated authenticity, even though the tools (the camera, the joins of the script, the 'staged' situation) are laid bare? *Mnemopark* both poses and problematises each of these questions.

Mediatisations and Simulations

Rimini Protokoll turns the process of copying into an artistic process. Along with the special features the experts bring to the performance, the architectural, historical and anecdotal meaning of a particular space is central as a "starting point and as structuring factor" (Matzke in Dreysse and Malzacher 2007, 105). Simulation allows both the 'theatricalisation' of a non-dramatic process and compression to a manageable level. While talking about Switzerland, the country is produced, in front of the audience, as both a demonstration object and a theatre set, standing in for the aspects of the real thing that have been chosen as the topic of the production. Stefan Kaegi, who is mainly responsible for *Mnemopark*'s concept and direction, talks of the Swiss landscape looking like a film set when travelling through it by (real-sized) train, raising the sense in the traveller that the idyll is constructed and arranged in this "extremely concentrated form of naturalness" (in Rathmanner 2005).

The set shows, amongst other things, the participants' homes, parents' homes, workplaces, golf course, an unpainted partial model of Basle ("the future"), a meat mountain (to scale), a chicken cage (real size), a nursery, a stonemason's workshop and a cemetery, an industrial area, a railway bridge. The show starts with a video projection of a train journey onto the large screen. As we have no comparison of scale, we assume the landscape is real-sized until we see the heads of the participants resting at the side of the tracks. Only then do we realise that the camera is live, and that the screen is enlarging the miniature set.

Each of the experts tells their own story during the performance and performs a flashback section. At these times, the ensemble pretends that the storyteller has shrunk to fit into the 1:87 landscape, and it is made easy for the audience to concur, even though we can see the expert in question in front of the green screen at the side of the stage the whole time. The fact that we can see the storyteller's point of view, along with a seemingly convincing insertion of them interacting with the model landscape, does not entirely make for make-believe, but is pleasurable for an audience prepared to indulge in knowing illusion.

There is an ongoing strand of conversation and location scouting for a Bolly-wood film set in Switzerland (with two miniature model characters, Anjun and Priyanka Ghosh). The Alps are a highly popular Bollywood location, resulting in Indian tourist pilgrimages to the sites of filming. This strand of the plot contains plans for a pipeline, the insufficiency of oil coming into India, and a fundamen-talist blowing up trains. After underground activity, the two protagonists (about 3 centimetres each) decide to fight for India's inclusion in the UN Security Council. There are also excerpts of Bollywood films into which the model rail experts are inserted through footage, prepared in advance, showing them in a dance routine in alpine environments, while they dance live on stage as well. The miniature woods further resonate the theme of authentic copying: they are an area for mili-tary simulation by the army and by shooting clubs (Schützenvereine).

At the end of the piece the spectators are invited to come and see the model up close, talk to the performers, even take photos – so that reality and reflection, presence and revelation intertwine at yet another level.

Documentary Theatre and (Re)presentation

Rimini Protokoll's projects are shaped by documentary material, while simulta-neously commenting on documentary conventions. Documentary theatre is a ve-hicle for information, and drawing attention to its conventions and possible edits of this information might be seen to distract from its educational credentials. The main focus in Rimini Protokoll's projects is on the experts who, as explained above, are not just on stage because of the knowledge and skill they bring to the work. A lot of importance is given to the 'how' of the performance – how the story is told, how the experts present themselves, how, ultimately, they wish to be seen and how their performance as themselves leads to other narratives emerging for the audience. We learn about the 'what' of the story because the 'how' of the personal approach holds our attention. The approach also creates a theatrically rewarding tension between the self and the performance of the self. More dramaturgical than dramatic in character, these projects juxtapose fiction and 'reality', the theatrical and the everyday space, biography and performance, as well as research and performance. Rimini Protokoll has propagated new media technologies on the stage – in Mnemopark, these are the lipstick camera and the green screen technology – but the company never pursues an illusionist approach in its uses of it.

Rimini Protokoll adopts (or adapts) conventions of the media to the stage. Die-trich Diederichsen discusses different types of participants in the company's work: expert, person affected by the subject matter, witness, representative (Die-derichsen in Dreysse & Malzacher 2007, 159). And certainly, these distinctions are common within the non-fictional formats of television and radio news pro-grammes, documentaries and list programmes ("The 50 best romantic movies"). The fact that the experts are playing themselves in Mnemopark, but to a script, or protocol, means they don't have to invent their words for each performance, but the personalised stage script still has a flexibility that a filmed television or radio contribution cannot have (see Diederichsen in Dreysse & Malzacher 2007,160). As Kaegi explains:

> Our theatre events communicate a completely different directness in comparison to a filmed documentary. The decisive point is that the experts are not filmed, and that's it, but they're on stage every night. This means they have more say than they would have in a documentary film and are more open to this game of distorting reality (cf. Rathmanner 2005).

Mnemopark is labelled as a "film that is produced in front of the audience" (Dreysse & Malzacher 2007, 223) and has more filmic elements than other Rimini Protokoll's projects, but its liveness is its constituting element. While documentary content is part of the performance, the communication of this information is only one amongst its many foci. As Lindsmayer (2005) suggests:

> The social dimension is impressive, coming from memories of those involved, making the playing with models seem like an escape into an artificial and stylised world; a world between happening, Big Brother, lottery and memory workshop which could be seen as a representation of Switzerland and demonstrates how widely the borders of what constitutes theatre have been pushed.

Mnemopark is about technological ways of concretising memory (the insertion of the participants into their model rail landscape), and achieving theatricality without illusionism (the screen and the whole set up are visible to the audience). Where it is closest to documentary practice, it also dramatises otherwise unpalatable or inaccessible information through devising strategies of communication, and not least personalisation.

Portal: Time and Space

Other than notions of *the body*, perhaps no other elements receive as much scrutiny from collisions among theatre, performance, and digital culture as the resulting transformations of time and space. One of the most salient of these transformations has been the ability to access information outside progressive linear time and defined material spaces. Although refusals to conform to these dimensions date to the early twentieth century, the technological developments of the last 50 years have animated these concepts in startling new ways. If the metaphors of mapping and networking, frequently deployed throughout this book, have any effect at all, it is that they demonstrate the need for new relations among previously fixed dimensions.

This Portal thus seeks to examine these new relations through a recontextualisation of time, space, and the changing dynamics among them. As key reference points, Bay-Cheng and Wiens first examine the ways in which notions of time and space (also referred to as the *here and now*) of theatrical performance respond to and influence the effects of digital culture in temporality and spatiality. Drawing on critical theory and a history of defiance toward the *here and now* as a pre-condition for performance, both draw parallels to the historical avant-garde and modernist theatre theory as sites for the emergence of a conceptual intermediality that would become more fully realised in the latter years of the twentieth century.

The Node of Dimensions outlines the salient terminology for these shifts in time and space including: displacement; deterritorialisation; glocalisation; and telematic. These first two terms by Groot Nibbelink point to the ways in which digital technologies perform a destabilizing function in culture by undermining the conventional sense of place. Citing Martin Heidegger's work on the concept of *Unheimlichkeit*, Groot Nibbelink briefly surveys the ways in which intermedial performance prompts a subconscious defense mechanism, while simultaneously it allows for a reorganisation of connections by unmooring elements from their traditional locations. Wiens points to a similar phenomenon in glocalisation when she describes the effect of the 'spatial turn' on the (re)definitions of 'global' and 'local'. Finally, Bay-Cheng notes that the means by which these reconfigurations of space and time occur may be found in the specific effects of digital telematics, a concept of informatics that emphasises process and infrastructure over data and content.

These terms inform the instances: three noteworthy examples of international theatre and performance artists who engage the destabilisation of time and space as the basis for production. For example, Christopher Kondek's *Dead Cat Bounce* uses the real-time stock market as a performance against which the other actors and spectators must react. In her analysis, Wiens notes the ways in which Kondek reworks theatrical space as both material and virtual: an interplay of real places, such as a physical theatre in Berlin, and ethereal locations, such as the ubiquitous instances of global capital and information. Such deterritorialisations of traditional theatre space allow Kondek to stage an absent yet ubiquitous performer, the stock market itself. Though not concerned with the staging of ephemeral financial data, Arfara's analysis of Romeo Castellucci and his Socìetas Raffaello Sanzio adaptation of Dante's *Purgatory* similarly points to the ways in which intermedial disturbances of time and space allow live performances to explore the imperceptible and the unseen. Rather than globalised information diffusion, Romeo Castellucci and the Socìetas Raffaello Sanzio focus into the bourgeois family home as an unstable site of intimacy, horror, and the uncanny. Specifically, Arfara analyses Castellucci's use of digital surtitles, grotesque vocal amplification, and monumental stage dimensions as techniques for complicating the relations of time, space, and action. She then relates the experience of personal trauma to the functions of digitally-enhanced memory and the ways in which digital media both enhance and disturb these repetitions and revisions. Perhaps not surprisingly, both Wiens and Arfara refer back to Bertolt Brecht – that modernist intermedialist – as a means to historicize the effects of displacement, deterritorialisation, and defamiliarisation in contemporary culture. From their work, we can see that these effect pervade this digital culture from the most pervasive global context (international financial systems) to the most intimate (a child's bodily violation in the home).

The final Instance by Scheer focuses on the work of Granular Synthesis, particularly their production *Modell 5*, within the larger context of contemporary performance art and its emphasis on human perception of the *now*. In particular, he engages Mark Hansen's theories of new media temporalities and the ability of digital artists such as Bill Viola and Douglas Gordon to reveal the previously imperceptible moments of human experience, such as those emphasised by Marina Abramović and Mike Parr. Linking these developments in durational aesthetics to the modernist psychology of William James and contemporary cognitive theory, Scheer suggests a new conception of the temporal and spatial self that further connects to notions of the cyborg and the posthuman paradigm.

Temporality

Sarah Bay-Cheng

Theatre is perhaps the first and most enduring time-based art. Indeed, for Aristotle, the compression of dramatic time – "to exist during a single daylight period" – was one of the distinguishing characteristics between the form of tragedy and epic poetry (Aristotle 1970, 24). Although the emergence of Happenings and other performance art of the 1960s and 1970s drew new attention to the manipulation of time in performance (perhaps most famously in John Cage's silent durational work, *4'33"*), theatre and drama had long bent the dimension of time into a range of performance conventions. Photography and cinema made such manipulations of time newly visible to the observer, while playwrights devised techniques to convey past occurrences, memories, and simultaneous events. These experiments suggest an early twentieth-century proto-digital foundation, in which the concepts that inform current digital technology and networks first appeared via photography, cinema, and theatre. For example, theatre historian John Fell notes that melodrama functioned as a precursor to cinematic temporality: a "main structural problem confronted by melodrama was that of simultaneity. The stories turned so often on coincidental appearances of characters at unexpected times and on rescues in the face of imminent danger that staging had to facilitate two or more playing areas at the same time" (Fell 1970, 27). When Michel Foucault identified the postmodern period as "the epoch of simultaneity" and juxtaposition, he articulated the emergence of a condition (*per* Lyotard) that had its roots in early twentieth-century theatre.

Foucault, of course, was responding to earlier instabilities of time as articulated in Henri Bergson's considerations of duration and his designations of "pure time" as opposed to "mathematical time" (cf. Bergson 1910). Whereas classical theory conceived of time as progressive and linear, modernist and later postmodern theory fashioned it as a kind of constellation, or as Gilles Deleuze later called it, a rhizome. Such time-bendings followed new developments in theoretical physics, first by Albert Einstein and later by Max Planck and theorists of quantum mechanics. These theoretical advances transformed the conceptions of time and space from fixed entities into dynamic, responsive systems. Such transformations affected domains from philosophy and mathematics (cf. Edmund Husserl) to psychology (cf. William James). Later advances in technology would bear out these philosophical assessments of time and its relation to technology. Paul Virilio (1995), for example, cites the rise of time-sharing and real-time networks, such as linking the computer and telephone, to create the basis for present-day telematics ($\rightarrow$ TERM: TELEMATICS).

Such technologies, even those of the mechanical pre-digital era, affected notions of time and perception. Philip Auslander in his influential *Liveness: Performance in a Mediatized Culture* (1999) argues that live performance emerged not as a condition of physical proximity and co-presence (though this is a common usage), but as a correlate of time. Specifically, he cites the invention of broadcast and recording technologies. Although the radio was first a technology to bridge a spatial gap – listening to a musical performance in one's living room instead of a concert hall – recordings spanned a temporal dimension as well. One could listen to a recorded Friday-night concert on Saturday. Identifying this temporal confusion as a "crisis", Auslander thus locates the origin of liveness: "The response to this crisis was a terminological distinction that attempted to preserve the formerly clear dichotomy between two modes of performance, the live and the recorded, a dichotomy that had been so self-evident up to that point that it did not even need to be named" (Auslander 2002, 17). Similarly, Lev Manovich draws clear parallels between cinematic, temporal montage (a composite of multiple images in a single moment in time) and digital compositing. Noting the pervasive shifts in modern conceptions of temporality, Manovich notes that digitization – the transformation of media into data – was part of a much larger project of "cultural transcoding" (→ TERM: TRANSCODING) in which new media act as a precursor for a "more general process of cultural reconceptualization" (Manovich 2001, 47). Mark Hansen further explores this reconceptualisation of time, space, and the body in his influential *New Philosophy for New Media* (2004). In particular, Hansen explores how non-perceptual neurological duration correlates to new "machine time" made visible in media art (→INSTANCE: GRANULAR SYNTHESIS).

From the Ontology of Space to the Performance of Time

Perhaps most radically, performance theorist Alice Rayner describes the shift from material performance into cyberspace as one from the ontology of space to the performance of time. In her essay "E-scapes: Performance in the Time of Cyberspace", Rayner notes the ways "in which performance aligns with digital technologies to resist landscapes and geometric space, and to resituate space in the fugitive dimension of time" (Rayner 2002, 350-51). For Rayner, performance in cyberspace occupies no place, but rather ontologically exists *only* in a time, the perpetual now. In this sense, time is the most dynamic and yet most intractable element of digital theatre and performance. While the notion of time has always been a fluid one, in the "new temporality" of digital media (as Manovich calls it), theorists have positioned time in digital culture as many things simultaneously: constructed (Lyotard), digitally compressed (Dixon and Smith), regressive (Baudrillard), elongated (Virilio) and annihilated (Huyssen). For his part, Manovich traces the evolving temporality in digital media to Sergei Eisenstein's experiments in cinematic montage which followed a similar pattern to radio: changing from spatial montage (the first use of the cut in early cinema) to temporal or rhythmic montage, in which the very same edits could be used to create not only the simultaneity that D.W. Griffith developed from melodrama in his parallel editing, but also a new cinematically dependent rhythm that articulated a space and time exclusive to the cinematic experience. This dependence on mediated time would recur in digital art and performances in which, as Anne-Marie Duguet notes, "Time emerged not only as a recurrent theme but also as a constituent parameter of the very nature of an artwork" (cited in Rush 2005, 12). Chiel Kattenbelt in his essay "The Role of Technology in the Art of the Performer" argues further that the presence of recording technologies – both video and audio – disrupt the traditional reception of time and space, such that, "The expansion of the principles of the theatrical imagination through the use of live video and recorded sound can be characterised most concisely as a temporalisation of space and a spatialisation of time" (Kattenbelt 2006, 24). Kattenbelt grounds this shift in his reading of Kant's *Critique of Pure Reason*, specifically Kant's notion that "different times are not simultaneous but sequential (just as different spaces are not sequential but simultaneous)" (qtd., Kattenbelt 2006, 24). In the experience of digital media on stage, Kattenbelt's formulation of Kant suggests that time adheres to spatial properties as juxtaposition, while space becomes temporal and sequential. Akin to the synaesthesia embraced by the historical avant-garde, such confusions of temporality and ontologically disruptions of space thus become essential to our understanding of contemporary performance practices and their responses to digital media.

Ironically (and rarely noted by contemporary critics), the temporality of performance and its response to the change in technologies was perhaps first considered in detail by Gertrude Stein in her 1934 lecture, "Plays". Drawing on her early training with William James and his investigations into perceptions of time, Stein articulated her theory of the "continuous present" in relation to drama. In particular, she described the theatre and its manipulation of time as creating a sensation of "nervousness" due to its syncopation with the individual viewing experience. This nervousness, she wrote, "has perhaps to do with the fact that the emotion of the person at the theatre is always behind and ahead of the scene at the theatre but not with it" (Stein 1935, 103). Stein traced this experience of temporal syncopation to the cinema. Although she claimed "never to go to the cinema or hardly ever", Stein argued that the cinema was trying to solve the problem of modern time; that is, how to create art and performance in "the actual present, that is the complete actual present" (Stein 1935, 104-105). In this sense, Stein's approach resonates with Henri Bergson's spatialisation of time, and perhaps even more closely with Rayner's articulation of cyberspace as the perpetual *now* of time without space. In Stein's own plays, this meant articulating a temporal stasis that was nevertheless imbued with action – a duration of now in word play to replace the syncopated dramatic time and action. In digital contexts, temporality – which had originally referred to time as within the sphere of human life and the material world, that is, terrestrial as opposed to heavenly – came to represent a displacement of material space. No longer based in linear progression, external measures, and materiality, time in digital contexts evolved into a dynamic, dispersed, yet coherent network of temporal points – a time that could encompass, as noted by Foucault, many different points simultaneously; what Stein might have recognised as a further realisation of the continuous present.

New Temporalities of Theatre

It is not hard to find dramatic examples (and postdramatic, to cite Hans-Thies Lehmann) beyond Stein. Samuel Beckett and Heiner Müller in particular deploy radical reconceptualisations of time in their writing. In Beckett's case, the permeability of time finds an outlet in the technological (though analog) apparatus, as in *Krapp's Last Tape* (1958), a revisiting of the past played simultaneously in the present (and, it must be noted, inspired by a BBC radio broadcast from 1957). Indeed, Beckett's play relies on the recording device to create the construction of memory invoked by Bergson. Bergson's description of memory is striking for its notion of simultaneity and his technological metaphor. In his chapter, "Of the Survival of Images. Memory and Mind", he writes that in act of memory "we detach ourselves from the present moment in order to replace ourselves, first in the past in general, then in a certain region of the past – a work of adjustment, something like focussing a camera" (Bergson 1911, 77). Beckett read Bergson, and as others have argued, he drew on notions of time from Marcel Proust in much the same way that Deleuze would decades later. And yet, Beckett's attention to the singularity of the individual, of the particular, even when used to represent potentially larger groups follows the model of modernist time.

To understand these relations among different temporal constructs better, it may be best to start with the classical notion of time as a line, one that extends horizontally and progressively. This model is replaced by a modernist, Steinian/Bergsonian notion of time in which the horizontal line is replaced by a vertical stack, in which any particular moment in time is suffused by the past, present, and future simultaneously. Einstein's theories of relativity rejected the notion of an absolute time; emphasizing only dynamic, subjective relationships. Lehmann describes this development as the "loss of the *time frame*" (Lehmann 2006, 155, original emphasis). Although theatre artists such as Robert Wilson drew on Stein's theories for his own postmodern theatre (using her notion of the continuous present in particular to justify the extended duration of his theatrical actions), this is fundamentally a modernist temporality, one rooted in individual subjectivity. One need only adjust one's perception "like the focussing of a camera" as Bergson suggests, or replay a moment as Krapp does, to explore the past and future in the present moment.

The temporalities of the network similarly draw from this notion of the simultaneous, continuous present, but whereas the modernist conception relied on a singular consciousness in a moment of time, the postmodern, networked model draws not from a single perspective or memory, but from many multiple points simultaneously. As Deleuze points out in his imagery of the rhizome, there is no centre, no fixed point of entry and no singular consciousness to adjust (just as the camera has given way to digital imagery without a singular point of reference). The experience of time, the new temporality, is one of many simultaneous experiences and memories capable of being stored and accessed in random order, just as a computer deploys RAM, or random access memory, as the essence of data cognition. It is this change in processing structures – random instead of linear; simultaneous instead of sequential – that thus reorders time in digital media and changes our perception of past, present, and future. Beckett's fascination with tape was, after all, a fixation on an analog technology, but the contemporary Krapp can access not only the moments of his own recorded memory, but also everyone else's.

This change in temporalities came slowly to theatre, seemingly decades after philosophy, art, and cinema had engaged new temporal modes of expression. Although integrating mediated images in theatrical performance was nothing new, these techniques followed older conventions such as simultaneous actions in melodrama and linear memory and flashbacks, as in Tennessee Williams' pro-to-cinematic suggestion of a screen in the opening to The Glass Menagerie (1944). Performance in the theatre had always been a linear, temporal experience, one explicitly defined by the performance's duration. As Lehmann observes, "The real time of live performance ... overdetermines all theoretically distinguishable levels of time" (Lehmann 2006, 153-54). It was this overdetermined, seemingly inescapable temporality that art critic Michael Fried disdained in his assessment of theatre as "the negation of art" (Fried 1998, 153) and theatre seemed little able to escape it. Even early explorations of new media and telematics in performance seemed temporally constrained. George Coates' 1994 Nowhere NowHere, for example, used live feeds from webcams at multiple global locations seemingly to pass a ball from screen to screen, thus confusing the sense of space. But this confusion of space inherently depended on the unification of potentially disparate time without either disrupting the viewer's sense of time or even acknowledging the time differences among the different locations. Performance, it seemed, would always follow a temporality determined by its duration.

Against such immutabilities, playwrights sought to subvert duration. Heiner Müller, for example, de-centres his human subject to allow for a more expansive conception of time and space. As Jonathan Kalb describes it,

> Müller's dissolving of dramatis personae results not merely from the historically shrinking significance of the singly human subject. It has to do much more, for him, with the reconnaissance of regions in which time, logic, space do not function, in which the subject does not experience itself as centered but

rather as a contradictory imaginary *landscape* (Kalb 1998, 171, original emphasis).

This concept of the landscape (another concept derived from Stein) offered a potential model for the rethinking of theatrical relations between time and space. Theatre groups following the example of the landscape thus attempted to spatialise time, using a variety of techniques designed to materialise time itself visible as an aesthetic object. Lehmann points to a number of these techniques in his *Postdramatic Theatre*, noting particularly Wilson's extension of time (what Wilson calls "natural time" after the speed of imperceptible changes in nature, but which Lehmann calls "non-natural" time for its extremely slow motion); the use of repetition in performance; the time-image (adapted from Deleuze's theory of cinema) in which an image forces the viewer into his or her own memories and thus requires an individual construction of time; and simultaneity, the perception of disparate actions or events in a single moment in time. In spite of techniques that draw attention to the temporality of theatre, it is unclear how performance itself might work its way out from under its overarching duration.

Conclusion: Performance in Networked Time

The answer may not come from performance that relies on a mutual simultaneous experience of an assembled audience in spatial proximity, but from performance that is created in tension and collaboration with an audience disparately assembled in different space and times and therefore outside of time; an audience constructed through the digital network of augmented realities connected through mobile technologies and alternative non-environments such as Second Life. If we return to Rayner's description of cyberspace, we see that the no-place of online digital environments becomes the unceasing time of *now*, the spatialisation of time as all-encompassing location. As she points out, cyber-temporality is always in the present moment. This present moment, like the continuous present and the rhizome, is enduring beyond any one individual experience of the moment. To put it in terms of the interface: the internet structure is 'there' when I log on and when I log off. My time online may register outside of the computer, but digital access means that anything created within its parameters is automatically subsumed into the constant now of RAM. The past is as accessible as (and perhaps indistinguishable from) the present and it behaves the same way temporally; its time depends only on the strength of my online connection. Theatre and performance in this context do not rely on conventional notions of duration and as such are not created in time (or real-time as is often required to distinguish between relays, delays and lags – not unlike Auslander's live radio transmission), but rather culled *from* time. This is the new temporality that digital media, networks, and connectivity offers and it is a formulation of time with which emerging forms of intermediality in theatre and performance must engage.

MAPPING INTERMEDIALITY IN PERFORMANCE

Spatiality

Birgit Wiens

Since the early twentieth century, space has occupied an important status in theatre studies, with Peter Brook's (1968) seminal definition of the empty space as a landmark in the ensuing debate. Since Brook, theatre and performance scholars have recognised the importance of space and spatial relationships in re-conceptualising theatre as a performative phenomenon, and theorists have developed a more precise vocabulary to discuss the multiple dimensions of the way space figures in performance. Notions of space and spatiality are used to refer not only to theatre buildings and stages (as "empty space"), but also as integral and, at times, determining, components of performative processes. Indeed, space is now seen to function as an "active agent" and co-player in theatre events (McAuley 1999, 41). Spatiality may be defined as interactions among: (1) theatrical space (architectural conditions of theatre); (2) stage, or scenic space (set design, scenography); (3) place of performance (the local, sociocultural context); and (4) dramatic space (spatial designs as evoked by the dramatic or postdramatic text, libretto, choreography etc.) (cf. Balme 2008, 48f.). The critical discourses of the 20th century broke open essentialist concepts of space and, over time, the modern relativisation of space gave way to the postmodern discourse on deconstruction and spatialisation.

In recent years, however, new spatial models have revised conceptions of theatrical space. At the turn of the 21st century, digital media and global communication networks heralded a new spatial turn. The exponential increase of interconnections and real-time contacts between individuals and societies that are spatially, even geographically, apart from each other leads to new concepts of, and experiences within, actual and virtual spaces. These developments pose a challenge for contemporary theatre that has made new connections by allowing the virtual qualities of other spaces, transmitted via digital media, to appear on-stage. As Christopher Balme notes: "The possibilities of integrating *live* radio, television or even internet links into stage action suggest that the question of stage space will become an important area of experimentation in the coming years" (2008, 56, original emphasis). Indeed, a new type of stage, the *intermedial stage*, has emerged, affording an exciting field of theatre practice and research.

Theatre Spaces and Media Variations: a Sketch History

At the beginning of the 20th century, the established concept of space changed. Notions of space as a fixed container, dating back to Isaac Newton, were revised in the wake of Einstein's insights toward dynamic and relativistic spatial concepts. This paradigm shift widely affected culture, social life and the arts: "One should not lose sight of the fact that in the same time period that Einstein annulled absolute space, Sigmund Freud dissected human identity, the Cubists deconstructed shape and form as a whole and Ferdinand de Saussure developed his structuralist approach" (Löw 2001, 23). In the realm of theatre, it was the Swiss designer, Adolphe Appia, who in the 1910s rejected the concept of the proscenium and perspectival stage in favour of an open, kinetic space. His experiments replaced perspective image construction, static scenery, and two-dimensional backdrops with moveable elements (platforms, steps) and "scenic modules". Electric lighting was a key innovation: instead of serving as a mere technical tool, light for the first time in theatre history was assigned an active role capable of altering the density, energy and atmosphere of spaces. The music, the actions of the performers and the changing of the lights turned the stage and its material elements into temporal, "rhythmic spaces". Appia influenced numerous artists of the time including Max Reinhardt and the protagonists of the Bauhaus. Remarkably, in his later essays he also discussed the relationship between inner and outer spaces for the theatre: "Dramatic art has burst the frame that had held it rigid for so long, and the very concept of theatre has so expanded that it gives us vertigo and a slight feeling of anarchy" (qtd. Beacham 1994, 264). Appia was patently committed to an open art conception of theatre, for which modern technology was the catalyst: "I shall bear in mind all the different possibilities for expansion and transformation that modern technology can supply" (Beacham 1993, 140).

Not only Einstein's insights but also early 20th-century everyday experiences with new types of mobility impacted perception. The new film medium led to new spatial experiences. It was Walter Benjamin who observed that film offers an "immense and unexpected field of action" which allows for options that transgress the "prison-world" of the space of nearness and to split these up into a "prism" of spaces through which "we undertake far and adventurous journeys" (Benjamin 1977a, 35f.). According to this formulation, space, in its capacity as communication and action space, was no longer perceived as something 'given' but rather as an occurrence. Propelling this change forward is the ever-increasing dissemination of the telephone as a medium that "like no other decisively forced open the formation of 20th century communication possibilities" (Münker and Roesler 2000, 12). For the first time, a medium allowed the transmission of audio/voice signals affording the sense of telepresence (→ TERM: PRESENCE). This transgression, experienced as a perforation of a stable here and now, offered a type of shock for contemporaries and was initially perceived as being frightful, or at least ambivalent. Nevertheless, in the arts, new communication forms subsequently became a hot topic. At that time, the telephone began to enter the realm of theatre and drama (cf. Jean Cocteau's piece La Voix Humaine, 1930). Slide projection and film also entered scenography – for example, it became part of the "epic stage" of Erwin Piscator and Bertolt Brecht. Based on the principle of "the separation of the elements", their stage forms aimed to demonstrate the constructedness of the world and thereby its changeability. Brecht's attempts artistically to interpret the radio not as a distribution but rather as a communication apparatus might also be noted in this context. Dynamic concepts of space thus began to transform the theatre. Later in his life, Brecht even called himself "the Einstein of the new stage form" (Fuegi 1972, 336).

Although numerous scientific and technical transformations led to shifts in the perception and interpretation of space throughout the 20th century, static spatial models remain tenacious. It was left to the neo-avant-garde to postulate that spaces (and especially places) are not determined as such, but rather are produced through performative multivectorial movement and action. Einstein's dictum "There are no fixed points in space" became a principle of experimental dance, performance art and performative installation since the 1960s (cf. Reynolds and McCormick 2003). The idea that there is not just one centre but rather a "multitude of centres" that "interfuse and penetrate each other" subsequently suggests an equal treatment of actors and audience (Cage 1981, 102). Spaces – in their complex relevance as material, corporeal as well as communication modes – turn out to be complex and dynamic components of culture and communication, in other words, they are always precondition and product at the same time.

According to Foucault, the 20th century might be defined as an "epoch of space", as "the epoch of juxtaposition, the epoch of the near and far, of the side-by-side, of the dispersed" (Foucault 1986, 22). Spatialisation in the postmodern debate became a model of philosophical thinking, and the rejection of diachronic in favour of synchronic concepts of space and time became a prominent concern. The question of the media was always implicit in this debate, and at the turn of the 21st century it gained attention again with the emergence of the so-called second media transition that marked the change from analogue to digital media and its plurimedial, interconnected and newly defined virtual spaces.

Spatiality and the Intermedial Theatron

At the turn of the millennium configurations between theatre and media spaces arise as new live events (→ INSTANCE: CHRISTOPHER KONDEK). These performances comply with the established spatial and temporal conception of live theatre – performed before an audience in the here and now – but in a form that reinterprets and extends these concepts. The question of space, in certain ways, becomes neuralgic here since the traditional medial specificity of theatre barely allows questions as to the participation of other media vis-à-vis its production. Often, spaces of other media, such as those within film, are categorised as *technical reproductions* and thus incompatible with theatrical space. The conception of theatre is thus troubled by intermedial practices.

In theatre theory, though not so much in theatre practice, this spatial exclusiveness has a long tradition. There is now a controversy about to what extent media spaces can be connected with those of the theatre, as the relations among them are rethought. Digitisation and the possibilities of interactivity allow media spaces to become dynamically inter-engaged in ways that modify understanding of the liveness criteria of real-time events (cf. Auslander 1999; Dixon 2007). Artists experiment with feedback loops (← TERM: FEEDBACK LOOP) between spaces in ways that extend the spectrum of the new stage from platforms located in real space to manifestations of cyberspace. The challenge of this approach is that it undermines established notions of real space actor-audience relations (cf. Dixon 2007, 462f.). A both-and model is, however, provided by the intermedial stage. At first sight, this platform is primarily located in real space, and from there – as a spatial configuration – it travels across different spaces, actual and virtual (→ TERM: TELEMATIC). According to this concept, the intermedial stage can be understood as an adjustable platform, or interface, in which real, imagined and virtual spaces can performatively reconfigure one another and create enlightening tensions. This stage thus becomes a discursive instrument that resonates with current social transformation processes brought about by digital media and interconnectivity as well as cultural and economic globalisation. As Chiel Kattenbelt puts it:

> If the expression "all the world is a stage" is (or seems to be) no longer just a metaphor, but on the contrary a characteristic feature of our mediatised culture, then we really do need a stage on which the staging of life can be staged in such a way that it can be deconstructed and made visible again (Kattenbelt 2006, 38).

The intermedial stage affords the exploration of performative configurations between *here* and other spaces, and experiments with simultaneous actions at different (locally or geographically separated) locations. These complex scenographies not only go beyond the bounds of theatre space in order to extend it within the local context (see Environmental Theatre and Site Specific Theatre since the 1960s) but also include what George Christoph Tholen calls the "playing space of media" (Schade and Tholen 1999, 17). In other words: the process of performance is no longer limited to the here and now, but rather transgresses local contexts and environments and playfully connects to telematic and other remote spaces (→ TERM: TELEMATIC). The space of intermediality, in this regard, is not already *there* but can only be understood as a temporal, dynamic and highly complex spatial configuration, which is created within the process of the performance.

'Spatial Turn': Redefining Space as a Category of Performance Analysis

Thus, the advent of the intermedial stage subjects the traditional definition of theatre to renegotiation and rethinking. The live phenomena of media spaces (virtual spaces, telespaces, networks) that emerge on stage are no longer constrained simply to the radius of the here and now. This signals a need for a fundamental revision that is challenging some of the basic premises of the Theatre Studies discipline. Among these is the assumption that actors and audience have to be present in one location ("corporeal co-presence"), a definition applied not only to traditional forms of theatre but also to postdramatic theatre and its scenographies. For all his reconceptualising of theatre and drama, Hans-Thies Lehmann continues to define a theatre event as a "time segment in one's life that is spent together by the actors and the audience in that *space* in which they both breathe and in which the theatre acting and the act of viewing occurs" (Lehmann 2006, 12). Meanwhile, it has been emphasised on numerous occasions that "the ontology of performance (liveness), which exists before and after mediatization, has been altered with the space of technology" (Causey 383). According to Balme, "the doctrine of media specificity...is becoming obsolete, and needs to be replaced by a more integrative concept" (2008, 205). As a consequence of this paradigm shift, the categorical ascertainment of space (and the concept of co-presence) has to be qualified. Definitions of space must be supplemented by a subcategory, *medial space*, the digitally-generated spaces in which theatre is composed.

As Dixon has pointed out, the term space in a digital context certainly includes virtual representations of space that show up on the surfaces of screens and other interfaces but is, in effect, even more varied than this. Indeed, its usages, especially in relation to the spaces of electronic communication and the Internet, are indistinct and "largely metaphoric" (2007, 462f.). Nor is it helpful simply to observe that the term "cyberspace" (Gibson 1984) has, in its short history, already undergone a remarkable change with regards to its interpretation. Far from early visions of a happy "global village" (McLuhan), more recent critical readings of electronic space conceive it as a domain of vast data transit and distribution, and of surveillance, commercialisation and exclusion. The ubiquity of the Internet in cultural and social spheres led to predictions that real space would lose its relevance vis-à-vis the virtual (cf. Paul Virilio, 1977). Following this discourse, the question of virtual space, during the last two decades of the last century, had been discussed mainly as a simulation problem. Then, at the turn of the millennium, another shift of perspectives happened. Decisive events such as 9/11 were interpreted as a collapse of the "non-geographic world view", and since then and in contrast to the simulation hypothesis, many point to the "permanences of space", to its materiality, to political and social impacts, and to geographic reference points (cf. Maresch 2003, 16).

These changes signal not a new essentialism, but an extension of the postmodern discourse of "spatialisation" which encompasses positions of postcolonial and gender-specific geography (cf. Edward Soja, Doreen Massey et al.) (→ TERM: DISPLACEMENT). In the meantime this perspective, inspired by Cultural Studies, has been extended by "media geography" which analyses the use and effects of media in a global and intercultural comparison (cf. Falkheimer and Jansson

2006). The underlying claim here is that the interpenetration of real and virtual spaces has to be analysed in a more differentiated manner than previous formulations allow.

Regarding the still unresolved question of space, academic Theatre Studies must attend to the "spatial turn" noted above. This means that media spaces have to be examined not only in terms of their semiotic and phenomenological characteristics, but also in terms of their technological ramifications and culture-specific usage. This affects the media tools as well as the software that is being implemented and, as far as this can be analysed, the technological infrastructure. In respect of theatre practices, a key concern is how actors and audience behave within new spatial and intermedial configurations. The challenge is really to understand the interpenetration of differently constructed spaces and the concepts engaged within them: connectivity; presence, telepresence and absence; perception and teleperception; and new performance modalities. The performativity of the intermedial theatron, in this respect, has to be analysed as a complex, heterogeneous and relational phenomenon.

MAPPING INTERMEDIALITY IN PERFORMANCE

Node: Dimensions

Displacement. Displacement may best be defined as a "travelling concept" (Bal 2002), one applied in a variety of fields, each emphasising a different accent depending on how the concept is used. In physics, displacement refers to the difference between the initial position and the final position of an object; in engineering it is used to measure the process by which an object immersed in a fluid pushes some of the fluid out of the way; in mechanics it is the distance moved by a particle or body in a specific direction. In psychoanalysis, Freud used displacement to describe a subconscious defence mechanism, in which dream thoughts about the self are decentred, appearing instead as Other, but still associated with the self. Because of its prominence in Freud's theory, displacement is often related to the experience of uncanniness, a concept that permeates contemporary studies of media and theatre. In the social sciences displacement refers to political or economical migration patterns and/or feelings of being displaced. Here, Heidegger's notion of *Unheimlichkeit* reverberates.

To analyse displacement in intermediality, a glance at mechanics may give insight, where it is understood as a vector quality, entailing both magnitude and direction. Magnitude could refer to the possibilities of experiential impact of displacement, where as direction may focus on displaced objects, bodies, and spaces and the different medial contexts with which they are connected. This type of displacement is often used to release creative potential. Displacing objects, images, and words, removes them from their original contexts, thus drawing new attention to the object. This use may be found in collage or in strategies of re-framing, as in Sergei Eisenstein's montage of attractions. Digital technologies that reconfigure the ontologies of space and time add to a sense of displacement that increasingly characterizes intersections of media and theatre. (Liesbeth Groot Nibbelink)

Deterritorialisation. Deterritorialisation articulates the undoing or destabilizing of a territory, an entity traditionally defined by geographical coordinates, as well as by cultural, political, or social phenomena. By definition, a territory has boundaries, and therefore installs an inside and an outside. Deterritorialisation is a concept closely connected to the theories of Gilles Deleuze and Félix Guattari. For Deleuze and Guattari, deterritorialisation refers to acts or movements that disrupt and destabilize rule, order or convention. In the field of anthropology, deterritorialisation often refers to the transcendence of territorial boundaries in current society, and may be seen to "untie the links between culture, place and identity, to understand fissures between language and cultural identity, to situate the notion of community in multiple locations" (Elden 2006, 49-50).

The concept of deterritorialisation is often partnered with its obverse, reterritorialisation. According to Ronald Bogue, deterritorialisation concerns the detachment or unfixing of elements, that are therefore given greater autonomy, whereas reterritorialisation implies the reorganisation of elements within new assemblages, in which components acquire new functions within the newly created territory (Bogue 1997, 475). This is a continuous process, an endless reconfiguration of spatial relations. The same might apply to intermedial relationships. The concept of de/reterritorialisation allows for studying disruptive medial constellations, in which the greater autonomy and newly acquired functions of media redefine territories of media, emphasizing process instead of final product. (Liesbeth Groot Nibbelink)

Glocalisation. Glocalisation was first introduced by the British sociologist Roland Robertson (1992). According to him, globalisation has led to a "compression of the world", in which increasing mobility and digital communication have changed spatial relations. The term suggests that communication today always involves both local and global networking (→TERM: NETWORKING) and exchanges of knowledge and commerce. This concept differs from that of McLuhan, who envisioned the "global village" as some sort of liquid space, consisting of "boundless random resonations", disconnected from real space (McLuhan and Powers, 1986). The concept also differs from Paul Virilio's "dromology" and his influential thesis that "the perspective of real time" will supersede the "perspective of real space and geosphere". Following Virilio, one cannot differentiate anymore between "global" and "local"; phenomena have become "glocal" in the infosphere and its "one-time-system" (1995). In this sense, the virtual "hyperspace" of media has been debated throughout the 1990s almost exclusively as a simulation problem (Baudrillard).

In the context of the so-called "spatial turn" (Nigel and Thrift 2000), these concepts became subjects of controversy. At the turn of the millennium, especially post-9/11 and the tensions of ongoing economic globalisation, the perspective of the local returns in the analyses of postmodern thinkers, such as Edward Soja and Doreen Massey who, after Foucault, deconstructed territorial delineations or demarcations to include marginalised positions. From this perspective, glocalisation draws attention to the "digital divide" within material space and to the so-called "cyber segmentations" within the digital space (Sassen 1996; 2001) and to the dynamics that happen among these spaces. Currently, the debate articulates global and local, space and place as being neither dichotomous nor revoked; instead, based on the assumption that space is a heterogenising relational term, we are seeing overlapping, couplings and breaks between spaces taking place. (Birgit Wiens)

Telematic. Telematic was first coined by Simon Nora and Alan Minc (1978) and now broadly describes digitally-mediated communications among the range of mediated network access through devices such as the telephone, computers, the Internet, and other data-processing systems. Nora and Minc derived the term from the combination of telecommunications and informatics, and their report emphasised the importance of transmission infrastructure over information content. Closely related to telepresence and virtuality, telematics provides a useful umbrella term for the dynamic relations among artists, participants, devices, and digital content of new media in performance. Indeed, telematics serves to explain performance in the spaces left by the description of theatre as the nexus of Space, Time, and the Body.

Telematic art began as early as the late 1970s with televisual and early email experiments by artists such as Bill Barlett, Liza Bear, and Roy Ascott. Notable performances include "Hole in Space" (1980), which connected visitors to shopping malls in New York and Los Angeles through satellite video, and Paul Sermon's "Telematic Dreaming" (1992) in which a single performer's image (dancer and media-artist Susan Kozel) was digitally projected onto a physical bed on which participants could interact with the virtual body. These projects contain many of the key elements of telematic performance: namely, real-time interactions mediated by virtual, visual projections linking disparate physical spaces and bodies. Telematic art also includes connected performances, in which multiple aspects of a single production occur in multiple locations simultaneously. For example, Wafaa Bilal's *Domestic Tension* (2007) explored the material consequences of virtual presence by inviting online participants to shoot at him with a web-controlled paintball gun, and Christopher Kondek's *Dead Cat Bounce* (2005) drew together geographically separate audience and performers to explore the tensions between virtual and real spaces (→ INSTANCE: CHRISTOPHER KONDEK). (Sarah Bay-Cheng)

Instances

Instance: Christopher Kondek, *Dead Cat Bounce* (2005)

Birgit Wiens

This instance considers how theatre extends into a *remote spatiality*. Christopher Kondek's intermedial stock market performance-game *Dead Cat Bounce* exemplifies a shift in the intermedial conceptions of time and space. Telecommunicatively linking spatially distributed and geographically separated actors and audience, *Dead Cat Bounce*, a project of Berlin-based American artist Christopher Kondek, allows for the creation of complex, dynamic interlacings and transitions with regard to distinct real and virtual spaces. Its intermedial scenography evokes new performance modalities and perceptions, one that simultaneously echoes the effects of financial globalisation, digital culture, and the tools of telematic communication.

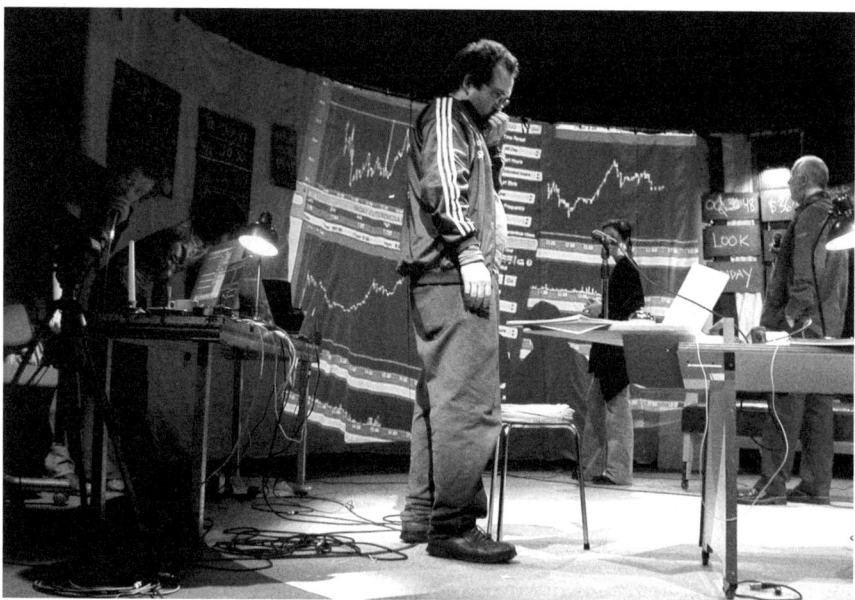

Fig. 1: Dead Cat Bounce, *rehearsal photo,* © *Christopher Kondek*

The project title describes a well-known stock market mechanism – the short, temporary price rise in the shares of a stock before its continuing fall – by referencing in short form the one-liner, "Even a dead cat will bounce if it falls from a great height". This allegory already has a spatial metaphor within it, although Kondek observes that he didn't explicitly plan a project on spaces when he started developing the idea for *Dead Cat Bounce* with his team in 2003. Having bought shares over the Internet, he initially wanted to do a piece on how the audience would hang on to the edge of their seat – as he had done himself as a share owner – in the face of the ups-and-downs of the share prices (interview with author, 2007). The complexity of the project makes this account something of an understatement. Kondek's description of it as an "interactive edifying play about the functional mechanisms of the stock market" leads us into a production that deals imaginatively with the shifts and rhythms of virtual financial transactions and the heated environments in which they take place (Kondek 2005).

The Intermedial Theatron

Dead Cat Bounce exists in different variations. This article refers to the performance in Berlin, 2005 (Theater am Halleschen Ufer, November 2005). For Kondek's stock market game, the stage designer Herbert Klitzsch constructed a system that can best be described, following Marvin Carlson, as a "ludic space" (Carlson 1989, 6). A round acting area (similar to that of an ancient orchestra) was featured in the centre of the room, surrounded by a semicircular auditorium, rising upwards. Behind the acting area there was a large, slightly curved projection screen in addition to a smaller screen. In the acting area were two tables with laptops and telephones, chairs, a sofa and a high desk with a clock on top. The arrangement evoked the classical Greek theatron, albeit an intermedial one. The actors logged on to the online trading programme "Interactive Brokers", which connected the theatre space live and in real-time with the New York Stock Exchange (NYSE). The theatre, then, has its eye on the virtual world of the stock market as if it were a peep show, a self-reflexive feature noted by one of the performers. The five actors, present on the stage throughout, were both traders – playmakers – and commentators on the action. The audience's entrance fee constituted the pot of money to be gambled for the evening and spectators were asked to vote on the buying and selling decisions. As explained in the show's programme, the audience thus became a "shareholder in the theatre production: the question as to the participation of the audience is being redefined here in a quite pragmatic and capitalistic manner" (programme 2005). The production had a 90 min. running time and was scheduled to end at exactly the moment that the NYSE closed trading for the day. The results of the day's trading were then presented via live television broadcast and the profits (or losses) in Berlin were calculated and – in cases of profit – shared with the audience.

After Brecht: *Dead Cat Bounce* – an "Interactive Edifying Play"?

Kondek's project taps into a phenomenon – global share trading – that affects everyone as demonstrated by the international economic crisis of 2008-2009. Such global interconnection is not only communicative and cultural but also economic. In the days of telegraphs and telephones, long before the advent of the Internet, it was the stock market that used the metaphor of the network, and thereby conceived as a spatial phenomenon. As André Kostolany, the grand old man of finance, observed:

> All stock markets function more and more according to the laws of the communicating channels. Someone somewhere presses a button – and five thousand kilometres away one can feels the effects. The Emir of Kuwait makes a decision and the gold mine shares in Toronto go up. A financial crash with a revolver shot in Paris and the pound sterling falls in New York [...] Behind it all is always the adventure with money (Kostolany 803).

In the 1980s, Kostolany envisaged that traditional floor trading would soon be replaced by the much faster and more speculative tele-trading: "Gradually the stock markets will disappear as they do not have presence any more. Everything will be replaced by telecommunication...by pressing a button" (2006, 811).

Kondek's project responds to this development. *Dead Cat Bounce* constitutes an experiment by both actors and audience to tune into the communication flow of global share trading in real time from the room of a Berlin theatre. The theatrical stage is turned into a platform from which to observe and comment upon the mechanisms of the stock market. The project sets itself the difficult task of producing and staging a performative space that has a functional relation to the virtual world of financial markets. Due to their complexity, size and dimension, not to mention their dynamic changes, these markets cannot easily be contained within representation. Their actions and movements can barely be apprehended, although their results – particularly, the rise and fall of share values – materialise in a real way, leaving in their wake consequences for their participants. The performance of the stage platform, with its artistic aspect, is put into tension with the performance of the stock market, that in turn functions according to other rules, namely those of the market: efficiency and quick decision processes in accordance with pecuniary interests. Can so complex a phenomenon as the global financial markets be broached with the tools and instruments of the theatre?

The comparison between the stock exchange and theatre, central to *Dead Cat Bounce*, was established well before terms such as performance and performativity were in vogue (Kostolany, 227). Kondek, however, does not present over-simplified analogies between the two. *Dead Cat Bounce* is rather a stock market theatre in which the market is both main actor and subject matter, and as such reveals itself as a blueprint. The piece is comprised of a fast-paced collage of stock charts, share curves and images from company websites. There is some storytelling, in which the performers give short reports about their own personal trading experiences, which remind the audience that market performances, though abstract, can have severe effects on people's private lives and working conditions. The show also integrates retrospectives on the history of the stock market, as well as documentary and interview clips, such as those featuring a banker from the Dutch Fortris Bank or the publisher of *Left Business Observer*. Short excerpts from relevant films are played, including the stock market scene from *L'Eclisse* (1962) by Michelangelo Antonioni. This type of staged montage attempts to encircle that which remains ultimately absent, the presence of the global stock market itself. The complexity of the stock market's mechanisms, dynamics and interlacings ensures that the subject remains elusive. The issue is partly one of articulating interconnected transactions rather than concrete and single locations, though Kondek is not the first to attempt such a challenge.

Bertolt Brecht, as Walter Benjamin noted, was already aware of the increasing complexity of social phenomena which art, especially in its traditional forms of expression, fails to represent:

> [T]he situation, says Brecht, is complicated by the fact that to a lesser extent than ever a simple "rendering of reality" reveals something. A photograph of the Krupp or of the A.E.G. plants tells us next to nothing of these institutes. The actual reality has slipped into the functional one. The reification of human relationships, e.g. in the form of a factory, is not given by the latter. Therefore something does actually have to be "built up", something "artificial", "contrived" (Benjamin 1966, 245).

As if he had followed this advice, Kondek set up something artificial and contrived for his stock market game. This decision was not without scepticism, and Kondek noted the futility of the undertaking from the very start. The performance begins with a video image of NYSE's front façade, with its massive columns and flags, on the projection screen at the back – a scene that could be interpreted as a Benjaminian reference and a comment on the attempt of trying to explain the complexity of the stock market or revealing something about it. Accordingly, Kondek's labelling of *Dead Cat Bounce* as an interactive edifying play (*interaktives Lehrstück*) – another meaningful reference to Brecht's issue-based *Lehrstücke* – seems almost malicious. With the help of the "Interactive Brokers" software, the actors and spectators become alsomost entirely immersed in the events of the stock market, an immersion that make it difficult to see through its mechanisms in a classically Brechtian sense.

A witting irony is in play. Just like petty capitalists, the actors and audience participate with their own stake and are immediately affected by the ups and downs of the financial market. Brechtian dissociation is not possible. That said, the experimental set-up of *Dead Cat Bounce* continually raises awareness of the ambivalence and finiteness of its own undertaking. The production's game-like interactive arrangement produces a sense of the strangeness of the event. This makes *Dead Cat Bounce* both a post-Brechtian edifying play *and* the rejection of an edifying play. The means, mechanisms and modalities of this particular piece of theatre relate to the performance of the stock market in a manner that is neither solely resistive nor wholly affirmative. The production does not negate one's own entanglement within the complex processes of globalisation but rather, as far as possible, turns its own engagement into the subject of the performance.

"Wait, Watch and See What the Market Does": Staging the Absent

Dead Cat Bounce features five actors on stage, all appearing under their real names, who take on different functions during the course of the play. Alex (Schröder) appears as a very alert host in a suit, interacts with the audience and leads everyone through the evening. Victor (Morales), a computer nerd, always has the latest hot tips and supplies updated stock market news and rumours, whilst recommending the shares of companies that have exotic-sounding names. Simon (Versnel), the oldest in the team, displays a more wait-and-see, sceptical attitude. As a native of the Netherlands he talks about the origins of the stock exchange in seventeenth-century Amsterdam, where the commodity was tulip bulbs, and home to the first failed speculation. Christiane (Kuehl), the only woman, is busy in a sober, business-like manner in front of her laptop. She triggers the mutually agreed purchase and sales orders via the "Interactive Brokers" programmme and announces the current share prices in a news presenter's voice. Kondek himself, sitting at another computer, acts as a sort of commentator who joins the game on various occasions using comments, company histories and background information. He gives the news behind the news, talking, for example, about a company that dismissed workers and how this affected the share performance positively. Meanwhile he searches the Internet for companies that could come into consideration and whose details are projected onto the screen from time to time. The game, limited to 90 minutes, is performed in a dynamic and fast-paced manner. The aphorism "time is money" continually comes to mind. The efficiency of one's actions and decision-making shapes the theatrical action to concrete economic effect. Indeed, spectators are continually reminded of their role as speculators and day traders, for instance, when they are photographed by Victor (using the command: "Say money!") as new shareholders in an Indian company that they have never heard of.

The main performer in Kondek's project, however, is the stock market. At regular intervals – and always when an order has been placed – the host announces in a mantra-like tone, "Now wait, watch and see what the market does". In these moments a change of pace takes place, and a period of waiting ensues to see what this absent performer will do. The time ticks by ever so slowly, a waiting that tides one over in manifold ways.

Again and again the actors make us aware of the fact that the whole thing is not just a game. Rather, the participants in Berlin are connected in real-time to the actual goings-on of the stock market and therefore find themselves implicated with a number of invisible speculators and traders as part of a globally interconnected event that is taking place right at this minute. This process has something phantasmal, something disembodied about it. In order finally to have something he can hold on to in this nowhere place – graspable counterpart – Simon tries to make a long-distance call to the PR department of one of the companies in order to have them explain to him how and why the shares of the company are performing as they do. He fails at the switchboard, however, and then only gets half-baked information. The stock exchange and its activities remain abstract and barely accessible. This inability to catch up with the main performer implies a distance that is metaphorical as well as spatial. This becomes especially noticeable when, over the telephone and Internet data lines, one can sometimes hear a far-off swishing sound.

Blind windows

There is quite a lot to see on the stage of *Dead Cat Bounce*. The dramaturgy and the scenography clearly evoke features of the spaces of postdramatic theatre. Images are treated in a manner that is collage-like, there are multiple framings, visual windows and a splitscreen aesthetic oriented by way of a computer-interface design. The effect on the audience is to privilege what Hans-Thies Lehmann described as the "seeing sight" (1999, 294). Kondek's previous work as a video artist and his collaborations with Robert Wilson, Laurie Anderson and the Wooster Group show their traces here. A plethora of film excerpts, interviews and documentary material is shown. Included is a cowboy who is steadfastly riding westwards – suggesting that even the Internet, conceived in the USA, is ultimately only one more expansion of western thought.

Notwithstanding such a spectrum of images, these images reveal close to nothing that is tangible by way of direct representation. The stock market is at best present in an atmospheric manner. The stage becomes an intermedial arena for an act of participatory witness. The acting area, as I have previously noted, deliberately reminds one of an ancient amphitheatre. This time, however, we are not surrounded by an open landscape and the sky, but rather confronted by a screen-filled horizon. On this horizon we view the images that are projected, but sometimes there are only projected red theatre curtains that shroud in secrecy all events happening behind them. What is staged here? The appearance of nothing. In one scene, when it is clear that nothing else will help, the performers call an alleged stock market saint and light a candle in the hope that through this magic the right impulses will be sent into the virtual casino of investors, players and speculators that seems so unfathomably large and incomprehensible. The stock market, the project appears to conclude, turns out to be an irrational sphere. As the programme note suggests, "The market takes on the role that the gods played in classical tragedy, whose arbitrariness humans suffered under. It plays with fortune and kismet, makes careers and breaks livelihoods just as quickly as it set these up" (Programme 2005).

Fig. 2: Photo of one of the scenes: Simon Versnel, film excerpt, © Christopher Kondek

Summary: Space, Connected Performance and 'Remote Presence'

From a stage in Berlin, Dead Cat Bounce invokes spaces that go beyond the localised here and now of theatre. Theatre scholarship has to date addressed these remote spaces only peripherally. Certainly the technical infrastructure of telecommunication and the Internet, distributed over large distances, allows for spatial interpretations. But the application of spatial terms onto the performative dimension of cyberspace, as Steve Dixon notes, is "largely metaphoric and conceptual" (Dixon 2007, 462). The virtual spaces of the Internet have promulgated a remarkable range of interpretations since their inception, from a naive vision of the global village to a current understanding of the Internet as a sphere of (self-)marketing and economic competition, exerting power and control (cf. Sassen 1997). In the meantime there is a tendency to analyse virtual space as a social construction and a communicative sphere where, in order to avoid generalising the cyberspace, local access requirements, media competence and user behaviour are gaining more attention.

Medial space of interconnected, digital communication is a space of *remote presence*, the immediate presence of something located far away or that takes place over distance. The transactions that this space contains may not entirely be present, but nor are they absent (Faßler 1997, 199). As observed by the spectators with money at stake, these transactions show their effects in the here and now. Remote spatiality has increasingly become part of cultural awareness and will become both a topic and a production mode for theatre. Thus, we need to understand, in a more exact manner, which spaces are forming within the Internet, what new forms of spatial experience and knowledge they cause, and how these in turn affect the spaces of the material world. Such issues go beyond the playful aestheticism of performance. It is not enough to interpret the Internet as the "largest theatre in the world" on whose virtual stages and platforms anyone can (re) produce herself. It is of greater importance to identify and analyse the emergent economic, social and political implications of the Net and its interactions with physical space and society. This could become a new, even explosive task for performance, exploring and staging the constellations, relations and dynamics of electronic spaces and the gestures and modalities of their interconnected phenomena. Kondek's *Dead Cat Bounce* does just that.

Instance: La Socìetas Raffaello Sanzio, *Purgatory* (2008)

Katia Arfara

This instance focuses on *Purgatory* (2008), which premiered at the Avignon Theatre Festival. *Purgatory* is the second part of La Socìetas Raffaello Sanzio's (SRS) triptych based on Dante's *Divine Comedy*, and it offers an exemplary instance of the company's anti-naturalistic treatment of space and time. Since its inaugural performance *Diade incontro a Monade* in Rome (1981), SRS has displayed a distinctive performance mode intermixing visual and theatre arts. Radicalizing the avant-garde conviction that art should evolve by breaking out of the canonical forms, the Italian company questions the very nature of representation while redefining the role of the spectator. In *Purgatory*, director Romeo Castellucci uses digital devices to collapse binaries, such as imaginary/factual reality or conscious/unconscious spectatorship, into a plane of hyperreality.

Since its beginnings, the Cesena-based SRS has worked on an expanded field of intermedial practices based on the concept of displacement (← TERM: DISPLACEMENT). Conceived by Castellucci as a transmigration of figures and forms, displacement is an ongoing process which involves practices of transition, transplantation or transposition from one discipline (visual arts) to another (theatre arts). In the process, correspondences between components of the same genre, such as its spatiotemporal conventions, are redefined. SRS is interested in mapping out patterns and symbols of a collective reality as it has survived in mythological and religious traditions and beliefs beyond western aesthetics. By displacing media devices (rather than the media themselves) from digital arts to the stage, the performance breaks with conventional perceptions of space and time while redefining, both literally and metaphorically, the very notion of intermedial theatre. In these new contexts, the media that are mutually implicated and repurposed are time and space themselves.

Uncanny Spaces

In Dante's *Divine Comedy*, purgatory is conceived as a lucid topography marked by an ascending spiral movement. It constitutes an active intermediary space which repeats and reverses Hell's structure, on both literal and symbolic levels (cf. Schapp 1993). Highly symmetrical, these levels constitute a realm of transformation, a negative double of life on earth that troubles the binary system of Heaven and Hell. Everyone here is changing, or waiting for a change that will allow one to enter the City of God. Despite the movement within many of his seven concentric terraces (each of which represents, in a decreasing order of gravity, the seven deadly sins), Mount Purgatory is a fortified city of *stasis*. Its movement is not progressive but useless and eternally repetitive (cf. Ryan 1993).

The opening scene of Castellucci's *Purgatory*, in contrast, introduces a rigorously framed interior of an ordinary world. We are in the high-ceilinged kitchen of a bourgeois family. A mother is preparing lunch for her son, an everyday task. Even though Castellucci establishes the codes and conventions of a naturalistic scene, the kitchen does not exactly correspond to a real, domestic interior. The set is cube-like: an enclosed and impermeable space, clearly de-contextualised and isolated from the world outside. The room remains spatially and topographically unspecific while its recessed, strangely cold lighting cannot be identified with any specific time of day. The displacements of time and space, coupled with the room's monumental dimensions and the spatialised sound created by unseen microphones, create an effect of hyperrealism. Visually and acoustically, it is impossible for the spectator simply to be drawn into this interior in the manner of dramatic theatre. Castellucci often conceives of space as a material, an enclosure that both implies and encases the transgression of its concreteness by an immaterial, yet precise, spiritual order. The cube belongs to the internal typology of SRS as one of the company's major framing devices. As an explicitly geometrical space, it reduces space to its primary elements (walls, floor, ceiling). Once the illustrative dimension of the scenery is banished, a question of theatre ontology is raised: *what sort of stage does the performer inhabit?*

As in every Castellucci performance, the opening scene does not so much inform the spectator in representational terms as install an energy field onstage: the short dialogue between the mother and the child creates the strange feeling that something is going to happen, something terrifying that happens here repeatedly. The domestic interior functions in counterpoint to the action that follows.

Hyperreality

The uncanny aspect of this familiar place is reinforced by the stage directions (*didascalies*) projected on a video monitor installed at the upper part of the proscenium. The text describes everything that is said or done onstage, appropriating the form, if not the function, of surtitles. This textual anticipation of the action continues throughout the second and third scenes, which are situated in the child's room and the living room. The technique of delay interpenetrates the hyperreality of these domestic interiors. Castellucci explicitly dissociates the 'real' space from the virtual one in order to displace dramatic tension from stage dialogues to the existential gap between physical and virtual time, the material and the immaterial.

Introducing on the video monitor a second, digital reality, Castellucci implodes established scenographic space and dislodges the here and now condition of the theatrical event. Instead of a present-time image we experience onstage a delayed and consequently *past*-time image. The delay further disrupts the action and contradicts the hyperrealism of the stage while at the same time multiplying viewpoints by shifting the emphasis to gestural details: taking off a jacket, sitting on a sofa, putting a plate on the table. The de-synchronisation of utterance and action alters the sense of immediacy inherent in both dramatic theatre and live video practices. Once our attention focuses on usually unnoticed activities, the instructions projected on the screen function as a microscopically zooming camera that creates close-ups on specific moments within the stage action.

This discontinuous video time makes for irruption within the spatial as well as the temporal continuum of the stage, blurring the performance's immersive effect and breaking with illusion. The stage instructions go beyond their cinematic origins. More than a commentary parallel to the action, the surtitles create a separate world of their own. The screen text attains the dramaturgical autonomy of a detached virtual self that observes the stage world from a distance and plays it back as if it were a closed-circuit video. It functions as an external narrator, with a personal identity and a virtual embodiment. The back-and-forward effect of the surtitles places the stage under more overt surveillance while simultaneously breaking the conventions surrounding the unpredictable 'real' event. The spectator is informed via the surtitles that the father is going to drink one more whisky, that he is going to turn on the TV while asking the mother if he can have dinner in the living room, that he will not finally touch his food.

Fig.: Pier Paolo Zimmermann as Second Star and Sergio Scarlatella as Third Star, © Luca Del Pia

Expanding Perception

Once the nature of the theatrical space is disturbed, perception is affected: the spectator becomes engaged with the stage action, and is at the same time a remote observer, without being psychologically involved. Castellucci appropriates a digital technique to introduce a kind of delay communication. This is a strategy of distantiation: the spectator is distanced from the phenomenological perception of performance as a real-time experience. In Castellucci's hands, digital devices create an expanded, intermediary space between the mental and the material, the intellectual and the performative.

The screen text thus gives visual form to the passage of time, making the spectator conscious both of the *process* of perception and of her privileged position as a witness-observer. An altered narrative form is in play, one that depends upon the spectator's capacity to combine and synthesize the double information. Because of the delay effect, the written text and the stage action become two parallel realities that relate to each other but never coincide (→ SEPARATION). The immediate present is distinct because it juxtaposes with the immediate future. This media art effect introduces a double articulation: it creates an in-between space – involving an awareness of gap, difference and relationality – and gives spectators the impression that they're watching the action from an elevated point of view, similar to an omniscient, or God's eye view.

The performance's climactic action, the rape of the child by the father, occurs offstage, recalling the dramatic conventions of ancient Greek tragedy and leaving the spectators to contemplate an empty living room while the amplified sounds of trauma fill the space. Just before one hears the brute grunts of the father and the plaintive screams of the son, the screens display contrapuntal descriptions such as, "The Second Star shows its drawings to the Third"; "They laugh together"; "The Second Star also laughs"; "The First Star plays a record of light music"; "The Second Star begins to dance and jump in the room"; "The First and the Third Stars are dancing together". According to the surtitles the stage personae do not have names: the mother is the First Star, the child is the Second and the father the Third. By juxtaposing these simple lines with the agony offstage, the text creates a layer of discordance between the visual banality and the sonic brutality that follows. By unsettling these relations of space and time, Castellucci also reshapes the ontological nature of the personae standing on stage. We deal more with figures than with characters.

"Figural Realism"

This technique is perhaps best understood in the context of Dante scholarship. SRS's *Purgatory* is conceived within an anti-naturalistic yet realistic frame which recalls Dante's "figural realism" as defined by Erich Auerbach. Auerbach describes the *Divine Comedy* as a flood of figural characters defined both as "tentative fragmentary reality and veiled eternal reality" (Auerbach 2003b, 72-73). Following

Auerbach's theological, yet historicised approach, we observe that Dante creates a figural reality that merges the ahistorical, eternal reality of neo-Platonism with the incomplete, concrete, historical present. Originally referring to a dynamic "plastic form" shaped by man, *figura* also appears in the writings of the Roman philosopher Lucretius in the sense of simulacra, effigies, dream images or ghosts. According to Auerbach, Lucretius uses *figurae* in the Greek philosophical sense as structures "that peel off things like membranes" and "float round in the air", a kind of *eidola* (phantom image) in a materialistic sense (Auerbach 2003b, 17). The simulacra provide structure without closure, an open process of displacements, discontinuities and transformations.

Digital devices allow Castellucci to intensify this trope of the *figura* in order to transgress the limits of a naturalistic representation. Detached from, yet embodied within earthly (corporeal) selves, Castellucci's figural bodies have common human afflictions such as hunger, fatigue and headaches. We are indeed in the Ante-Purgatory, a space that, according to Dante, lies in front of Mount Purgatory's ladder. It is a realm of imperfection, irregularity and degeneration, subject to turbulences of the weather and to all forms of natural mutability. Here, animal and plant life is decaying, clouds appear and disappear, their shapes changing continually. At the close of the rape scene, the child's forgiveness of his father is a tragic act that transgresses the Law and thus cannot be perceived within a realistic context. It is rather an allegory resonating within an ontologically distinct domain: here, in the Ante-Purgatory, souls need to be forgiven by their loved ones so that they may shorten their stay (cf. Le Goff 1981, 461-464).

Reconstructing Memory

Following the rape of the child, Castellucci transposes his stage action into an anti-naturalistic space where a number of anthropomorphic, gigantic flowers appear as in the Ante-Purgatory. They rotate in a slow, endless movement inside a circular frame. The strangeness of their shape together with oblique lighting reinforces the feeling of the uncanny, as does the extreme low-frequency sound penetrating the auditorium. In the last part of the performance, the living room shifts from being a hyperrealistic domestic interior to an almost empty, uncanny space where a disproportionately tall child faces a disproportionately short father who suffers from spastic tetraplegia, and the inversion of size reflects the inversion of power. Ante-Purgatory contains a number of what Rachel Jacoff calls "body-biographies", "stories of the placement or displacement of the earthly bodies of the souls Dante encounters, many of them killed violently" (Jacoff 2003, 128). According to Jacoff, these body-biographies "point in two directions, suggesting the gap between the fate of the body on earth and the soul in the Purgatory, but also insinuating a sense of ongoing connection with the material body through the observation of its earthly fate" (Jacoff 2003, 128). Punished in an infernal unceasing movement, the deformed figures of the father and child in

Castellucci's Purgatory jar their bodies against the floor as if re-experiencing and perhaps deliberately re-enacting their traumatic past. Their convulsions are doubly framed by a circle clearly marked on the floor of the stage and another made of glass that hangs in front of their action. Castellucci's Purgatory is shaped in the form of a circle. As the suffering, deformed bodies of father and son escape our balanced, symmetrical way of seeing, the circular shape disturbs the geometry of the stage. Contradicting perspective, it also implies a circular movement: here, punishment is being materialised. The ongoing suffering of malformed or transformed bodies intensifies memory.

Reflecting the Divine Comedy's internal circular structure, Castellucci's Purgatory becomes a performance based on a memory system, a doubly structured space that preserves the memory of the father's sin through the remediating operations of digital practices. It is commonplace to suggest that the digital image has become the privileged medium of memory. In Castellucci's use of digital references (including the surtitles, the screen through which we view the monstrous flowers, the amplified sounds), the boundaries between recorded and live time become blurred: digital culture alters not only the way that we perceive reality but also the way that we record its expansion of our memory field. The obscurity of the second part of Purgatory could now be (re)considered as a never-ending present, with the hyperrealistic scenery of the first part operating as a flashback that activates memory. The focus shifts from the stage presence to the (painful) act of remembrance.

Castellucci's theatre of memory is based on a strikingly individual topographical system that is rhythmically articulated and that reconsiders, through the effects of digital culture, relations between figures, time and space. Both space and time in Purgatory are treated as concrete and suspended, literal and symbolic, historical and theological. The estrangement produced by this spatiotemporal structure reflects the intermedial nature of the performance itself. Underlying both the limits and the possibilities of technological devices, Purgatory lies neither in the real nor the un-real, is neither illusionary nor actual. We are given to see an aspect of realism that echoes Dante's particular perception of the after-life. As Auerbach suggests, even if we are no longer in a "purely earthly realism ... yet we encounter concrete appearance and concrete occurrence", the figures being at the same time changeless and ephemeral, eternal and phenomenal (Auerbach 2003b, 51). Once the double articulation of time and space enters representation through digital devices, the actors become figures of remembrance whose punishment is to re-enact what happened. Castellucci brings the spectator closer to the lucid intimacy of a vision – an ontological experience capable of expanding perception beyond the sensorial limitations of the present moment.

Instance: Granular Synthesis, *Modell 5* (2001)

Edward Scheer

This instance concerns the ways in which digital sound and video processing affect our experience of the 'now' in performance. It addresses the installation *Modell 5*, by Granular Synthesis, and locates this work in relation to other installations and performance art pieces where the present moment is peculiarly durational, or fragmentable, and mediatised for intensity. Specifically, it asks: has the digital age, with its profound changes to machinic processes and technological systems, really (as Mark Hansen puts it) "altered the infrastructure of our contemporary lifeworld in ways that directly impact our embodied temporal experience?" (Hansen 2004, 235).

Modell 5 and Audiovisual Presence

Granular Synthesis was established in 1992 by audiovisual artists Kurt Hentschläger and Ulf Langheinrich, and is named after a technique of sound synthesis "that operates on the microsound time scale...[where samples] are split into small pieces of around 1 to 50 ms [milliseconds] in length...called grains. Multiple grains may be layered on top of each other all playing at different speed, phase, volume and pitch. The result is no single tone, but a soundscape, often a cloud, that is subject to manipulation in a way unlike any natural sound" ("Granular Synthesis" 2010). *Modell 5* is described by the artists as a "live performance featuring a choir of cyborgian clones". *Modell 5* premiered in Hannover in 2001 and was seen more recently in Melbourne in 2004 at ACMI in an exhibition of new media work entitled *Sense Surround*. The piece features a pulverisingly phat-bass-driven techno soundtrack that feels like it is doing permanent damage to your hearing even through the ear plugs provided. Apart from the audio shock, the work has a four-channel video component featuring digitally re-edited footage of the Japanese performer Akemi Takaya. Shot in extreme close-up, the video was reworked using non-linear editing and motion-control videotape systems to create the effect of a stammering or stuttering image in which the face can be seen in-between durations. The facial gestures are re-ordered at a micro-temporal level so that even the blink of an eye is disrupted and a scream is fragmented into component intensities.

Apart from the cyborg clone choir on screen, the live component of the performance consists in the mixing of images onto the four screens and the sound into the speakers and controlling the levels of sub-bass. The presence at the mixing desk of one of the group is hardly the stuff of conventional performance aesthetics. He sits at the rear of the space manipulating the EQ on the mixing desk, altering levels of different channels so that what one hears changes according to the presence of the operator, but there is no overtly visual component to his performativity (← PORTAL: PERFORMATIVITY). This kind of performance is commonplace in musical contexts such as electronica in which the focus is not primarily visual but is determined by the audio track and oriented to the experience of the spectators, to their own rhythms and their movements rather than to the performance of the artists. Often images are projected to enhance the visual experience of these events. Similarly, Granular Synthesis draws focus to enormous screen projections that threaten to exhaust the visual field in the space. Although any connection to notions of the presence of the artist, which is a *sine qua non* of much performance, may seem tenuous at best, presence remains a key thematic for this installation/performance in unusual ways. In *Modell 5* presence is broken down into its constituent entities: space/time and the sensorial experience of the body that registers them (← PORTAL: CORPOREAL LITERACY). This latter experience that grounds and guarantees presence is both reinforced by the power of the sound, and serially subverted by the temporal disintegration and restructuring of the audio and visual data. It is a performance based on the digital recomposition of presence, in which micro-durations, smaller than the experiential present, are endlessly repeated and phased in and out. Constructing the event as a performance also means that the spectators stay for the entire duration of the work so the component phases of the work can be experienced in all their visual subtlety and sonic brutality.

Like all non-narrative-based performance art *Modell 5* occurs in the present and returns the sense of the audience to the immediate moment of the *now*; but this work also broaches the question of the limit of durations of which we can be aware. To put it another way, it questions how technical means of presentation can influence our perception of durations. If the domain of performance is the present tense then how can technical, digital and intermedial processes alter this fundamental reality?

Performance and the Now

Modell 5's turn to micro-duration and its extension of the present calls to mind works such as Douglas Gordon's *24 Hour Psycho* (1993) and Bill Viola's *The Passions* (2003), especially his *The Quintet of the Astonished* (2001), which slow affective (intensive) speeds down to the point where previously undetectable moments become visible. As Mark Hansen suggests, these relatively simple aesthetic functions of extreme slowness "bring the properly imperceptible, microphysical machinic inscription of matter (time) into the sphere of human experience" (Hansen 2003, 266).

Performance artists such as Marina Abramović and Australia's Mike Parr have always returned to the present and the body as the base chronotope of their art form. Abramović says of her piece *Nightsea Crossing* (1981-86):

MAPPING INTERMEDIALITY IN PERFORMANCE

Fig. 1: Granular Synthesis – in the excess of the visual, audience members do not know where to look, © Modell 5 04 photo videostill (c) granular synthesis

> We didn't want the public to see us begin or end the performance but only this permanent moment of "now", present time, to stay in their minds ... and that moment now is the most difficult for us in the West because we're always reading the past or projecting the future and "now" doesn't figure in this. We are in a tv time which is always the future, the direction is always forwards which is why performance is important to freeze the moment "now" (Abramović 1998, 34).

Similarly, Parr, who over a long career has made body-based, durational and video/performance works, has said that "I always had this idea of the performance occurring right at the edge of the present tense, myself and the audience being dragged right up to the edge of the present tense so that there was no gap between the behaviour and the response...." (Parr in Bromfield 1991, 68). But what would this have meant in effect? How would this present tense have been perceived? A better question is perhaps how could it have been perceived?

In the catalogue of Machine Times, the Dutch Electronic Art Festival DEAF_00 (14-26 November 2000), organiser Joke Brouwer states the answer emphatically:

"Now" lasts for approximately 0.3 seconds. This is the time it takes the various centers and sections of our brain to find a synchronous rhythm which we experience as the present. As cognitive research into the phenomenon of time progresses, it is becoming more and more obvious that time is not an objective quantity which can be measured by chronometers and divided up into seconds and everything beyond. Time is a personal and therefore emotional experience, controlled by social rhythms – a process which starts in the womb. Time is never only natural or only historical, only subjective or only objective: it is always both at the same time.

What is important to clarify is not the exact duration of the present but whether or not the present has a meaningful duration to begin with. William James posed this problem in terms of what he called the specious present", which he defines as "the prototype of all conceived times ... the short duration of which we are immediately and incessantly sensible" (James 1890, 631). James further argues that, "We are constantly aware of a certain duration – the specious present – varying from a few seconds to probably not more than a minute, and this duration (with its content perceived as having one part earlier and another part later) is the original intuition of time" (James 1890, 642). This definition poses some problems since it claims that the indivisible present contains duration of sufficient length to include a sub-division of a present and a past moment within it. In this sense James's present is itself "specious". The importance of this aspect of James's argument, however, is that the perception of the present is fundamental to the "intuition of time" in that it encodes the experience of temporality more generally. James suggests that a meaningful experience of time cannot occur without the perception of the present and that temporal perspective is not possible without it.

This also suggests why artists like those discussed above might take this as a central issue that determines experience, a perception which governs others and forms individual behaviours and perspectives. By creating art works that facilitate the perception of the present moment, they assemble a frame around this notion so that the chaotic temporal perception of quotidian life can come into focus and be reordered. To translate a perception of the present to a spectator or viewer of a work is also therefore to facilitate the process by which a viewer can experience a reordering of her own sense perception.

Neurobiologist Francisco J. Varela argues in words oddly reminiscent of Abramović:

Only when you break away from the spell of time as a sequence of instants one can measure by the clock, and you come back to your own depth of experience, you realize that what you live right now is almost like a cloud, like a whole, like a span, like a flash, which is far from a dot. The now is like an enormous matrix from which you can grow the quality of who you are. If the quality of that now is flat, your life is flat, and you have a life in which one appointment follows the other. It's hurry here and hurry there; it has no depth. Everything that has quality requires the reassessment, the reinvention of the now, whether it is in aesthetics, in love, in sensuality, eating or playing or sport ("The Deep Now", published in Brouwer and Mulder 2000).

The revelation of the span, the flash, is the peculiar characteristic of performance art, and it plugs a very real gap in the symbolic since, in rendering the present, it explores something for which other art forms and discursive modalities cannot provide an exhaustive account. For the artists under discussion, the present is the time of realisation. The time it takes to cut into your stomach, brand the word artist on your arm, or drop a brick onto your foot or nail your arm into a wall is the duration of breaking away from the things that inhibit creativity, empathy and intuition. It is also the time taken to produce the effect of presence, whether through filmic or video media or live action, so as to focus perception into an intensity that excludes the contemplation of the passage of time and focuses the gaze inward, as Varela says, "to your own depth of experience."

However, Althusser's argument that "each mode of production generates its own unique and specific temporality" (Althusser and Balibar 1970, 99) might require us to take another look at this chronotope. If now is 0.3 of a second, then, in the digital age now is looking quite slow. The "tv time" Abramović decried is now the machine time of informational speeds measured in microseconds, which we cannot observe but which structure "our living and working environments, our social and cultural life" (Brouwer). The now of the living body in the digital mode of production is the specious temporality of what roboticist and new media artist Simon Penny once described as these "slovenly biological peripherals" (Penny 2000).

New Media and the Now

Has the now itself been altered in ways which leave performance art behind as a tactic for rendering the temporal substratum of lived experience? Intermedial performance provides perhaps the most efficient means currently available of posing questions about the constitution of temporal experience. What it does with the present, as the basis for the experience of presence, is not simply to make it appear. It also provides both a concept for it (that can engage with aesthetics and a variety of discourses that shape the historical moment in which the work is unfolding) and an overt mediation of it (that draws attention to the produced and contingent nature of time). In this sense the conception of the present in intermedial performance is functional rather than descriptive. An experience of the present may be construed as the revelation of the transhistorical, ever-changing, durational flux that guarantees all experience of time – but in intermedial performance the breakthrough into real duration is framed as one phase of a performative act, not as a unidirectional escape from reality. It therefore provides a way to intensify our engagement with the world.

If we consider new media art in its performative modality we might approach the question of its appropriateness as a vehicle for the now right at the interface between intensive machine time and what Hansen describes as "human temporal experience". He asks of media art an important question: "How can it broker an opening of embodied experience to the subperceptual registration of intensive time?" (Hansen, 235).

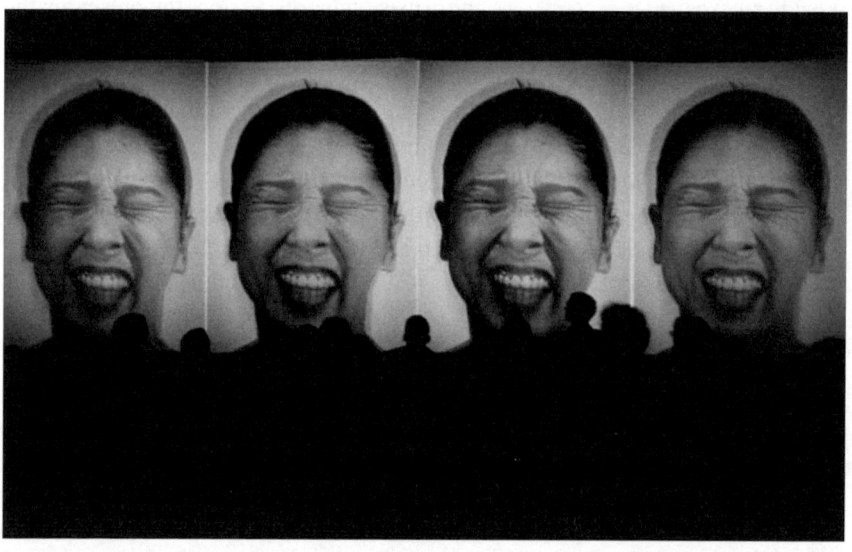

Fig. 2: Audience and all four channels at MAK Museum of Fine Arts Vienna 1995, Modell 5 03 MAK Vienna, © Komfar Sengmueller, Bruno Klomfar & Gebhard Sengmueller

To answer he goes back to Varela's own neurobiological account of the thickness of the now, specifically the multiscalar structure in which the now contains multiple layers within it: beginning with the affective microphysical event of which we are unaware but which is collected into packets of sense data which can be cognitively processed in the moment of perception and which itself occurs in the context of a larger temporal structure of cultural meaning, such as the narrative account, which is properly external to the organism itself.

Varela describes this model of the now as a "frame or window of simultaneity that corresponds to the duration of lived present" (Varela in Hansen, 250). The now is an "incompressible duration" (249) of present time consciousness in which microphysical elements are combined and framed into aggregate cognitive acts. This is an essentially organic human function internal to the body. For Var-

MAPPING INTERMEDIALITY IN PERFORMANCE

ela it is the "origin of duration without an external or internally ticking clock" (250). The similarity here with Bergson's real duration suggests to me that the now of performance art is still in play as Hansen also suggests: "the now itself must be accorded a lived quality that makes it more than a mere point or temporal location though (sic) which an object passes, and indeed, more like a space in which we dwell, 'a space within time itself'" (250).

What happens to this model when it is placed in the context of machine time, when the micro temporality of digital information intervenes into this space within time? For Hansen, a kind of cybernetic temporal mechanism emerges in which 'machine time can in some sense be said to enlarge the frame of the now itself. For if the exposure to machine time functions to stimulate neural dynamics and ultimately to trigger the emergence of new 'nows', then it might be said to contaminate the now with "elementary elements" that are properly inhuman (251).

New nows anyone? Husserl blinks his cyborg's eye and human presence flickers and stutters. Of course it couldn't remain the same. Bergson's cinematograph of perception has become digital video which, as Hansen argues, has been "invested with the task of expanding our experiential grasp of the complex embodiment of temporal perception" (236). Ultimately for Hansen it is embodied human experience which provides the frame in which mediatised imagery makes sense. Without embodied perception (that of both spectators and artists) we don't have art, we have patterns of unrendered code.

Hansen's examples (he discusses Gordon's 24 Hour Psycho and Viola's The Passions) are both classical and restrained. Both artists refrained from hacking the original performance and instead allowed the space of the now to dilate, placing technology at the service of human perception but not challenging that perception, which remains unchanged. But if we can accept a model of time as cybernetically enhanced then surely we can expect artists working at the speedy end of machine time to reconfigure the performance of the body so that a spectator can witness the action from the point of view of the machine? Artists such as Martin Arnold and Granular Synthesis take samples from the audio-visual field of performance and synthesise them. In doing so they heighten time consciousness and the perception of time but they also create a different picture of the results of the operation in which new media technology "oversaturates the now with information and enlarges it" (Hansen, 266). This new now feels more constricted and compressed.

The time signature of Modell 5 is not a cuddly anthropomorphised rhythm but emphasises differential speeds and affords a glimpse of machine time. In this sense Modell 5 does not deprivilege the technical frame in the way Hansen suggests of Viola's Quintet of the Astonished, but it does "bring the properly imperceptible, microphysical machinic inscription of matter (time) into the sphere of human experience" (266). But a human performance here is almost unrecognizable. In this work a more self-consciously cybernetic performativity is evident in which the body's movement in time is not fluid and extended but intensive and granular. In this kind of remixed performance, actions are no longer returned to their constituent gestures in a Brechtian sense but into micro-gestures which bear no direct relation to the originating action. Like Bill Viola and Douglas Gordon, Granular Synthesis uses the mediatised image to "contaminate the perceptual present", but not by way of "the material infrastructure of the enlarged now" (259). Instead the group produces a less sympathetic and more critical take on human affect. The now is not extended and enlarged but fragmented into grains and pulses of information. We glimpse the edges of our perception of the temporal, the genotype of chronometric time.

What remains is something posthuman (→ PORTAL: POSTHUMANISM), or at least something pre-individual, as the song of Akemi Takeya becomes a shriek. In presenting this perspective these artists certainly 'contaminate the now' with 'elements that are properly inhuman' and this now, much more than those of Gordon or Viola, suggests a new chronotope structured around a different assemblage of machine time and the virtual body.

Portal: Digital Culture and Posthumanism

This section of *Mapping Intermediality in Performance* is concerned with digitality, and its reworking of a theatrical currency of bodies, spaces and co-presence. It looks at ways in which digital technologies help to shape intermedial performance, but beyond this it responds to paradigmatic aspects of digital culture that effect the way in which performance events are created, shared and experienced. In particular the authors examine a key characteristic of digital culture – the fact that apparently separate media, phenomena and categories are in play simultaneously, so that they are productively interrelated.

At the portal, Lavender addresses paradigm-changing characteristics of digital culture, including altered perspectives of time and space, and developments in the way that artefacts and events are created and consumed. He suggests that the notion of the binary (0:1) provides a partial metaphor for the various interrelations that run through digital culture, then argues that the model of the network offers a more supple means of expressing the plural and shifting interrelations of the digital age. In this analysis intermedial performances are increasingly hybrid in form, and entail (simultaneously) fragmentation and synthesis, immediacy and mediation, personal engagement and separation. Remshardt expands on this theme in relation to the 'posthuman'. He presents the case that bodies (which are present and material) can also be thought of as parts of a system (dynamic and interrelational). He explores the premiss that we are now engaged in a "post-biological 'era'" (Ascott) where notions of embodiment and the real are troubled – or usefully expanded – by virtual realms and distributed performance. As far as the individual is concerned, Remshardt suggests, "a digitally hybridised or nomadic subjectivity" is at large within digital culture's "new performance ecology".

The subsequent node explores the interrelation of actual and virtual in this ecology. A triad of terms – 'materiality', 'transparency' and 'virtuality' – help to shape some parameters. In each case the author notes paradoxical distinctions between potential meanings – where, for example, 'transparency' denotes either making visible or making invisible, or 'virtuality' suggests both distance from and closeness to material bodies, objects and phenomena. There is a sense, here, that fixity of meaning is continually in jeopardy.

The four instances in this section look in detail at relations between the actual and the virtual. Hübner discusses his piece *Thespian Play*, in which a performer mimes to a saxophone-based soundtrack that he has helped create. Mimetically accurate, the musician nonetheless plays without his instrument. His performance, then, is both substantial and immaterial, whilst the piece throws presence, pastness and absence into relief, theatricalising phenomena that are evocatively fragmented. Klich, writing on The Builders Association's *Super Vision*, draws (as Remshardt did earlier in the section) on Hayles's account of "a condition of virtuality", which argues that a dialectic of pattern and randomness (characteristic of computer-based systems) exists in interrelationship with – and is beginning to take precedence over – a dialectic of presence and absence (characteristic of the material world). In Klich's analysis, the virtual realm in *Super Vision* is not subordinate to the material, but involves a "complex and dynamic intermingling of presence, absence, pattern and randomness". Petralia illustrates a 'both-and approach' as the director of *Virtuoso (working title)*. He describes a scenic space that is both theatrical and screen-oriented, where performance is simultaneously corporeal and mediatised in order to effect drastic combinations of proportion (a large hand in a doll's-house, a big-close-up of a performer's lips) and underscore live presence by way of its multiple re-presentation. Bay-Cheng discusses ways in which Richard Foreman's pieces *The Gods Are Pounding My Head! (Aka Lumberjack Messiah)* and *Deep Trance Behavior in Potatoland* evoke techniques pertaining to telepresence, fragmentation and simultaneity. Telepresence takes its place amid the distinctly multifarious stage world that Foreman creates, whilst at the same time extending this world from theatre space into screen space.

The section as a whole suggests that the digital is foundational, for it has changed our experience of time, space and bodily implication; but also part of a continuum whereby cultural production becomes increasingly hybridised. There is a sort of inexorable refunctioning at work – of the spaces, bodies and media of performance, and not least of our own expectations and experiences in the face of such developments.

Digital Culture

Andy Lavender

This section outlines some of the underlying features of digital culture, in order to see how they apply to – and help shape – intermedial theatre and performance. We begin with three different events. If you had been in, say, Paris in July 2008 (or several other cities that year), you could have sat in a container pulled by a truck, and listened to the musings of two Bulgarian truck drivers, as you watched video projected on the side of the container or looked through its glass side at the urban landscape through which you were travelling. Nearly a year earlier, you could have jumped on a bicycle and taken your own route around the streets surrounding the Barbican Centre, an arts complex in London, responding to suggestions, requests and prompts from a device connected to a server and attached to your handlebars. If you were in Berlin (or Brighton or Groningen) in 2006 you could have watched a show featuring actors in the same room as you, who performed via the Internet alongside others in similar rooms for similar audiences in the other two locations.

These shows – respectively, *Cargo Sofia*, presented by the Berlin-based company Rimini Protokoll, *Rider Spoke*, by the British interactive media group, Blast Theory, and *The Other Is You*, by the London-based performance company Station House Opera – are quintessentially products of a digital performance culture. The digital signature, of course, is more widely inscribed across areas of our lives. Since 2001 you could lie in an operating theatre in Europe and have your gall bladder removed by surgeons operating a robotic arm (with its scalpels and all) from across the Atlantic. You could work in a call centre in India or Africa, responding to European or American callers concerning their train timetable requests. If you had been travelling on the tube in London on 7 July 2005 you might have been involved in the series of explosions across parts of the network and, as a survivor, you might have taken video images on your mobile phone that were then broadcast to news agencies around the world.

Each of these instances is mediated by digital technology. Already a set of connecting principles is apparent, to do with mobility, speed and immediacy, interaction, task-specific communication and the apparent erosion of distance. All of which are (to use a fleshy metaphor) right at the heart of digital culture.

What is it to be "Digital"?
In the first instance digitality describes the use of binary code that uses the digits 0 and 1 in order to structure information. As Peter Lunenfeld explains:

Digital systems [...] translate all input into binary structures of 0s and 1s, which can then be stored, transferred or manipulated at the level of numbers, or 'digits' [...] It is the capacity of the computer to encode a vast variety of information digitally that has given it such a central place within contemporary culture. [...] The computer, when linked to a network, is unique in the history of technological media: it is the first widely disseminated system that offers the user the opportunity to create, distribute, receive, and consume audiovisual content with the same box (2000, xv, xvi, xix. See also van Dijk 2006, 9).

This information is produced, stored and manipulated by computers and shared across networks. The computer itself was first invented in the 1940s, but it was not until the 1960s that it became viable as a means of processing information, in the first instance in military applications and settings. The production of the personal computer from the 1970s onwards meant that individuals, as opposed to solely corporations or government-sponsored organisations, could access computing power. The availability of hypertext transfer protocols by 1991, enabling the relatively easy sharing of information across a network, along with the establishment of the Internet and the World Wide Web in the 1990s, meant that information could be shared rapidly and widely. The social networking sites MySpace and Facebook were founded in 2003 and 2004 respectively, marking the personal curation of such public sharings.

Take-up of digital technologies was relatively swift. PCs (personal computers), invented in 1975, were established in a quarter of homes in the US by 1991; mobile phones, invented in 1983, were likewise in one out of four American homes by 1996; the Internet, established in 1991, had achieved similar uptake by 1998 (Malecki and Moriset 2008, 27). By the mid-1990s, then, digitality was well on the way to being grafted into post-industrial societies, a process that has accelerated since then. (We should pause to note that a similar rate of growth applies to the "digital divide" – the gap between the technological haves and have nots. See van Dijk 2006, 177-186) In the nine years from 1995, for instance, the ownership of mobile phones rose from just over 90 million to over 1,750 billion (Goggin 2006, 1). Adams and McCrindle note that "If it is defined as any digital electronic device capable of performing automatic computation then there are now more computers in the world than people (consider that most people in the industrialised world own more than 20)" (2008, 31).

Digitisation is not simply a matter of technological advancement. It is profoundly cultural in its applications, not least since it makes information more quickly accessible, easier to handle and more swiftly adaptable. As Vincent Mosco explains:

Digitization refers to the transformation of communication, including words, images, motion pictures, and sounds into a common language. Providing the

grist for cyberspace, it offers enormous gains in speed and flexibility over earlier forms of electronic communication which were largely based on analog
techniques ... [D]igitization enables one language to govern practically all
electronic media. The fundamentals of translating, processing and distributing
electronic communication no longer distinguish among a page of newspaper
copy, a radio news broadcast, a CD recording, a telephone call, a television
situation comedy, and an e-mail message. Each can be sent at high speed over
various wired and wireless networks (2005, 155).

This turn to digitisation across media embraces the production of images, texts,
sounds (including music) and (through telephone systems) utterance – the stuff
that we share with each other by speaking, recording, showing. Digital technologies have changed the way that people, companies, organisations and govern-
ments handle information and manage communications. This is not simply to do
with the replacement of the older analogue technologies (images fixed on film;
voices converted to signals that travel along a telephone wire) with their digital
counterparts, although in itself this shift has enabled greater rapidity to the processing of information and greater capacity for its storage and speed of access.
Developments in information and communications systems have had a wider impact. They have changed the way that we manage our time and our exchanges as
participants within a culture. The digital domain of information and communication has been commodified (then re-commodified) in ways that have altered our
experiences of creativity, ownership and distribution. Peculiarly, these developments entail the convergence of media outputs into large corporations and the
growth of monopolies, but also the spread of ownership, authorship and segmen-
tation into small – and even individual – production and distribution agencies.

There are wider consequences to the ways that we imagine doing business and
taking pleasure. As Charlie Gere suggests, "Digital refers not just to the effects
and possibilities of a particular technology. It defines and encompasses the ways
of thinking and doing that are embodied within that technology, and which make
its development possible. These include abstraction, codification, self-regulation,
virtualization and programming" (2002, 13).

Those of us who remember life before computers are well aware of their rapid
incursion. However, digitisation did not happen all at once, nor is it disconnected
from previous cultural, technological and economic developments. The Russian
economist Kondratieff developed a theory of cultural "waves" to describe long-
term cycles of economic activity that significantly impacted on economic activity
and means of production and exchange. Following Kondratieff, some contemporary economic theorists describe the digital age as one such wave. Malecki and
Moriset adapt tabulations developed by Freeman and Louçã that argue for the
revolutionary consequence of the new digital paradigm. They list the following

waves of development, where digital technologies are the spur for a fifth Kondratieff wave:

Wave	Date
The Industrial Revolution	1780s-1815
Age of steam power and railways	1848-1873
Age of electricity	1895-1918
Age of mass production	1941-1973
Age of microelectronics and computer networks	1990s-

(Adapted from Malecki and Moriset 2008, 26)

As Malecki and Moriset point out, the latter wave is not exactly a radical break with existing technologies. Instead it depends upon an array of earlier twentieth-century innovations including the spread of electrification and the development of electronics, as well as earlier advances in telephony and computing. Further, it maps alongside the spread of post-Fordist production methods, in which services become at least as prevalent as goods, and where monolithic factory-based production is overtaken by a move towards a diversification of products, markets and customer preferences (2008, 27-8).[31] These developments are not exactly determined by digitality, but are consonant with and enabled by it.[32]

The notion that digital technology underpins a revolutionary turn to cultural production also has its advocates in the discipline of performance studies. Steve Dixon, author of the compendious *Digital Performance*, for instance, notes that he and co-contributor Barry Smith are "unequivocal that the conjunction of performance and new media has and does bring about genuinely new stylistic and aesthetic modes, and unique and unprecedented performance experiences, genres, and ontologies." (2007, 5) Before turning to the relationship between digitality and artistic production, let us consider more closely the suffusion of the digital in the warp and weft of contemporary culture.

Cultural Production and the Digital Reach

Digitisation has transformed the means of recording and distributing the things that we watch and listen to. Its processes underpin the way in which cinema films, television and radio programmes, photographs, newspapers, books, magazines and musical recordings are produced. It also, evidently, facilitates the spread of 'new media', not least in and through a direct interface with computers, used to surf the Internet, send and receive e-mail and process and publish anything from documents to databases to films. It brings with it an accompanying array of devices and gadgets that enable individuals to participate in digital culture – the silicon mountain of personal computers, laptops, notebooks, PDAs,

GPS devices, mobile phones and portable music players that looms in the junk-yard of the digital age.

Such devices have emblematic cultural status and effect beyond their technolo-gical function. Gerard Goggin describes the mobile phone (or the cell phone), for example, as "much more than a device for phone calls – it has become a central cultural technology in its own right ... associated with qualities of mobility, port-ability, and customisation" (2006, 2). As Goggin suggests, mobile phones, as with iPods and other MP3 players, betoken not just a means by which to speak or listen, but sets of cultural activities, cultures of use and constructions of personal identity.

This tendency to inter-articulation (here, personal gadget and private identity) underlies one of the characteristics of digitalisation – an ongoing drive to conver-gence across devices and applications. This can be seen in the uses to which a device is put – Apple's iPhone, for instance (along with competitors in the cut-throat smartphone market) is simultaneously a music player, web browser, games console, location finder, camera and telephone. Convergence also applies to the modes by which information is presented. Klinenberg and Benzecry, for example, note that "News companies can repurpose 'content' ... across platforms, adapting a single digital file to suit a newspaper article, Internet publication, or teleprompt-er script. This is a significant transformation ... since it changes the meaning of cultural products" (2005, 8).

Such convergence takes us ever closer to what Gere describes as a "seamless digital mediascape" (2002, 10), which is also profoundly personal, even bespoke. We can shop interactively, send invitations by way of unique mailing lists, draw on open source programmes to design our own artefacts, while playing in the background music that we have downloaded, or keeping an eye on a live webcam feed of our favourite participant in a reality TV programme. Yet digitalisation is more promiscuous than merely pertaining to mediascapes. As Taylor and Harris suggest, "a crucial dimension of the digital is its ability to change whole environ-ments into areas ripe for informationalization" (2005, x). Digital technology has impacted upon the financial sector (banking, insurance and stock trading), the services sector (in particular, from early on, the travel industry, and now retail commerce), transport and utilities. It is pervasive in offices and factories, and in many parts of the education system. Computers serve the manufacturing (auto-mobiles, aerospace) sector. They regulate the temperature of buildings, the speed of cars, the rates of return in gaming machines. And in a final ratcheting of sig-nificance, computing applications do not simply help to make things work, or help us to work with things. As Klinenberg and Benzecry argue, "the most funda-mental effects of digitalization on cultural production involve the restructuring of time, space, and place in daily work processes" (2005, 8) (← PORTALS: TEMPORALITY AND SPATIALITY). And, we might add, in the forms of creation and (re)presentation found in new theatre and performance.

The Digital Paradigm

In digital culture, devices, events and activities are mutually interdependent. This provides a structuring principle that helps to explain the paradigmatic nature of the digital, and that characterises the work discussed throughout this book. A number of commentators note, either explicitly or implicitly, the mutual opera- tion of opposites, conjoined terms or also-others in digital culture. We continu- ally come across couplings of different elements, and coinages of new terms. Taylor and Harris, for example, address "the digital's ... materiality and immateri- ality. These are not contradictory qualities but rather essential, mutually constitut- ing elements." (2005, 18) Their book elucidates what the authors term "the para- dox of this *im/materiality*" (x, original emphasis) (→ TERM: MATERIALITY). The term "glocal" is coined to describe the phenomenon of being both global and local (→ TERM: GLOCALISATION). Latham and Sassen note that both "[v]ariabil- ity and specificity are crucial dimensions" of digital formations (2005, 6). In *Net- work Culture* Terranova suggests that "To think of something like a 'network cul- ture' at all ... is to try to think simultaneously the singular and the multiple, the common and the unique" (2004, 1). In *Theatre and Performance in Digital Culture* Causey addresses "the (dis)appearance of theatre" in virtual spaces. He discusses the relationship between digital simulation and embeddedness, the latter a pro- cess "that seeks to infect information from within while colonizing the body through science and technology" (2006, 180). The resonant couplings of virtual and actual, corporeal body and incorporeal information run through the analysis (← PORTAL: CORPOREAL LITERACY; → TERM: VIRTUALITY).

Customarily, then, analyses of the principles and artefacts of digital culture are shot through with this notion that distinct or even contradictory elements are productively combined. In a similar vein we can sometimes add counter-terms that help to expand upon the concepts and practices under discussion. In *Digital Practices*, for instance, Susan Broadhurst remarks upon "the centrality of non-lin- guistic modes of signification [in digital performance practices], since in much of this performance significatory modes are visual, kinetic, gravitational, proximic, aural and so on" (2007, 10). Of course the performances that Broadhurst's book describes are also centrally determined by digital code, language and writing of different sorts. In his book *Multi-Media: Video – Installation – Performance*, Nick Kaye begins with a bald proposition: "In performance, video amplifies division, differ- ence and multiplication" (2007, 9). He could as easily have said that video ampli- fies synthesis, overlap and convergence.

The degree of counterpoint and simultaneity in digital culture is striking. This calls to mind the originary binary of digitalisation – the zero and one, the on and off of digital code-making. In its classic binary structure, the digital is comprised of entities that are irresolvably different and yet always conjoined in relation to each other. I do not want to argue for a direct correlation between system form (at the level of functioning hardware) and cultural form across a wider set of

0	1
Access	Gatekeeping | Password protection
Agency	Receptivity
Authorship	Readership (scanning, surfing, receiving)
Automation	Agency | Authorship
Code	Transparency
Communication	Isolation | Encryption
Connectivity	Insularity | Disconnection
Convergence	Dispersal
Cyberspace	Space
Distribution	One-to-one
Embodiment	Disembodiment
Globalism	Localism
Hybridity	Media specificity
Hypertextuality	Textual specificity
Immersion	Detachment | Distanciation
Interface	Individual
Intertextuality	Non-matrixed
Liveness	Timelessness | History
(Co)Location	Dislocation | Placelessness
Modular structuring	Sequential structuring
Multiplicity	Singularity
Navigation	Flow
Networking	Individual authorship
Non-linearity	Pathways
Numerical representation	Felt experience
(Co)Presence	Absence
Process	Product
Repeatability	Uniqueness
Sampling	Compositing
Self-absorption	Self-projection
Seriality	Rhizomic patterning
Simultaneity	Here and now
Social networking	Solipsism
Spatialisation	Borderlessness
Textuality	Noise | Hypertexts
Transcoding	Mono-functionality
Transformation	Transference
Variability	Repeatability
Virtuality	Actuality
Voyeurism	Exhibitionism

manifestations. However, the particular nature of the binary (0:1 in endless difference and dependence) provides a metaphor for the proliferating interrelations of digital culture. I shall argue shortly that this metaphor is only partly useful and that we shall require a better one. Firstly, however, let us consider some of the key terms of digital technologies and cultural practices, and their beguiling co-relation with contiguous counter-terms, as indicated in the table above.

These terms are inherent in the systems, protocols and operations of digital culture. In keeping with a model of binaries (which is also a peculiarly poststructural model), each term is meaningful by way of its definition according to its Other. And yet this will not quite do. The Other is (usually) not absent, not 'off', but also-present (← INTRODUCTION, where Nelson introduces this concept of simultaneity).

The model of the binary is inadequate to describe the fluid imbrication of terms and counter-terms, and their shifting and reconstituting relationships across digital phenomena and activities. It is peculiarly two-dimensional. A turn to a different shape – but one that is also umbilically connected with digitality – provides a more flexible model. That shape is simultaneously (unsurprisingly, characteristically) shapeless, a form without end or boundary – the network. Manuel Castells describes a network as:

> a set of interconnected nodes. A node is the point where the curve intersects itself. A network has no center, just nodes. Nodes may be of varying relevance for the network. ... The relative importance of a node does not stem from its specific features but from its ability to connect to the network's goals. However, all nodes of a network are necessary for the network's performance. ... The network is the unit, not the node (2004, 3).

Whilst expressing caution at the "exaggerations" of Castells, van Dijk concurs that "social and media networks are shaping the prime *mode of organization* and the most important *structures* of modern society" (2006, 240, original emhasis). In van Dijk's analysis, the network is characteristically a "dual structure" where oppositions combine (241) (→ PORTAL: NETWORKING).

If we return to the terms in the grid, above, with this in mind, a different set of relations immediately suggests itself, one based not on parallel tramlines and separate columns, but on constellations that can shift endlessly into new configurations, where some terms loom large and some recede, with some in equal balance with their counter-term whilst others predominate over theirs – as figured in the diagrams of terms that precede the nodes in this book. The constellation itself is a network, and the network is fluid, not finite.

Digitality and Intermediality

How do such considerations matter to intermedial theatre and performance? Firstly, we can, in specific instances, address the interrelation between media in intermediality, which itself tells us something about both the aesthetic construction and phenomenal effect of intermedial form. Here are three models of that relation.

1. Hierarchical (dominant / dominated)

   One medium – or mediating effect – is preeminent. This is the position Auslander takes in *Liveness* (1999) and reiterates in his "Afterword" to Broadhurst and McMahon's *Performance and Technology* (2006).

2. Inter-relational, but structured by (and opening up) spaces, gaps and 'fissures'

   This position is taken by Chapple and Kattenbelt in their introduction to *Intermediality in Theatre and Performance*. It is characterised by the notion of the 'in-between', which the present book problematises, preferring to argue that increasingly the inter-relation of media entails productive fusion rather than separation.

3. Hybridised, and producing effective (affective) inscription through (new) mergings. The instances in this book tend to exemplify this model.

In *Mass Mediauras*, Weber argues for:

> a mass movement of collection and dispersion, of banding together and disbanding. In this movement ... something both very old and very new makes itself felt: the irreducibility of a certain separation, of a stage which is not simply the setting of a picture or the scene of a glance but at the same time a scenario of inscription (1996, 106).

Weber's case entails a sort of necessary conjunction: an irreducible "separation" (a gap, void, disconnect) and a "scenario of inscription" (concrete manifestation). This itself is another binary – the void; and the thing that is written in and through the void. As with the partner-terms above, the two sides are effective insofar as they are synchronous. However, this synchronicity doesn't, in and of itself, produce or depend upon new in-betweens, new voids. Instead it operates by way of overlaps, doublings and fusings – phenomenal configurations in time, space and perception, whereby the operating principles of different entities, ontologies, media are simultaneously in play to produce a richness of effect (→ TERM: HYBRIDITY). I am reminded of Lehmann's suggestion that a feature of the postdramatic is that "A scenic *écriture* captures the attention" (2006, 74). As far as the performances that are the subject of this book are concerned, inscription (*écriture*) takes place in a way that is medium-specific – which is to say, media-rich.

Intermedial work participates in – is structured by – such fusions, hybridities and interrelations, not only of different media, but also of discrete phenomena. Let us go back, briefly, to the three examples of intermedial performance with which I opened this section. *Cargo Sofia*, *Rider Spoke* and *The Other Is You* offer both detachment and a sense of engagement, are geographically specific and entail a sense of unmooring from geography, engage with a field of meaning and are also contingent and determinedly open. They are immersive to different degrees, but also require that the spectator-participant looks and listens carefully. They are formally heterogeneous, but also evoke specific styles and genres (the road movie; the transaction; the game; the soap opera). They are open to chance, but also depend upon tightly organised conceptual and time-based structuring. They are not dramas with characters (albeit that *The Other Is You* flirts with characterisation across its three locations), but are propelled through a witting evocation of the dramatic encounter, the scenario and the persona.

In these examples, as with many others, audiences are also agents and participants, consumers of time and presence. This, then, is a sensuous consumerism, marked by transactions that place the body in the moment. The intermedial offers what, in a broader context, McCarthy and Wright describe as "a new way of seeing experience with technology: as creative, open, and relational, and as participating in felt experience" (2005, x). And yet these pieces are not necessarily, or not only, awash with the sensuous effects of full phenomenal engagement. They are also systemic and programmatic. This is part of their embeddedness within digital culture. They are inherently multiform. Intermedial theatre and performance entails systematicity; plurality of (re)presentation; compound action; multi-modal *mise en scène*; and a disposition to affect.

The effect is that of a network in which interrelated elements and phenomena coexist. The network is not (only) abstract and remote, but (also) inhabited and experienced. Productive doublings and connections abound. In the interrelation of digital culture and intermedial performance, coherence is produced in the face of fragmentation, gathering through plurality. Media are both distinct and synthesised. Bodies are involved and apart. An intermedial dramaturgy 'inscribes' presentation with mediatisation, form with feeling, and evokes the always-other in the here-and-now of performance.

Posthumanism

Ralf Remshardt

Mapping Posthuman

In spite of its many inflections by intermedia and digital technology, performance as a centrally human practice remains anchored in the humanities, and it might be expected that a term whose meanings are as shifting and occasionally contradictory as "posthumanism" can do little except adumbrate the debate about its nature and future.[33] Carefully unfolded, however, the term can become an interpretive matrix – there is no singular 'posthuman condition' – that resonates constructively with the multiplicity of intermedial performances and allows for a liberatory sensibility that can serve to reimagine the body, spectation, and performance. In a posthuman performance paradigm, spectator and performer both relinquish their positionally determinate (dialectical) claims to presence and reconfigure themselves as dynamic, interdependent parts of an emergent system.

The term derives its provocative potential partially from its contested semantics. In the discourse of robotics and cybernetics (theorised for instance by Marvin Minsky or Hans Moravec), posthuman designates an evolutionary or morphological step towards a synthesis of the organic and mechanical/digital, and may indeed portend an apocalyptic and deterministic techno-scientism culminating in the subsumption of human consciousness into the binary code of cyberspace so that, as Katherine Hayles paraphrases this position, it will no longer be "possible to distinguish meaningfully between the biological organism and the informational circuits in which it is enmeshed" (1999, 35). Against this teleological and dystopian view of posthumanism, Hayles posits an open one:

> [T]he posthuman does not really mean the end of humanity. It signals instead the end of a certain conception of the human, a conception that may have applied, at best, to that fraction of humanity who had the wealth, power, and leisure to conceptualize themselves as autonomous beings exercising their will through individual agency and choice" (Hayles 1999, 286).

As a term of cultural criticism, posthuman aims at dismantling the many binaries endorsed by Western dualism: body/mind, self/other, culture/nature, gobal/local, and so forth. Such a view is indebted not least to Donna Haraway's bold "Cyborg Manifesto," in which she envisions adopting the "ironic mythology" of the cyborg in order to cut through the "maze of dualisms" that structure and entrap us; today, she argues, "we are all chimeras, theorised and fabricated hybrids of machine and organism; in short, we are cyborgs. This cyborg is our ontology; it gives us our politics" (1991, 150). It may also give us our performance, to the degree that we extend Haraway's boundary-dissolving cyborg metaphor to the stubborn binaries of performance discourse: presence/absence; fiction/reality; performer/ spectator; liveness/mediation. Deployed in performance theory – as for instance by Steve Dixon (2007) and others – posthumanism signals the new confluence of physical materiality with performative consciousness resulting from immersive virtual reality environments, telepresence, distributed performance and so on, which increasingly trouble the traditional notions of embodiment and presence (← PORTAL: CORPOREAL LITERACY).

Performance and the Posthuman Body

Given the discursive appropriations to which it is subjected (psychoanalytic, post-structuralist, constructionist), it is tempting to try and salvage a kind of pure body out of the white noise of mediated transmission, a body phenomenologically 'in-the-world' whose salient feature, if not quite freedom from signifying practices, is at least an elision of the economy of reproduction and circulation. So Peggy Phelan: "In performance, the body is metonymic of self, of character, of voice, of 'presence.' But in the plenitude of its apparent visibility and availability, the performer actually disappears and represents something else – dance, movement, sound, character, 'art'" (150). In such a formula, even if marked by disappearance, the body still has its determined place in an operation of metonymic 'translation'.

But intermedial practice, especially if it involves some manner of feeding back the living body through digital representation, telepresence, or virtual reality, de-stabilizes the spatial, temporal and communicative relationships implied by such a translation. The performer's body (as indeed the observer's) already exists inside what Anja Klöck has referred to as "a conceptual a priori mediality of all representational practices" (117) for which there is no longer a natural or natura-lised body as external referent. If we indeed have entered what Roy Ascott calls the "post-biological era" then bodies not only no longer represent some 'natural' fixed point of the real, but on the contrary the very place (or scene) at which the real comes undone: "the site of bionic transformation at which we can recreate ourselves and redefine what it is to be human" (376).

One of the performers who has most radically explored these bionic transformations is Australian performance artist Stelarc who in works such as *Fractal Flesh* (1995) and *Exoskeleton* (1998-) has created robotic extensions of his limbs or surrendered control over his body to remote manipulation via the internet, in some cases himself becoming the avatar of a dispersed, often chaotic, sometimes self-regulating system. Insisting that "the body is obsolete," he writes: "We have always been prosthetic bodies. We fear the involuntary and we are becoming increasingly automated and extended. But we fear what we have always been and what we have already become – Zombies and Cyborgs" (Stelarc).

Such profound cultural anxiety arises any time posthuman hybridities are brought into play because they potentially put performance itself and its cognates, the (human) body and (organic) presence, into doubt. The question "who performs?" leads directly to "what is human?" Current practices range from the mere digital doubling of the live performer – which some critics have described as "uncanny" – to experiments along the bionic/cybernetic continuum. Perth-based collective Tissue Culture & Art fashions human and non-human cell cultures into objects called "semi-livings" which "purposely subvert binary positions such as human/animal, life/death, nature/culture as well as performer/performed" (Catts and Zurr 2006, 155). Conversely, the digital avatar in Susan Broadhurst's *Blue Bloodshot Flowers* (2001) was programmed with an "emotion engine" that called forth a range of autogenic performative behaviors. In investigating how each of these is present and embodied in their respective performance contexts, it helps to recall that in the posthuman analysis, as Hayles remarks, the conceptual dyad of presence and absence in the material sphere is complemented (and potentially substituted) by the informational dyad of "pattern" and "randomness" (1999, 247-9).

The Experiencer as Cyborg

Today a spectator, or experiencer (← TERM: EXPERIENCER), of digital performance comes into the realm, site, or space of the performance already as a thoroughly initiated citizen of the cyberworld, conversant with the raft of devices she owns and/or manages, some of which are still attached to her body, steeped in the mythology of techno-culture (is she Mac or PC?), flexible in extending herself locally and globally, practiced in dividing her attention simultaneously between screened and non-screened versions of reality. That is, even without being fitted with any prosthetic gear connected to the *specific* performance at hand – a walkie-talkie, VR helmet, datagloves, and so on – the experiencer is already a cyborg. This is literally true to the extent she relies substantially on any portable technology to fulfill social functions of locomotion and communication, and figuratively inasmuch as she has incorporated Haraway's cyborgian ethos (now mutated from an ironic-resistive stance to one of necessity). "In our cyber-universe," writes Rosi Braidotti, "the link between the flesh and the machine is symbiotic, creating a bond of mutual dependence" (2009, 249). Not only has her life as social cyborg habituated her to shifting her perceptual focus from representation to simulation and from mimesis to the play of signifiers (to cite only two performance-relevant categories of "transitions" Haraway enunciates [1991, 161]), it is likely that technology has even changed how she embodies her encounter with the performance in many subtle ways (I am thinking here of my students whose reflexive texting has made them *physically* a fundamentally different kind of audience). Thus any theatrical production running today, intermedial or not, already contends with the posthuman subjectivity of its audience, a dislocated and distributed subjectivity Braidotti has called "nomadic."

The gradual "becoming-cyborg" of the audience (as well as powerful commercial interests vying for dominance in communications and entertainment) are perhaps what will push immersive (← TERM: IMMERSION) technology out of the mode of a separate and solitary novelty-driven experience and shape a new communal posthuman sense of performance experience. Even though experiments with technologically mediated immersion and augmented or virtual reality environments in performance date back to at least the 1980s (see the histories provided by Giannacchi and Dixon), the concurrent presence of an audience whose identity is at least partly constituted by a digitally hybridised or nomadic subjectivity, a techno-self that habitually extends itself through a multitude of channels, from social networking sites to 3-D simulated environments with avatars (← INSTANCE: SECOND LIFE), is a recent phenomenon. Blast Theory in the UK is one performance group that uses a quasi-cyborgian model for its participants/experiencers and whose imaginative locative media projects are acutely concerned with the social transformations occurring at the intersection of urban space, its virtual mappings, the ambulatory human body, and communication technology. In Blast Theory performances (which are structured similarly to games), participants are typically equipped with prosthetic extensions, both low-tech (bicycles) and high-tech (hand-held computers and GPS systems), and appear simultaneously as avatars on screen to other participants. The often simple quest narratives Blast Theory initiates (for example in *Uncle Roy All Around You*, 2003 or *Rider Spoke*, 2007) trigger potentially complex meditations on reality, orientation, memory, trust, surveillance, and the limits of performance. In this very contemporary iteration they seem to fulfil a definition of posthumanism given more than a decade ago by Judith Halberstam and Ira Livingston: "Posthuman bodies are not slaves to master discourses but emerge at nodes where bodies, bodies of discourse, and discourses of bodies intersect to foreclose any easy distinction between actor and stage, between sender/receiver, channel, code, message, context" (Halberstam and Livingston 2).

Emergent Performance

How does a posthuman ethos function in the creation and reception of performance? Posthumanism dispenses with categorical separations that constituted an older model of performance premised simply on presence, or what Robert Pepperell calls the "boxed body fallacy" (Pepperell 13). In fact, if *the body* was the locus *sine qua non* of a performative fallacy that privileges notions of agency, semiotic transactions, and being *present to*, the locus for posthuman performance theory is consciousness. Performance, especially in mediated events, is not so much the result of a clearly defined transaction as an *emergent structure* that becomes extant under certain conditions. Writing on virtual reality performance,

Johannes Birringer contends that human performers are not separate from the software system or programming environment; "the entire interface environment can be understood as digital performance process, as emergent system" (Birringer 44). The transition into posthuman performance is to be found where digital media are transformed from simply providing channels streaming a version of physical reality, or being a vehicle for digital doubling and representation, to being constituents of a new "condition of virtuality", to invoke another of Katherine Hayles' coinages. Seen this way, a posthuman reading of performance allows for the raising of an emergent consciousness, for a new performance ecology. Posthuman refuses to close down the available connections, intersections, and nodes; rather it insists on making them visible and articulating the need to (re) connect with them.

telematic

intertextuality deterritorialisation displacement

experiencer **transparency** hybridity

recursion glocalisation connectivity

actuality-virtuality

virtuality presence **materiality**

immersion interactivity embodiment

feedbackloop separation

intimacy

Node: Actuality-Virtuality

Materiality. Material is a term fraught with historical connotations and contradictions. Within 20th-century media studies, certain theorists (e.g. McLuhan, Kittler) have typically, though not incontestably, drawn upon a concept of materiality to emphasise the physical characteristics of communication media, rather than focus on the minds, spirits or souls of individuals. Cultural expression, this line of thinking argues, always has a materially embedded character, from processes of inscription (writing, painting, printing) to practices of iteration (performances, recitals, rituals). In order for meanings to be produced, communication processes require complex arrangements of material forms including technologies, human bodies, languages, buildings, and environments. "Materialities of communication" can thus be defined as "all those phenomena and conditions that contribute to the production of meaning, without being meaning themselves" (Gumbrecht 2004, 8). This understanding of materiality has two implications for researching theatre and performance. First, theatre and performance can be studied in terms of media history, since the introduction of new mechanical and technological possibilities – from lighting and sound effects, to set and costume design, to today's digital technologies – have contributed to the capacity for theatrical invention and production in any given era. Second, theatre and performance can further be regarded as a form of "exteriorisation", a material embodiment (← TERM: EMBODIMENT) which, when the performance is over, deposits cultural expression in cultural memory and also leaves any number of material traces (programmes, posters, reviews, blogs, images, sound bites, interviews), all of which can return to affect later performative work (→ TERM: FEEDBACK LOOP). (Michael Darroch)

Transparency. In media contexts, the term transparency has two potentially contradictory accents. To draw upon Bolter and Grusin's distinction, one denotes immediacy, a neutral perceptual impression made in the process of notionally immediate transmission; the other, hypermediacy, denotes the drawing of attention to the devices of composition. Classical philosophy provides us with the concept of the "medium diaphanum", which refers to the merging of a medium with the purpose of transmission, such that it is not recognised as an object itself. In Aristotelian aesthetic theory, media are considered innately invisible and transparent, which enables this merging to happen. But Aristotle does not neglect the material aspect of the medium completely and therefore we can trace the philosophical awareness of the materiality (← TERM) of media in the transmission process back to Classical aesthetic theory. Paracelsus even provides the medium with a "corpus" – a material body.

The first explicitly subject-oriented perspective dealing with media transparency can be found in the cinema analyses of Apparatus theory in the 1960s and 1970s. As theorised by Baudry and Comolli, a cinema audience would not perceive the apparatus of the projector but would experience only the visual frames and filmic narration. The cinematic medium thus turns into an ideological apparatus secretly normalizing its communications for the watching subjects. By way of this process the cinema dematerializes as an apparatus, with both technical production and cultural norms concealed by representative strategies. Current discourse on transparency draws on both notions of the apparatus (technological and ideological). Current discourse on media art and intermediality, however, emphasizes precisely the opposite position; namely, the critical potential of intermedial art and its ability to break the "transparency illusion" of conventional media by making the medial structures themselves visible. (Meike Wagner)

Virtuality. Amid the significant and growing discourse surrounding intermedial and mixed reality performance, the term virtuality has emerged as a fundamental term, perhaps even the key term for the contested space between live events and mediatised parallels. Derived from the Latin *virtalis*, virtuality first referred to moral virtue and the potential for action: "Capable of producing a certain effect or result; effective, potent, powerful" (c. 1432; OED). Transcending disciplinary boundaries, the virtual currently applies to any number of contemporary media performance contexts, including virtual worlds such as Second Life and other multi-player online games, virtual selves as expressed through internet social networking sites and digitally constructed avatars, virtual pets, virtual sex and even the somewhat paradoxical "virtual theatre", as coined by Gabriella Giannachi in her book of the same title (Giannachi 2001). In all such contexts, virtuality suggests a distance from – as well as an engagement with – the actual, material, and physical world, real life (← TERM: MATERIALITY).

Virtuality thus occupies a crucial space between what is imagined and actualised, between potential and realisation. It is in many ways the essence of intermediality, "a lived paradox where what are normally opposites coexist, coalesce, and connect" (Massumi 2002, 31). In a theatrical context, virtuality suggests an indeterminate status between the potential of the performance and its actualisation. As such, it provides a crucial bridge in contemporary debates regarding the ontology of performance and the effect of digital technology and telematics (← TERM) in the material and phenomenological experience of theatre. (Sarah Bay-Cheng)

Instances

Instance: *Thespian Play*: Synchronous Differences

Falk Hübner

This instance concerns the process of devising my fragmented work-in-progress, *Thespian Play* (2008/2009), a performance piece for a saxophone player (without saxophone), soundtrack and video.[34] It also looks at the nature of presence and performance in the production, in relation to some of the key features of intermediality (← TERM: DISPLACEMENT). What interests me as a theatre maker is the multi-faceted way the audience can perceive a performance. I am therefore interested in fragmentary structures that need to be negotiated by everyone who experiences them (← TERM: EXPERIENCER).

Thespian Play is a kind of mime or playback performance, on the borders of music, choreography and installation. A performer mimes the playing of a saxophone. Everything the musician has traditionally trained in for years – playing his instrument and controlling both the sound and timing he produces – is denied him. He does not make any sound at all during the performance; every sound is pre-recorded, partly processed by electronics and played back through two loudspeakers. However, every sound, pure or heavily processed by electronics, has its origin in the musician and his instrument. During the rehearsal process all basic sounds were recorded, so the performer well knows the soundtrack that surrounds him acoustically. He also knows the origin of the processed sounds, which enables him to produce the movements in his body to mime these sounds – though without his instrument. Different medial layers of the performer's body – especially movement (through the live body) and sound (through loudspeakers/ electronics) – are extracted and used as separate entities and elements.

It is a conceptual and conscious choice to make separate, pre-recorded audio and video tracks instead of using live electronics, motion-sensors or live video.[35] Usually sound and movement are produced by a musician inseparably at the same time,[36] but in *Thespian Play* they are separated, with the result of a fragmentation of the different elements that, as Walter Benjamin would say, are made visible, stay separate, and at the same time complement each other to create a new, tessellated 'whole'.

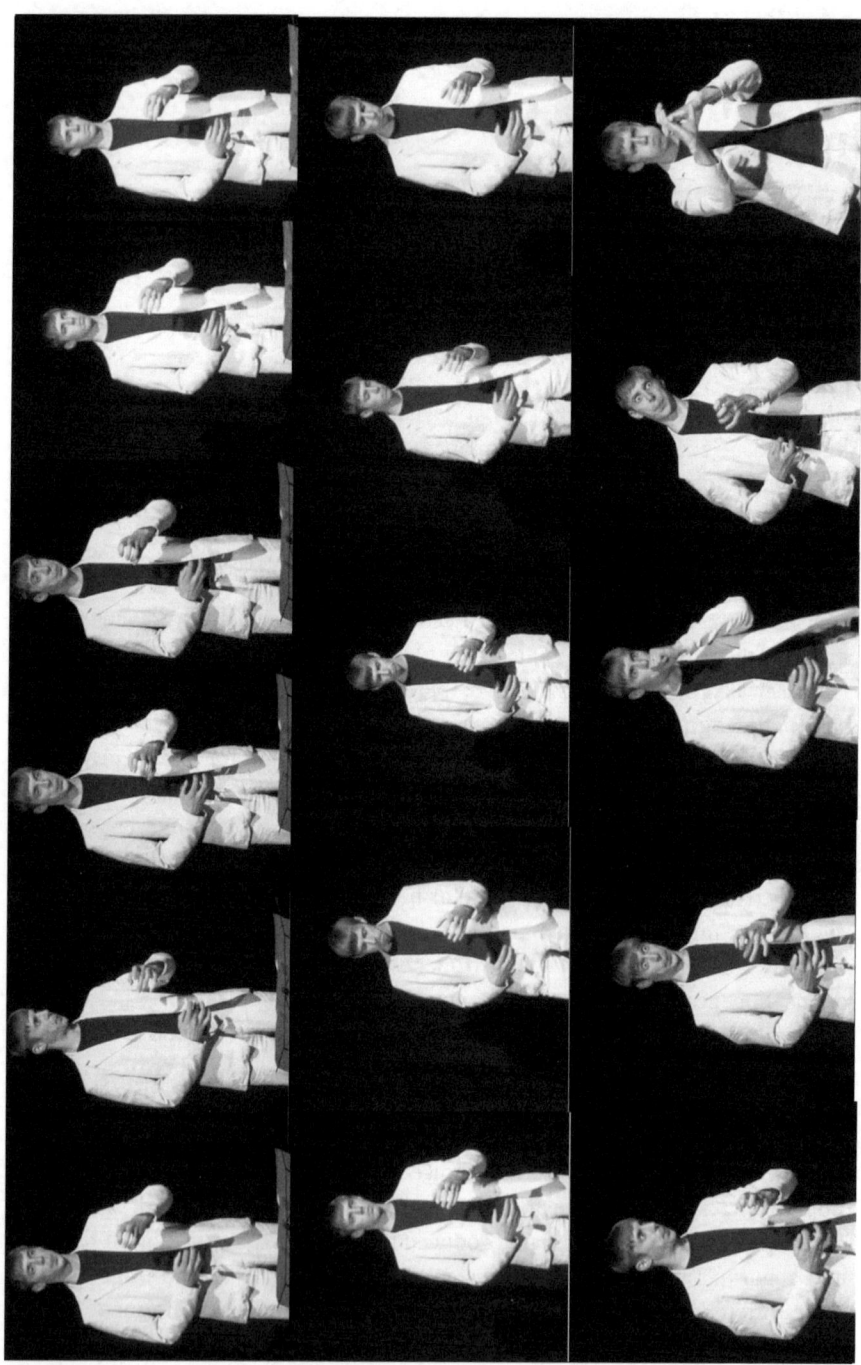

Fig.: Thespian Play *collage,* © Falk Hübner

MAPPING INTERMEDIALITY IN PERFORMANCE

Idea and Concept

When I began conceptualizing the piece, the main idea was the fragmentation of the performer – the separation of the different means of expression. I wanted to create a polyphony of different means of expression and an intermodality of rhythms:[37] I questioned whether the rhythms of sound and moving body are the same, whether there is a polyphony of two (or more) independent rhythms, or if they add up to one compound rhythm.

Furthermore I was interested in the identity of the performer on stage. I wanted to dislocate the central parameters of the profession of a musician – on the one hand the possession of his instrument and, even more strikingly, his ability to control and decide what to play and when, and his ability for timing. On the other hand, I wanted to create a piece that can only be performed by a musician, as it uses crucial abilities of the musician such as breathing and finger technique and the ability to perform and remember complex musical rhythms. As techniques of task-based performance these requirements also prevent the musician from any necessity to 'act'. The bodily movements cannot properly be performed by a dancer or actor; they have to be performed by a musician, even specifically by a saxophone (or possibly a clarinet) player.

A musician generally has control over his appearance on stage, and both the space and time of performance (see also Kattenbelt in Havens et al. 2006, 22). This does not apply to the performer of Thespian Play, who seems to be only a human 'at rest' in the acoustic ecology of the performance, surrounded by an audio and video environment that he has (co-)created but cannot control. All audio signals have been prerecorded, processed and produced in advance, so the performer has no control over any musical parameters. As a live performer he is the centre of the performance as perceived by the audience, but bound to the control of the electronic system.

From Process to Product

In the opening passage of the piece I composed the player's finger movements and doubled them by prerecording key sounds of the saxophone, thus fragmenting two elements that usually belong together and are produced at the same time (finger movement and corresponding key sounds). Having recorded the key sounds with the performer, I started composing a choreography. I loaded the sounds into a sampler in order to be able to react most flexibly to the movements, and to readjust and reorder them if necessary. For rehearsal purposes I composed several études to test and learn about the relationship between sound and movement in this specific setting. We rehearsed these examples over and over again and I changed sounds until we arrived at a movement-sound-relation that I liked most. In general, on both hands I chose to use lighter sounds for the pinkie, the ring finger and the middle finger, and heavier, bass-like sounds for the thumb and the index finger. Thus, in the actual performance of this passage there is no longer any logical connection between the technique and the original sound this technique usually produces.[38]

The experience of this passage is still one of separation and difference, although every movement is precisely doubled in time by sound. As one possible example of displacement (← TERM: DISPLACEMENT), the sounds are taken out of their original context (some of them can hardly be perceived as key sounds if the listener does not know their origin) and confronted with movement, raising the awareness of the viewer and allowing for new experiences of relationships between movement and sound. Without digital technology this process would not have been possible, since only contemporary audio software offers advanced interfaces, direct and fast access to recording, enhanced manipulation, live performance and production capabilities.

When I was planning the piece, I wanted to use the auditory and visual elements separately, in a polyphonic and intermodal way. However, during the process this approach did not prove to work best: movement and sound seemed weak and uncoordinated, somewhat arbitrary and without a strong coherence. There are two conceptual and practical reasons for this. If movement and sound were presented as autonomous elements, the sound would be perceived more as the soundtrack to a minimalist choreography. The difference between the two would paradoxically almost disappear, because they are presented as autonomous elements, whereas in fact they are not. Although fragmented, both are different *performative* aspects of the act of making music. When placed at the exact moment in time, the difference becomes most experienceable, because one perceives them as separate elements that usually belong together. Here the concept of intermediality as the conjunction of "phenomena across medial boundaries that involve at least two conventionally distinct media" (Rajewsky 2002, 13, my translation) is reversed. In *Thespian Play* aspects not usually perceived as distinct are separated and thus perceived as distinct after the process of separation, with the effect that one becomes aware of the art form's mediality, of the different elements of musical performance.

The second, more practical reason is that the musician needs some sound relationship to his movements in order to be able to perform these movements convincingly. Since sound as the effect of his physical bodily processes is already taken away from him, he has to be able to connect his movements to something he knows. As a musician he does not think and act in reference to pure bodily movement like dancers or mime performers, but he needs at least some kind of acoustic reference in order to be able to fill his movements with meaning and intensity.[39]

Surprisingly, the most striking and interesting relationships between movement and sound occur when the rhythms of both are exactly the same. By placing movement and sound exactly together in time the differences between them (and their mediators, the live performer and the soundtrack and loudspeakers) are most accentuated. This phenomenon of unison is not new in contemporary theatre. In many performances movements are repeated (Christoph Marthaler), or performed in slow motion in unison (Robert Wilson). Even the smallest differences become observable and come to the fore. The difference in *Thespian Play* is that I use different medial materials that are not necessarily directly connected to each other (as, for example, the video doubles in Guy Cassiers' work of performers who are at the same time present live on stage), yet they still match each other in the experience of the here and now of the performance.

In many theatre and performance works since the 1960s, rhythm has been used to de-synchronize the audience. The individuality of different medial elements has been accentuated by giving them their own autonomous rhythms (or leaving them in their own natural/organic rhythms), instead of supporting each other's rhythms and joining each other to a summing-up of more or less the same. Leading to a dislocating experience for the audience, this approach has become a powerful tool for the liberation from logocentrism in the context of postdramatic theatre, as well as for shifting the attention from character and narrative towards timing and polyphony of the various media (Roesner 2008). Other approaches work with repetitions, in which a particular element changes every time it occurs, even if the differences are very small (Fischer-Lichte in Brüstle et al. 2005, 238-239). In *Thespian Play* it is neither the individuality of the different media nor repetition that makes the small differences experienceable and accentuates the individuality of sound and movement. I use exactly the same rhythm for both and hold a strong coherence between both visual and auditory rhythms through the whole performance.[40] It is the exact appearance of visual and auditory elements, placed together in time, that communicates their difference.

According to normative conventions, we expect sound and movement to match, even if we already know that they are separately produced. In *Thespian Play* the perception is twisted because movement rhythmically matches with sound, but the instrument on which these sounds may possibly be produced is missing. What makes this experience more radical, however, is that I manipulate and combine prerecorded saxophone sounds in ways that do not just re-inform the possibilities of the instrument, but that are not possible in reality. By means of digital technology the saxophone player seems able to perform something impossible, which makes the difference between his movements and the sounds become even more striking. Although the technical processes are obvious and made visible (← TERM: TRANSPARENCY), in some passages of the piece one could almost believe that the performer really produces the sounds, although one knows that this is not possible due to the absence of the instrument. The experience constantly shifts and oscillates between knowing and believing.

Nearly all artistic decisions during the process made the piece simpler and clearer – and at the same time more radical. The experience of difference is greater; the difference of origins of the displaced material more experienceable, the fragmentation more obvious and clear. In my experience from creating this performance, to plan to design difference, fragmentation, displacement or separation is not necessarily the best approach. In Thespian Play, the most striking experiences emerge from the simplification and rhythmical parallelisation of the different elements.

As a result of the staging, the audience experiences more immediately the live body of the musician-as-performer than a musician performing a piece on his instrument. As the instrument is missing, the focus of attention shifts to the body. The musician becomes a performer, and becomes theatrical without acting, which has important implications and possibilities for future techniques of task-based performance.[41] As all actions have at least some reference to the performer's professional practice as a musician, the movements themselves become theatrical, and may be further developed into an independent yet musical movement language.

However, for the performer the piece demands an enormous amount of concentration, and he must struggle anew with it at every performance. Precisely because the instrument is missing, even standard musical movements become new and challenging; no matter how often the musician plays Thespian Play, performing without his instrument will never belong to his professional daily practice. For me as a director watching his performance in the theatre, the experience remains challenging, sitting on the edge of my seat as the performance can never be safe. Though he is physically there, the performer is displaced from his habitus; his customary mode of making airwaves vibrate has been digitally displaced through time and space. The player's attempt to reconcile these separations in performance is both futile and seemingly possible simultaneously, and this is what makes Thespian Play an intermedial performance for the saxophonist and experiencers alike.

Instance: The Builders Association, *Super Vision* (2005)

Rosie Klich

This instance explores the position of the human in the space of technology by examining *Super Vision*, The Builders Association's ninth major work since the company's formation in 1994.[42] Under the direction of Marianne Weems, the company, based in New York, unites text, sound, architecture, video and performance to explore the impact of technology on human presence and selfhood. Created in collaboration with multimedia company dBox, it explores the concept of "data bodies"; the versions of ourselves that exist as the collation of all the data files that collectively store our information. Three intertwined stories of human-computer relationships explore the diverse ways digital information technologies record, reflect and refashion human identity. Characters in a range of social and geographic situations interact with the world of cyberspace information, and their social lives are both overtly and inadvertently affected in a variety of ways. *Super Vision* highlights how "With every cctv image, credit card swipe, email and phone call the technological evidence of our existence grows" (Liverpool08 Arts and Culture Website) and in our digitally saturated environment our data-identity is often recognised as more 'authentic' than the physical or subjective self.

Virtuality and Intermedial Performance

This perceived supremacy of information has altered our social, economic, and creative practices and the concept of the "data-body" explored in *Super Vision* epitomises the contemporary cultural tendency to perceive information as dominant over the material world. This case study will explore how *Super Vision* presents the human as positioned within what Katherine Hayles has labelled "a condition of Virtuality" (← TERM: VIRTUALITY), defined as *"the cultural perception that material objects are interpenetrated by information patterns"* (2000, 69, original emphasis). Here information and materiality are not viewed as discrete concepts. The shift into virtualisation, though gradual, may be viewed as a cultural shift embedded in our cognitive and social processes. Virtuality, Hayles argues, is predicated on the dissolution of the separation of the real and the virtual, and the perception that informational pattern is displacing and pre-empting materiality (← TERM: MATERIALITY).

It is the tension between information and materiality that is the defining dialectic of our current state of virtuality. Information consists of data bits that have been sequenced to create recognisable forms. It relies on the organisation of otherwise random units and, as such, information may be characterised by the interrelation of pattern and randomness. Materiality implies physical presence, the existence of matter, and may be characterised by the interrelation of presence and absence. So in our condition of Virtuality, Hayles asserts that the dialectic of pattern/randomness, the basis of information, is beginning to develop prominence over the dialectic of presence/absence. Using these two dialectics she develops a framework for understanding the "semiotics of Virtuality", in which the axes of presence/absence and pattern/randomness are arranged not as opposed, but as complementary and interactive (Hayles 1999).

Recent debate surrounding the relationship of the live and the virtual in the field of performance has tended to focus on the inherent difference between these forms, the effect of one upon the other, or the elements of change that have shaped these allegedly opposite phenomena. Matthew Causey asserts that the "contemporary discourse surrounding live performance and technological reproduction establishes an essentialised difference between the phenomena" (Causey 1999, 383). Yet the efficacy of intermedial theatre is based on the audience's perception of the integration and interdependence of the live and the mediatised. Peter M. Boenisch explains that it was the original aim of discourse on intermediality to counter notions of "media-strategic purity" in the arts and he uses the term "intermedial" to imply the fundamental integration (← INTRODUCTION) of communication media (Boenisch 2003). Intermedial theatre, rather than reinforcing the discreteness or incompatibility of live and mediatised forms, foregrounds common denominators across media in its very combination of live physical bodies in actual spaces with virtual projections.

In intermedial performance, the relationship of the material and the virtual is thus freed from the hierarchical framework that subordinates the virtual realm and relegates it into a position of fabrication or copy of the real. To theorise the practice of intermediality in multimedia theatre it is necessary to avoid theories of performance that reinforce the binary of the material and the virtual. This instance uses Hayles' semiotics of Virtuality to provide a point of departure from which to address the complex and dynamic intermingling of presence (← TERM: PRESENCE), absence, pattern and randomness that occurs in intermedial performance. Such an analytical framework foregrounds the intersections of these dialectics and enables theatre analysis to avoid reinforcing the distinction of the live and the mediatised, and focus instead on the patterns and rhythms created across media.

Super Vision

A traveller, a Ugandan citizen of Indian descent, repeatedly enters the US on business. In each of his scenes he must pass through a security check, and as the checks grow more interrogative, the traveller becomes more frustrated and defensive. In a keystroke the security official can access endless personal details about this 'potentially suspect' visitor and these details are presented to the audience as swirling information patterns on a large screen. The traveller stands amidst spidery lists of purchased items, assets, travel documentation and family histories, and humour is often derived as the airport security officials believe only what is recorded in the traveller's passport and travel information, disregarding the person standing before them. The usually immaterial, informational 'identity' manifests not as a translation or extension of the material self, but as an-other presence.

Fig. 1: Super Vision, © *The Builders Assocation*

In a middle-class Seattle household John Snr. secretly conducts fraud via the Internet, using the identity of his young son to run up credit card debt. As his wife Carol and son John Jnr. play in the rest of the house, he hides away at his computer constructing a virtual identity and playing with virtual money. Yet the trails of information he leaves behind are recorded and stored and his actions in the virtual world of information have a very real impact upon his material existence. One could say that he 'steals' the identity of his child, though of course the identity in question is only a constructed pattern of information particles and does not directly represent the actual child. Interestingly however, John Jnr. is never materially present on the stage, rather he is shown as a video image. As such, the digital information manipulated by John Snr. is just as theatrically 'real' as his son; the digital information in this case is not inferior as a copy or representation of the real, but is constructed from the same bits and bytes as the material presence of John Jnr. in the performance space.

In New York, a member of the digirati, the burgeoning generation of young technology-obsessed professionals, communicates daily via webcam with her grandmother in Columbia, Sri Lanka. From the other side of the world, Jen is organising her grandmother's affairs, overseeing doctor's appointments, real estate problems, and financial arrangements. She is simultaneously building a family history, recording and storing information, photos and important documents on her computer. As she scans old photographs, the audience watches as the old medium of photography is remediated by digital technology and, as the grandmother in Sri Lanka narrates (via webcam) the memories each photograph evokes, we are reminded of other, older ways of locating one's identity. As the grandmother's mind begins to wander and slowly fragment, we see the importance the technology plays in allowing Jen literally to 'keep-an-eye' on her grandmother's health and state of mind. At the same time the image of the grandmother's pixelating mind serves to remind us that electronic systems too can cross their wires, slow their electrical impulses and create false information; randomness can disrupt pattern.

Super Vision explores different relationships between middle-class humanity and digital technologies. The work probes the issue of identity in a world in virtual transit, and depicts how the ubiquity of computer and communication technologies in Western society is refashioning our identities. The Orwellian omniscience of surveillance in a digital age is presented as unlimited, its impact underestimated. Director Marianne Weems explains that the work was created in reaction to other artworks that explore the issue of surveillance, because "in a post 9/11, post-private culture we all know we're under visual surveillance – this is not news" (Weems 2005). Rather what interested Weems was the idea of dataveillance as an "invisible form of surveillance that's actually much more omnipresent at this point and much more insidious ultimately", precisely because dataveillance is "compromising our sense of identity in a way that visual surveillance never will" (Weems 2005). Dataveillance is depicted as having enormous potential power, both as a means of corruption and as itself corrupt. Within the three stories presented we see the different ways dataveillance's power manifests. We see its positive potential to unite the distanced and enable the monitoring of those that require assistance; we see it manipulated both to commit and catch financial fraud; and we see its impact upon the boundaries of personal privacy as it is implemented in the name of security.

Fig. 2: Super Vision, © *The Builders Association*

In an introductory speech at the beginning of the show, a performer informs the audience that in our simple act of purchasing tickets we have inadvertently volunteered information about our personal lives. The performer declares that, based on our credit card purchases, the company has created a statistical profile of the audience demographic. Although the statistical profile she then proceeds to offer is clearly generalised and designed for humorous effect, this introduction implicates the audience as naïve participants in the process of data monitoring and the unknowing objects of surveillance. This also sets up a slightly disconcerted, defensive position from which the audience will view the rest of the performance. As the security official questions the Ugandan commuter regarding his travel, shopping and personal information, audience members may reflect upon their own personal information and its easy accessibility; as the onstage screens are covered in web-like branches of the traveller's statistics and history, the spectators are forced to ask themselves whether their own information should be so readily available and publicly displayed.

The story of the Ugandan traveller having to defend himself against the questioning security official also explores the idea that the information stored does not necessarily provide an accurate record of reality. The information that forms his data-identity is stored in separate files without an organising narrative, and it is the security official who interprets the information and connects the dots to establish a narrative pattern. To be relevant, information must be perceived by way of patterns, firstly on the level of bits and bytes, and then as constructed and interpreted by a human reader. There are many potential spaces here for randomness to enter into the equation. The perceived dominance of the information over materiality forms the basis for our condition of virtuality, which means that the random elements not only alter the informational pattern, but also affect the material world, mutating reality.

The onstage media architecture and slick sound and lighting effects create the sense of a world where digital technology reigns. It is not only depicted as a vital infrastructure allowing communication and access, but is a fundamental part of the performance environment. The integration of live performer and digital scenery is crucial in developing the themes of the work. In his study, the character of John Snr. sits at his desk surrounded by swirling patterns of information in which he appears completely immersed. Here the live performer does not appear in contrast with the digital environment but rather both appear inherently enmeshed. The scenography shows the virtual – the streams and patterns of information – as seeping out of the computer screen and completely encompassing the character's physical self. While the actor is recognisable as a material form within the virtual environment, the patterns of information that flow over his face and body create the effect that he is only two-dimensional, a shape and not a being. The boundary between his body and the virtual environment seems fluid, insignificant and potentially permeable. The actor's face is often amplified through a webcam image projected on another screen, and this image is more visible than the actor himself. These visual effects create the sense that information is leaking out of the computer-based world and colonising the material space.

The computer-generated performance text should not be read in isolation for it only develops relevance through its conversation with the live. Weems suggests that the media in Super Vision make up half of the dialogue with the actors performing the other half, and each is meaningless in isolation from the other. The efficacy of the work lies in its utilisation of the "intermedial mise en scène" (Wagner 2006, 129), and it is the configuration, the arrangement that generates meaning. The organising framework relates all the elements non-hierarchically so as to produce intermedial patterns. These patterns consist of both live and mediatised elements, and the convergence of the live and the mediatised onstage reflects the thematic concerns of the production: the interaction of information and materiality, and the cultural perception that information is displacing materiality.

This work explores the idea that humans are not only being mediated by communication technologies, or even simulated within media, but that they may potentially become *translated* into digital patterns and replaced by their virtual counterparts. As the traveller is accosted at airport checkpoints, his material self is perceived as lacking credibility, while the security official deems his informational version more authentic. The character of John Jnr. appears to have absolutely no control over his own data-identity, as his father constructs a pattern of actions in the virtual world that will exist as the authoritative version of the child's identity. The production suggests that this 'data-identity' will inevitably be viewed as valid by the authorities simply because it exists in digitalised form. When this occurs, the child's data-identity will have become a substitute for the material child.

At its heart, *Super Vision* poses the question: are humans more than the sum of their digitised statistical information? As the character of the grandmother begins to show signs of senility, the giant webcam image of her face slowly breaks apart. The fragmentation of the image suggests that the breakdown of the machine and the gradual interjection of randomness into the pattern of the media image may correlate with the disintegration of the human brain and the disconnection of organic electrical impulses. While this image may also remind us of the complexity of preserving human connections, it also suggests that we are now truly posthuman, that human beings now function not only *through* technology but also *as* technology. Our actions and impulses may correspond to those of the digital computer, and yet computer-generated information is illustrated as more authentic in today's society. Unlike material human computation, digital information is recordable, objectively classifiable and almost permanently retrievable.

Both in its intermedial staging and its dramatic content, *Super Vision* foregrounds how the dialectic of pattern/randomness is now dominant over that of presence/absence. Visually and thematically the production suggests that both the material and the virtual may be viewed as equally divisible into information particles, constructed from the same elementary bits. As bits become bytes, and particles are pixelated, they come to form recognisable patterns or 'presences'. In this instance presence in no way relates to material existence, for material actuality is not a concern. Rather presence is simply the result of human response towards the formation of constructed patterns. From this perspective presence may be viewed as translatable, as patterns of information particles to be deconstructed and reconstructed in another medium. In this sense, presence is not limited to its traditional domain of the live, nor is pattern limited to the mediatised; the boundary between the real and the virtual is porous.

Instance: The Fragmented Stage of *Virtuoso* (*working title*)[43]

Peter Petralia

With specific reference to *Virtuoso* (*working title*), this instance seeks to illuminate my company Proto-type Theater's 'both-and' approach to fragmentation in a practice which otherwise affords wholeness. It looks particularly at live co-relations of actors with each other and the audience, simultaneously in stage space and screen space – with these distinct spaces and media in necessary inter-relation. As science constantly miniaturizes and reduces the world into its component parts, we have become capable of seeing the material world both as unitary particles and as joined together. In contemporary culture it is hard to imagine life without screens that isolate aspects of experience. We use them as a communication tool, for entertainment and as barriers to human contact. In *Virtuoso* (*working title*), television screens fulfil all these functions, but they also act as a membrane that separates performer from audience member while simultaneously bringing the fantasy of the piece's fiction – and indeed the performers themselves – *closer* to the audience.

Along the front edge of the performing area are three black, flat-screen television monitors, facing the audience. Behind them is a white taped-out square, within which are a variety of scenic elements, properties and cameras. Four live-feed video cameras are connected to the three flat-screen television monitors[44] and, during the course of the eighty-minute performance, three performers arrange and rearrange the materials within the space to create a series of increasingly complex shots for the cameras, and by default the televisions. The live audience witnesses both the creation process that happens in the theatre *and* the images that the performers create on the television monitors. The space the performers work within (the area behind the screens) is arranged like an abstracted, live television soundstage, with mapped-out spaces that represent particular fictional locations within and around a suburban home (represented on stage and on screen by a doll's-house). When developing the piece, the company was drawn to the photography of Gregory Crewdson, famous for his decadent, colour-saturated photographs of suburban America vividly capturing often-private domestic moments. The production stills included in his monographs reveal complex stages surrounded by lighting equipment and cameras; within the centre of the stage everything is perfectly ordered but around the edges a chaos of equipment reins. This juxtaposition became a central inspiration for the visual aesthetic of *Virtuoso* (*working title*) and as a result all of the on-stage action takes place within the taped-out space behind the televisions.[45]

When the audience enters the theatre, the three performers (Mark Esaias, Gillian Lees and Andrew Westerside) are within the taped area, and popular music from the 1960s plays through the theatre speakers. The television screens do not relay any images; they are black. Gillian, Mark and Andrew are odd figures whose oddities become more pronounced upon examination: they each wear wigs, and Mark wears only a yellow button-up short-sleeved shirt, underpants and slippers. The obviousness of their wigs is one of many devices used to create the theatrical wonderland that *Virtuoso (working title)* explores on stage, calling immediate attention to the constructed nature of the performances (← TERM: TRANSPARENCY). The wigs also relate to source materials that were explored in rehearsal, most explicitly the film *Grey Gardens*, echoes of which abound throughout *Virtuoso (working title)* without being made explicit.[46] The three performers smile at the audience, apparently enjoying the kitsch music. Once the audience has settled, the music fades out, the lights shift, and the performers stand up and prepare the stage.

They turn on the cameras that are positioned around the space before moving to the doll's-house far upstage centre. They place themselves around the house, although what they are doing is not immediately apparent. A soundscape starts playing at the same moment that Andrew opens the shutters on a camera focused on the door of the house. This image is transmitted to the three television screens. A five-minute sequence follows during which the audience sees the saturated miniature world of a doll's-house being filled with furniture by an oversised hand (Gillian's). Gillian's hand on screen is out of scale with the tiny furniture that fits into a *realistic* arrangement, and this is exaggerated by an eerie soundscape made up of household noises that have been processed and stripped of their context.[47] The camera pans, zooms and repositions itself until a complete kitchen is compiled in the doll's-house and on the television screens. At the end of this sequence, Gillian walks to the downstage edge of the stage and turns on an LED flashlight that she aims at her face, where she speaks directly to the audience (and to herself), not on camera. She is recalling a dream that sets up a number of themes that are replayed and rehearsed throughout *Virtuoso (working title)*, most notably, to paraphrase David Lynch (Chocano 2006), the notion of the house as a place where things can go wrong.

The performance thereafter is structured as a series of fragmented scenes between Andrew, Gillian and Mark staged for the cameras and involving a game of playing house where the rules are constantly shifting, but where the dangers of the outside world seem always to offer threat or seduction, depending on the performer's perspective. The game-playing evolves throughout the performance, drawing inspiration from the endless game-playing that the two Edies busy themselves with in *Grey Gardens* while their house literally falls down around them. These scenes are technically complicated and require the performers to stand in awkward positions, to face left or right to camera in order to affect the proper directional looks between the three screens, and to place the cameras/backgrounds in precise positions without substantial preview to ensure the shots are correct. When a performer is speaking to another performer, they speak via the screen, turning to face the other performer in the place that they are on screen. This means that sometimes the live performers who stage these images are standing next to each other (or indeed, nowhere near each other) but not *facing* each other in the live space, thereby disturbing the conventions of naturalistic performer interaction.

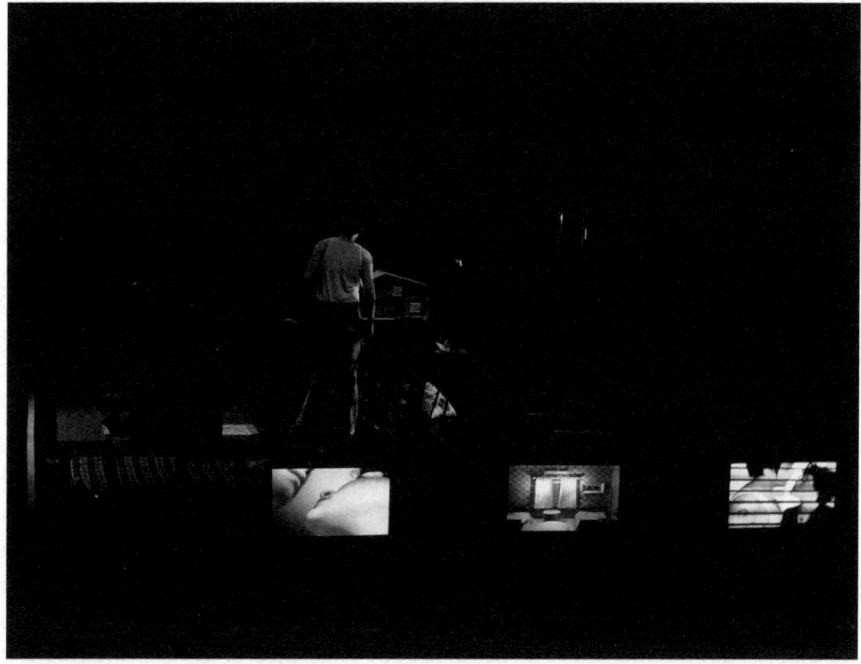

Fig. 1: Virtuoso (working title) *The television screens offer contrasting angles amidst a chaotic theatrical landscape (Photo © Proto-type Theater LTD)*

The scenes are broken by sequences at the doll's-house where the furniture from one room is removed, the camera repositioned and new furniture placed in a new room (indicating a shift in time/space) all by the articulate hands of the performers which seem to offer varying commentary on the objects via their subtle muscular shifts. For example, in the first instance of setting up furniture at the very beginning of the piece, Gillian's hand moves slowly and contemplatively into the doll's-house (and thus the frame of the camera/television), sometimes stopping midway in her task to make a small adjustment or to use the side of her finger in an overly delicate manoeuvre. Later, Mark dumps the entire contents of a room into the frame and then sorts out their arrangement. This progression of approaches to the doll's-house furniture tracks along a similar path to the narra-

MAPPING INTERMEDIALITY IN PERFORMANCE

tive destruction that is occurring in the piece: a general weariness with 'playing the game' and a desire (on the part of Andrew and Gillian) to end the game entirely that is accompanied by a growing awareness of the fragility of their own fiction. These sequences are a play of scale where objects on stage are loosely represented by objects in the doll's-house. In the live space, the doll's-house is a doll's-house, but on screen it is also a representation of a fictional scenic world.

A series of soliloquies (as in Gillian's first speech) that further the narrative and reveal the inner thoughts of the characters breaks the flow of the camera-play in Virtuoso (working title) since they are never delivered to camera. Structurally, they function to alter the pace of the performance and allow narrative progression. While one performer delivers a speech, the others are on the fringes of the visual space, listening in. In one speech, Andrew describes his desire to be John F. Kennedy before detailing his sexual exploits with Mark and Gillian. This revelation encourages a flirtatious exchange between the three that is only visible off-screen in the live space. Later, Gillian describes her journey out of the house to the edge of the subdivision where the forest lies, which ultimately results in an end to the game-playing in the subsequent scene. These interactions extend the fragmented narrative offscreen, creating a narrative tension with the televised scenes that places the screens firmly in the context of a live performance.

In Virtuoso (working title) the actions of the performers are duplicated and fragmented – they can be seen live and (generally) on the screens simultaneously. The performers are also, of course, fragmented on the screens themselves; their full bodies are never completely revealed in the shots being staged. The cameras work as a kind of microscope, focusing in extreme close-up on mouths, eyes, feet and hands or cutting off a performer's body halfway. This invasive operation of zooming into the minutiae of the performer allows us to see their pores, their structural components, much like an Adobe Photoshop image that has been magnified to several hundred percent its original size. When Mark asks to be kissed by Andrew in a scene near the climax of Virtuoso (working title), he approaches the camera until only his lips are in view. At such a close perspective, his lips lose their relation on screen to a face. It is only by raising your gaze to see Mark standing in front of the camera that the lips make sense. The viewer may know implicitly that the lips are Mark's but the seduction of the close-up makes them also simply colour, form, shape, and texture.

But the process of fragmentation does not end in this one-way exchange from live to screen: the macroscopic lips are out of scale with the image on the centre screen (of Andrew seated on the floor next to a chair, shot from a steep top angle) and in conflict with the other onstage performer (Gillian, who watches from centre stage, encouraging Andrew to kiss Mark). As is often the case in Virtuoso (working title) there is a multiplicity of image scales (both live and on screen) that creates a visual tension for an audience member: the eye of the spectator is delivered images, bodies and objects whose scales should preclude them from sharing a singular space. What we each see when we look at Virtuoso (working title) will undoubtedly vary depending on how we look, but there is a possibility for the spectator who takes in the *whole* scene, both on screen and not, to unify the stage in a fragmented image whose component parts are laid bare. By visually suturing the on-screen image with the live process of image construction, an audience member witnesses the straddling between the material and immaterial, and has agency in completing the image.

Fig. 2: Virtuoso (working title) *The use of extreme close-ups alters the spatiality of the performance space and the depth of the screen language* (Photo © Proto-type Theater LTD)

A play with identity and reality is also at work in the narrative and form of Virtuoso (working title). From the beginning, the narrative suggests an uncertainty of identity, with performers constantly turning to one another and asking, "Who are you?" The answer to this question turns out to be incredibly complicated as the structure of Virtuoso (working title) forces a confrontation between the performers (who move the cameras), the characters (who talk to us in their monologues), and the characters-within-their-characters (who are *performed* by the characters for each other). It is never quite clear who these people really are. Is Andrew, for instance, a visitor as is suggested by the earliest scene in which he speaks? Or, since he is onstage from the beginning and seen moving out of view of the live

MAPPING INTERMEDIALITY IN PERFORMANCE

cameras until his entrance on screen, is he *performing* as a visitor? Is Mark the *Marble Faun* as Andrew calls him, and have they really had sex in the back of a Buick, or is this an invention created to incite some tension between Gillian and Mark? Did Gillian really go to the edge of the subdivision? Is Mark really Jacques Cousteau?

The performers become unable to agree on the narrative, on who they are, and even on the condition of their world. The possibilities offered by the narrative accumulate and become increasingly implausible until Mark is coerced into performing his final role as John F. Kennedy on his way to the Dallas Trade Mart with his wife Jackie. Gillian and Andrew cage Mark in a triangle of cameras so that his image appears with a scenic background on the centre camera (and television screen) while two other cameras capture fragmented versions of him that include the theatre as a background. The fragmenting of the images accompanies a breakdown of character: Andrew and Gillian seem no longer to wish to perform their roles as suburban stereotypes and see a restaging of Kennedy's assassination as the final play to end all plays. Mark has become stuck here, operating as if the narrative progression that leads Gillian and Andrew to alter the rules of the game had never occurred, and he is left as the only image on screen as a result. This sequence escalates until a series of three gunshots are articulated by Andrew, simulating the assassination of JFK and, by extension, ending the game. These shots are accompanied by the television screens returning to black.

Further complicating matters is that the performers are all British and do not adopt American accents despite the narrative of American suburbia in which they exist. In creating *Virtuoso (working title)* the question of accents was perhaps the single most debated issue. In the end, I felt that by not having American accents the falseness of the world was more evident; this is not, after all, meant to be an accurate representation of an historical moment, nor is the audience meant to believe these people are who they say they are. By maintaining their own accents, the performers strengthen the theatrical distance that the structure of the cameras and screens provide; the characters are rendered immediately in inverted commas through the maintenance of accents that would not belong in an accurate representation of American people. These accents do not belong in the narrative of *Virtuoso (working title)* except to call attention to the falseness of the situation.

In *Virtuoso (working title)* there is nothing better for the performers to do than to play at television. McLuhan (2004, 346) has said that "TV tends to be a close-up medium," where the performance of actors needs to be more nuanced. The performance style of Andrew, Gillian and Mark is simultaneously in synch with and at odds with McLuhan's statement: they do explore the close-up extensively but they also use a heightened performance style that draws attention away from the screen and back into the live space. This heightened style is a hybrid performance language that was drawn from watching early American cinema, which built on the performance style of theatre, and from watching television, which also drew on theatre. The result is a form that occasionally calls attention to itself, inviting audience members' eyes to lift from the screen and observe the live space. This movement between the theatre space and the screen suggests a complex dynamic is at work bounded only by our ability to suture the fragmented images (← TERMS: PRESENCE; DISPLACEMENT).

Cognitively, this process of suturing stretches the brain's perceptive function because, as Semir Zeki has explained, "the primary law dictating what the brain does with the signals it receives is the law of constancy" (2006, 244). When we see images, these image signals are transferred to the brain and the brain processes them into meaning. In that process, the brain seeks to "eliminate all that is unnecessary for it in its role of identifying objects and situations according to their essential and constant features" (245). When the choice for the brain is simple, a *solution* to its stimulus happens quickly. When the brain is presented with more complex situations, or ones where there is no immediately apparent way of understanding, the brain goes through a process by which every possible outcome/answer is presented as equally correct. In essence, the brain handles multiplicity by recognizing the potential for there to be more than one way to interpret a situation: the brain does not require a single correct answer to any problem (Zeki 2006, 245).

So, when an audience member is presented with the spectacle of a live body facing a camera (in profile to the audience but visible from at least the waist up) and a screen that appears to display an image of that live body, as happens in the close-up lips/kiss moment described above, the brain knows that the image of close-up lips on the screen relates to the body in space, but it also knows that the image on the screen is equally an abstract series of colours and textures. These two ways of understanding the image are not mutually exclusive; they can exist simultaneously. Furthermore, the same "circuitry" in our brains that controls our movement also engages when we *imagine* movement (Lakoff 2006, 158). The implication in this instance is that when the screened image is present at the same time as a physical presence on stage which appears to relate to that *image*, our mirror and canonical neurons engage in the brain allowing us to *imagine* what is happening physically in front of us by feeling "what it would be to perform that motion"; a transference occurs between the physical body of the performer and the body of an audience member via the screen (Lakoff 2006, 157). Hence *Virtuoso (working title)* is at once fragmented and coherent, though it eschews the realist disposition to make sense of the fictional world it constructs.

Instance: Richard Foreman, *The Gods Are Pounding My Head! (Aka Lumberjack Messiah)* (2005), *Deep Trance Behavior in Potatoland* (2008)

Sarah Bay-Cheng

This instance concerns the use of telepresence in the work of American theatre director-writer-designer Richard Foreman, as a technique (and phenomenon) that supercedes theatre whilst retaining some of its core characteristics (← TERM: PRESENCE). It focuses on what might be thought of as a series of recent theatre pieces in Foreman's *oeuvre*, and particularly on *The Gods Are Pounding My Head! (Aka Lumberjack Messiah)* (2005) and *Deep Trance Behavior in Potatoland* (2008).

In late 2004, immediately prior to this phase of work, Foreman acknowledged his ambivalence toward the theatre: "I've always claimed that I have a love-hate relationship to the theater. And it's reached a point where I think this is probably the last sort of play like this that I'll be doing" (quoted in Sellar 2004). This announcement came as a shock to many who had followed Foreman's long thea- tre career. After all, this was a playwright who had long been acknowledged inter- nationally as an important figure on the experimental theatre scene in New York and a noted international director. Even as Foreman made his announcement, his Ontological-Hysteric Theatre in the East Village functioned not only as a venue for his plays, but also as an incubator for emerging theatre work by groups such as Elevator Repair Service and Temporary Distortion. Despite having made a career of challenging and rethinking the American theatre, Foreman seemed poised to depart the theatre.

Nonetheless, in the years following his announcement in 2004, Foreman con- tinued to make spectacles that more or less followed his earlier techniques in theatre, involving nearly constant dialogue with media (which had always been an important part of his theatre work), including his own technically distorted voice, recorded music, photographs, and ubiquitous references to film – although he subtitled these new productions "Film/Performance Projects". What changed in his most recent work (post-2004) is the integrated techniques of telepresence, fragmentation, and simultaneity made newly possible with video and later digital editing, whilst creating environments aesthetically similar to those of his pre- digital work. For all of its cultural acumen, Foreman's theatre aesthetic draws from a modernist high-art tradition that manifests itself in a philosophical cri- tique of mediated forms within theatrical contexts. These later works both in- voked a new perspective on telematics (← TERM) and illustrated the potential of telepresence to open up the space and text of the performance (→ TERM: INTERTEXTUALITY).

From Intermedial Theatre to Film/Performance

Although Foreman's supposedly final play – *The Gods Are Pounding My Head!* (Aka *Lumberjack Messiah*) (2005) – was not quite so final, the avant-garde theatre director was clearly moving in a new and, I would argue, intermedial direction. First appearing as background to the live actors, video images gained prominence in Foreman's productions from 2005 onwards. Against these video backdrops, the live performers increasingly took on the appearance of moving props, saying fewer and fewer lines in each successive show and articulating far less complexity than the video images that played above them. Whereas Foreman had previously layered his stage compositions in densely constructed physical spaces filled with strange objects, strings, oversized props and outlandish costumes that drew visual attention to the live performers, increasingly he shifted this compositional attention to the screen, leaving the theatrical bodies as static figures. This might seem a minor addition, a video screen and performers upon it simply adding another element to the saturated stage space. But, as I argue below, Foreman's inclusion of video radically transformed his theatrical enterprise.

Richard Foreman's plays had always been unmistakably recognizable as his own. Produced initially in lofts and other found spaces, Foreman's theatre productions emphasize a density of space, filled with unique objects such as oversized hammers and wheels, in which no part of the theatre, however small, was left unaltered. The walls of his current theatre, the Ontological-Hysteric Theatre in St. Mark's Church in the East Village of New York, are nearly always covered in layers of images, letters, printed texts, and geometric lines (often painted in red, white, and black) cutting across the walls. The floor is always painted in shapes and cryptic designs and objects hang from the walls and ceilings into the playing space, sometimes falling during performances, sometimes serving as additional props for actors to manipulate, including seemingly functional items such as lamps and levers. In many of his productions, Foreman constructs a barrier between the playing space and the audience – sometimes clear Plexiglas or bright lights aimed at the audience's eyes, other times, string. He is fond of string, often dissecting the playing space with crisscrossed string, painted in an alternating white and black pattern so as to appear to create dotted lines across the stage. Although every production is unique, the frequent viewer will note Foreman's recycling of images, objects, and costume pieces from one show to the next. His use of language is no less idiosyncratic, including repetitions, puns, and monotone deliveries interspersed with bells, buzzers, and crashing sounds. Ever a philosopher, Foreman saturates his plays with voice-over expositions that posit central terms, almost like a *leitmotif* for the production. In *The Gods*, for example, a whispered voice over a loudspeaker repeats the word, "Tendency". Elsewhere in the play, characters quote seemingly extant texts ("Remember when Victorian poet Alfred, Lord Tennyson wrote – 'MY HERO'") and unknown verse: "The Busy Bee/Has no time for sorrow". The central character, the titular Lumberjack, is augmented with a child's-sized tie, fingerless ladies' gloves, pearls and a Folies Bergère headdress. At the end of the show, a giant red bird enters.

The Gods Are Pounding My Head! thus displays many of Foreman's recurring ideas, such as the confusions of contemporary society, noting the division between materiality and the culture of the moving image. Always a bit at odds with his actors, Foreman articulates in this production a growing division between the agency of live actors and the more malleable, yet potentially superficial, media forms that might replace them. As the Deep Voice (Foreman's own recorded and distorted voice) summarizes in the conclusion:

> Suppose it was the case that you woke up one morning into a world in which the depth and intricacy of your fellow human beings was replaced by a different world, in which human beings were – you know – thin, somehow – just surface only – Even if that surface seemed clever and quick about the ways of this brand-new, paper-thin world. (Foreman 2005, 45)

The flat, monotone delivery of this voiceover reinforces Foreman's separation of elements, the splitting apart of the theatrical Gesamtkunstwerk into the fragmentations of images and bodies. He thus sets the stage for his own video-enabled exit.

Foreman's investigation into the limits of the "paper-thin world" (perhaps, as thin as a screen?) continued in his next three performances, reaching its climax in his 2008 Deep Trance Behavior in Potatoland, subtitled A Richard Foreman Theatre Machine. In this production, Foreman invoked the many meanings of medium by covering his set in nineteenth-century spirit photographs, images thought to capture the presence of ghosts and spirits invisible to the naked eye. Mostly stripping his live actors of text, the figures on the screen became another kind of super-medial presence, ghosts from another time and space made material through the unique properties of technological processes. The screen actors were the most distinctive and they performed most of the dialogue, often to the camera but occasionally to each other, while the live actors (five women and a man in a suit with fangs) carried on props and assumed a series of tableaux, punctuated by the occasional outburst. The live actors said very little, often chanted in unison and occasionally spoke a single line of dialogue over and over again. Positioned as larger, louder, and also palpably slower embodiments of a performance far away, the video performances as technological spirits became the focus of the piece. Hovering above the space on a large upstage screen (which dominated the visual sphere in Foreman's tiny theatre), the video characters seemed more important, more vibrant, and, ironically, more human than the live performers labouring under the weight of Foreman's objects and physical set. Whereas the screen characters talked and moved in visually striking (if hardly naturalistic) ways, the rigidity of the stage performers offered a striking counterpoint. They moved mechanically and talked in stilted phrases. Foreman thus created an environment in which the living actors became mechanical, while the digitally projected performances emerged as dynamic and ethereal.

If Foreman's physical objects functioned as the materialisation of his philosophy (over-sized Gordian knots, for instance) and his experience in an over-saturated world, his video imagery suggested an escape from it. Foreman recognizes this impulse, suggesting as much in his notes to the production: "Within this setting, the mind is asked to jump from world to world, Japan to England, filmed world to live stage world. The mind is also asked to jump to new ways of relating to reality, a reality in which ideas and behaviors, when viewed correctly, are also askew" (Foreman 2008). Foreman has often seen the project of theatre as a way of re-viewing; the reality he refers to is not the world outside the theatre, which he confesses "does not interest me very much" (interview March 2009), but rather the reality of his own imagined world. His works were always idiosyncratically coded in highly personal imagery, suggesting a 'reality' recognizable to no one but himself. As he described one performance in his "Visual Composition, Mostly" (1992), "giant checked walls in the rear evoked an abstract 'mental space', and random letters glued to the walls formed word fragments suggesting the inside of a book" (Foreman 1992, 63). Within Foreman's notebooks, one can see his evolution of composition from that of painting (framing), to textuality (punctuation), to theatre (staging), and, finally, to film (editing):

> Activity of framing
> & punctuation
> & staging
> & editing (Foreman 2008).

Foreman's theatre is in both theory and practice at the intersection of multiple forms, genres, techniques, and references.

Into this context the video characters in Deep Trance appear. Filmed on location in Japan and England as part of his Bridge Project with Sophie Haviland, they are in abject relation to the live performers. At times, they glare silently at the camera as if judging not only the physically present performers, but also the audience. Foreman imagines them as having control over the live actors, an idea that fits nicely within his notions of technology thinning people and their relationships. Certainly the poses of melodramatic fear exhibited by the live actors as horrified faces turned upwards toward the screen reinforce this notion. However, the power that is most clearly extended is his own. Mixed live during the show (a technique Foreman has been using throughout his career), the sounds and images subject the telepresence of the video characters to the here and now of performance, the continuous presence that Foreman adapts from Stein. Moreover, the telepresence of performances from a different time and place brings not only the immediate present under Foreman's control, but also suggests that his artistic control extends beyond the theatre, as he mediates the connections among his characters, texts, images, and audience.

Telepresence In and Beyond Theatre

For Foreman, telepresence is not just about bringing multiple spaces and characters into dialogue with one another, but also, and perhaps more significantly, about extending his own work beyond the confines of the physical theatre space. The slow gestures and meticulously constructed screen compositions suggest parallel performance creations. We watch the immediate performance aware of its utter dependence on a performance construction from yet another time and place; that is, watching the live production, one becomes aware of the live performance as incomplete without the video performance (acted, filmed, and edited prior to the live performance). The live performers can have no effect on the video figures who have already been captured and manipulated by Foreman. Liveness, as Philip Auslander argues, is always contingent upon mediation (Auslander 1999, 14). Similarly, Foreman has constructed an intermedial theatre in which the live performance necessitates the (tele)presence of the virtual performers. Although it seems like a recent discovery in Foreman's oeuvre, in fact it may be the fulfilment of Foreman's earliest theatrical impulses. As he wrote in 1972:

> Most art is
> created by
> people trying to
> make their idea,
> emotion, thing-
> imagined, be-there
> more. They re-
> inforce. I want
> my imagined to be an
> occasion wherein the not-imagined-by-me can be there. My work= to deny my assertion (imagined) is true (is there) (Foreman 1976b, 76).

As Foreman makes work that is there and not-there and asserts his own impulses within a context that invites a range of interpretations, the immaterial connections bring these questions of presence and absence to the forefront of his performance practice.

In 2009 Foreman concluded his work in the Ontological-Hysteric Theatre in St. Mark's Church with *Astronome: A Night at the Opera* (2009), a rock opera collaboration with composer John Zorn. Even while *Astronome* opened in New York, Foreman was already thinking beyond the theatre, shooting footage for his newest media project in Buffalo, NY as part of his Bridge Project with Sophie Haviland (Figure 1). Rather than arrange live actors in relation to video projections, Foreman in these recent film projects now concentrates his compositional attention to the framing of actors exclusively for the screen. Whereas he formerly imbued his theatrical productions with cinematic attention (as seen in his framing, for instance), he now works theatrically exclusively within video technologies (see Figure 1).

Fig. 1: Richard Foreman (right) and Sophie Haviland discuss a shot for his video performance project. Image courtesy Center for the Moving Image, University at Buffalo (2009), © Liz Chow: all rights reserved

In fall 2009, Foreman directed what he claimed is his last theatrical performance, *Idiot Savant*, a collaboration with former Wooster Group member and film actor, Willem Dafoe, for the Public Theatre in New York. This production was in many ways a 'pure theatre' piece that had little to do technically with telepresence or intermediality and, tellingly, it was performed away from Foreman's theatre at St. Mark's. The production was in many ways a farewell to the theatre, as Foreman simultaneously developed his new film and video projects elsewhere.

Throughout his career, Foreman's theatre productions were meditations on an ever-refining process as much as they were finished products. He produced one play a year, taking time to build the set, design and re-design the costumes, lighting and sound, and rehearse carefully controlled and crafted performances over several months. Until recently, film editing required special and expensive equipment that could only be used for a short period of time. Now, Foreman can do in his computer what he used to do in rehearsal: refine, re-work, re-edit. Watching

MAPPING INTERMEDIALITY IN PERFORMANCE

Foreman in 2009 filming his newest project (currently untitled), one can see his old techniques in process.[48] Actors are given text and Foreman carefully constructs his compositions in the frame, exploring different bits of texts in different positions. Looking at his actors primarily for their physical attributes, he arranges them carefully in space, moving one closer to the camera, another farther away. (See Figure 2.) He will watch their assigned movement and texts through a monitor, refining bits of movement or speech and occasional, dismissing the entire scene and starting from scratch. His emphasis is decidedly on the frame composition, a construction that feels very much akin to his careful framing in his St. Mark's theatre space.

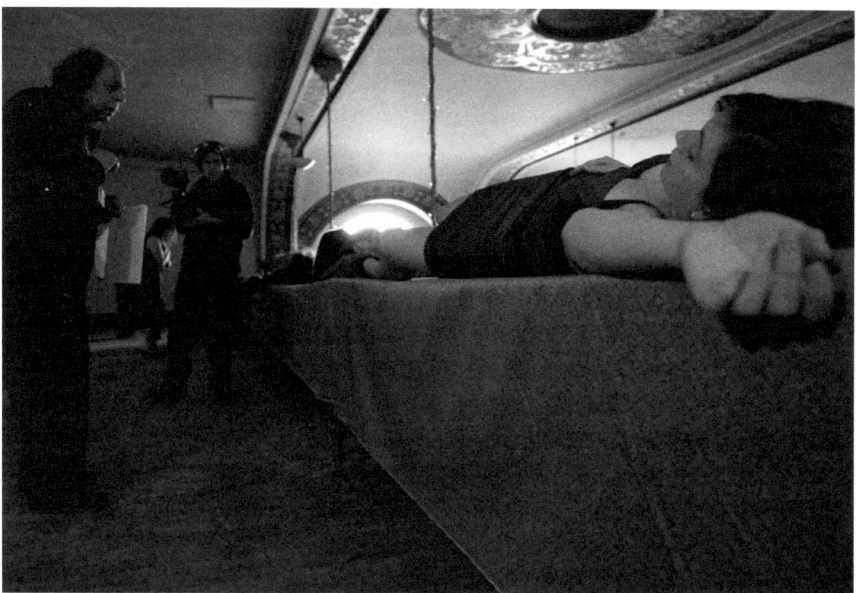

Fig. 2: Richard Foreman (left) positions an actor for his video performance project with filmmaker Elliot Caplan (center). Image courtesy Center for the Moving Image, University at Buffalo (2009), © Liz Chow: all rights reserved

The real difference between his earlier theatre projects and his current film work, at least as it appears to one outside the process, is the editing. Digital technologies have moved the key process of reworking and revising out of the rehearsal hall and into Foreman's laptop. Always distrustful of theatrical presence, he has traded it for perpetual telepresence. It remains to be seen whether Foreman's film work, which must eventually emerge as a finished and (at least temporarily) fixed art piece will retain the dynamic ambiguity of either his theatre work or his intermedial theatre machines.

Portal: Networking

Two key strands weave through the networking portal and its related node of terms and instances. The first is a network conceived as a complex of inter-relationships between mediums in which there are various ways of coming together of perceptibly discrete elements (even though the boundaries between them may be porous). The second is networking conceived as a complex of dynamic inter-related activities, always in interactive process.

At the portal, Wagner and Ernst are concerned with "the phenomenon of networking as performance". They note several consonances between notions of emergent networks in digital culture and expanding notions of performances which might equally take place on YouTube as in a defined theatre space. Re-marking on the anti-essentialist drift leading to an "intertwining of method and object" in both conceptual domains, they highlight "a conceptual shift from rather static ideas of time, space and subjectivity toward dynamic ideas of formation". Drawing on Latour's Actor-Network Theory (ANT), they propose that the actor-network changes in the process of its analysis through performative actions which are not driven by intentions (as traditionally understood) but are themselves an effect of manifold inter-relations. They illustrate the use of a combination of ANT and performance theory with a short account of Schlingensief's *Ausländer Raus! Bitte Liebt Österreich*.

The terms "connectivity", "feedback loop", "hybridity", "interactivity", "intertextuality", "recursion", "separation" and "transcoding" address some of the key inter-relationships between mediums which are identifiable in themselves and which remain discernible (though on occasion only just) in the process of making various kinds of inter-connections. The instances foreground the aspects of their chosen example of practice which illuminate key terms. For example, Pluta recounts, in respect of that particular inflection of hybridity Lepage calls *métissage*, how digital culture affords a specific mixing of the conditions of theatre (the immediate presence of an actual body) with those of cinema (the capacity to superimpose imagery) in the morphing of one persona into another by merging body and device in real time. The imbrication of one system within another leaves traces of each just about visible in the moment of its experience to produce an 'intermedial effect' (← PROSPECTIVE MAPPING).

The 'inter-'relationships between media in the dynamic network of possibilities illustrated by the instances are many and various. A distinctive feature, highlighted in this book's mapping, is evident where two systems, or two states, or two modes of being are simultaneously in play without affording any easy means of reconciling their discreteness (as traditionally understood). In the term 'separation' and in Pluta's account of Lepage's *décalage*, it is made apparent that 'both-and' hybrids arise from this feature of multi-faceted and multi-tracked contemporary culture.

Accelerating the interactive manipulation of words, visuals, sounds and gestures, digital culture contributes to the simultaneous presentation in performance of many modes and mediums and the creation of multiple modes of experience. Boenisch's instance brings out Castorf's distinctive theatrical 'both-and' treatment of Dostoevsky stories which, in the process of transcoding, remain at once "faithful to the source material" and yet contrarily anti-narrative and improvised in production. Whilst various techniques of collage and bricolage pre-date digital culture, the latter's technologies are disposed to compositing such that an actual stage set may be augmented by means of digital projection of virtual constructions of space beyond the theatre, to create what Boenisch calls "the also there". This notion resonates with the idea that the inter-connectedness of digital culture promotes a range of 'also-other' relationships (← PROSPECTIVE MAPPING) in social networking, for example, and in digital doubling as used in many contemporary performance practices. Ernst's account of Gob Squad's *Room Service* highlights the dual state of necessarily being a participant whilst being a member of the audience, communicating not face-to-face but by means of feedback loops in networks within networks, both digital and social. Callens recounts a series of recursions, remediations and transcodings of Cindy Sherman's already intertextual performative practices which destabilise space (gallery-theatre), medium (dance-photography), and ontology (horse-woman) to invite a "critical reflection upon the media codes determining representations of the body on stage and in everyday life".

Networking

Meike Wagner and Wolf-Dieter Ernst

Introduction: Networking and What a 'Network' is Not

This portal affords access to a relatively new approach to performance analysis especially designed for reflecting upon net-based practices. The verb 'networking' might seem self-evidently relevant to a scholarly book on intermediality in performance and digital culture. Indeed, as the Internet and the use of mobile computers have been commoditised, networking has become almost a synonym for a postmodern urban life-style, indicating many modes of being inter-connected, actually and virtually.

The term networking can take up at least three different accents of meaning:

1. within management procedures, it signifies a soft skill. It suggests the strategic use of a network of personal contacts to meet certain objectives. As such networking and an active network is a must to have success in business and industry;

2. it refers to technical networks, such as the railway system, power systems and communication systems. Here, networking describes the technical and material process of connecting a number of entities, to coordinate the flow of information, data, electricity in a complex, non-linear structure. A lot of the metaphors around networking, such as the fast-track, access, station, actually derive from the anthropomorphic interpretation of older mechanical networks;

3. it is a poststructuralist philosophical model, influenced by the Deleuzian concept of the rhizome, aiming to analyse cultural processes. Under this accent, it bears a strong relation to the notion of performance, in as much as both approaches share the critique of ontology, intention and presence and foster the idea of continuous citationality, repetition and relationality.

In what follows, emphasis is placed upon the philosophical model of networking to take a closer look at how this accent relates to both digital culture (← PORTAL: DIGITAL CULTURE) and the performative turn (← PORTAL: PERFORMATIVITY) as outlined in other portals of this book.

Three aspects of networking, loosely connected to the grid of concept and visualisation, will be explored. First, we take up a recent example from social sites, namely a YouTube community, to introduce networking as a *phenomenon*. Secondly, actor-network theory is introduced, pointing out its similarities to performance analysis by looking briefly at the Butlerian notion of the un-intentional act and McKenzie's performance paradigms. Thirdly, some benefits and problems of

ANT (Actor-Network Theory) are explored through a discussion of provocative performance praxis, namely the network of German director Christoph Schlingensief.

The subtitle of this introduction, indicating the implicitly absent, requires further explanation. In the listing of accents on networking, point one and two pretty much sustain the Cartesian matter-mind split. In the first instance we have a social network and, in the second instance, the materialised network. For two reasons, the approach here goes beyond this binary in addressing the third point, the philosophical implications. First, the focus of this book is on digital culture. The digital, as has been observed, blurs the boundaries of mind and matter. Many of the discussions on this issue, however, have suggested that in digital culture matter and reality were on the losing end. Computers became associated with mind and were seen to cause the loss of matter, reflected as virtual reality. As we now have learned, however, the Internet is also real. It is closely related to systems of power supplies and material resources and it causes materialised effects such as certain modes of embodiment in theatre and performance or, for that matter, the loss of jobs and real estate in the economy. Given this experience, to think of the Internet as something either real or virtual is to underestimate its complexity – which is in fact 'both-and'.

The second reason to cut through the Cartesian binary is an ethical one. Any attempt to relate the concept of networking to the concept of performance, demands an engagement with the critical impact, the latter has had on cultural analysis, gender studies and theatre studies over the last two decades. As Marvin Carlson has remarked, performance is a "contested concept" that is as necessarily debatable as the concept of democracy. If the usage of the concept does not provoke a discussion, it carries no value for the issue in question. This is not a preliminary remark since it is already part of a mode of thinking which lays the burden of research on the design of its method before actually starting to look at the body of research. The challenge of anti-essentialist and critical ontology is simply that there is neither a clear-cut problem or object of research, nor an objective perspective to adopt. Rather, there is an intertwining of method and object. The concept of networking might seem to answer this problem since a network (and a performance) is not a thing or an object, and an actor-network analysis is not simply a nuts-and-bolts tool for digital culture. The question is not what a network is, but rather what it does or, put differently, what it performs.

Networking as a Hybrid Phenomenon

In her YouTube video, Patricia G. Lange interviews several people, asking them if they consider YouTube a community and if they do, why. The video, having been posted on October 3rd 2007, received about 555,053 hits within two weeks. Among the people having viewed the video, 1607 commented on it and 16 members of YouTube chose to post a video message as a reaction to Lange's initiative.

MAPPING INTERMEDIALITY IN PERFORMANCE

Indeed, the moving image is framed by continuously evolving comments and statistics such that it is almost impossible to look at the video clip as a singular piece of cinematic art. On YouTube it becomes an object of discussion, a motive for starting a conversation, thus somehow stabilizing the group as a community by way of communication. The interaction in the chat room bears evidence of the self-conception of its members that also entails a certain ironic view on the virtual character of their encounter. "If youtube is a community, then if you post a video and don't charge others to watch it, is that considered community service?" (treelandhaha, 9 Oct. 2007).

Consider the characteristics of the phenomenon of networking:

1. *Participation*: The beholder as user. Watching videos online is more than just looking at moving images. Already the index page of YouTube offers manifold features for the user to get involved with the platform and to become an active participant. The log-in routine appears to be a threshold to active participation in a community that exchanges colourfully previewed film trailers, shorts and homemade movies among its members. Participants signal their approval by rating the films using little stars; their comments create new links and communicative relations and finally culminate in the posting of new films and video clips. The users' activities are tracked in real-time so that in the category "Videos being watched right now..." for example, one can observe and also follow the perceptive habits of other viewers. Every mouse click alters the number of views displayed which is, besides title and YouTube name of the person posting the film, the most important information for potential viewers (→ TERM: INTERACTIVITY)

2. *Feedback-loop* (→ TERM: FEEDBACK LOOP). Perception becomes production: On the YouTube site, participants are always invited to give an opinion, to write a comment, to engage in the evaluation process of the posted items. The figure of the passive onlooker or receiver does not exist in YouTube. Instead, participants instantly become aware that their own actions – multiplied by the feedback of other users – change the structure of the Internet site. In this sense, social and technical feedback-loops maintain the network in a process of co-evolution.

3. *Net-based community*. The process of networking sketched out in the above example of a social networking site calls into question conventional notions of the community. One click on the "Community" button pops up several calls for competition. The community is looking for the best music clip, the best stop-motion movie, the best amateur video and so on. "Be a part of our community, let us discuss your personal contribution!" is the credo of YouTube. Community-building traditionally associates face-to-face communication and ritualised forms. Net-based communities in contrast rely on mediated communication and employ contingent and continuously changing forms to achieve group-identity.

This example is telling for contemporary theatre and performance. Theatre makers and performance artists, such as Gob Squad (← INSTANCE: GOB SQUAD, ROOM SERVICE), Rimini Protokoll (← INSTANCE: RIMINI PROTOKOLL), and Christopher Kondek (← INSTANCE: DEAD CAT BOUNCE) discussed amongst the instances of this book, feel attracted to experiment with social sites, on-line games and pervasive gaming. Even more important, the audience carries the experience of networking into the theatrical space. Networks are on today's agenda. Virtual communities pop up like mushrooms. Email, mobile phones and the Internet have conquered our traditional intimate sphere and have out-performed the older distribution media, radio, TV and cinema.[49] Any attempt to play an active role in what has been termed 'thumb culture' relies on an email account or mobile phone. Abstinence from these items immediately annihilates the personal image unless one propagates absolute 'media asceticism' similar to that cultivated by Guy Debord or Thomas Pynchon. This change of personal lifestyle is paralleled today by a growing awareness of social and political engagement grounding in a new idea of 'community'. One of the best examples to illustrate this interrelatedness of new media and political activism can be found in non-governmental organisations and the Attac!-Movement. But also performances by, for example, the Yes Man, Billionaire Against Bush or Christoph Schlingensief attract attention through their networking and campaigning.

While phenomena such as the YouTube community clearly influence contemporary theatre and performance, the conceptualisation of these phenomena raises further issues. Networking appears to cut through traditional notion of theatre as determined in time, space and a more or less local community. While traditional stage interactions are controlled and carefully prepared, the interactions in (virtual) communities are not. Quite contrary to a theatrical script, they are uncontrolled and self-generating. Additionally, the presentation of technological competence pertaining to interactive theatre is less important in virtual communities. Instead the interplay of gain and loss of control becomes part of the game: Any interaction in virtual communities relies on a careful and meticulously programmed and controlled software while at the same time, this software would never come alive and allow for (→ TERM: CONNECTIVITY) without the 'wild' and 'uncontrollable performance' of various users. In short, participation feedback and net-based communities call for a conceptual shift, from rather static ideas of time, space and subjectivity toward dynamic ideas of formation and process. It might thus be more productive no longer to proceed with traditional notions of actor, beholder and art-work, but rather to look from a different methodological angle at the phenomenon of networking as performance.

Actor-Network Theory and the Performance Paradigm

From a theoretical point of view an analysis of networks and cultural performance can benefit from approaches relating to the Actor-Network Theory. Two main characteristics are particularly important here: the question of agency and un-intentional acts replacing subjectivity, and the intertwining of social, economic and technological performance.

In cultural studies, the noun network refers to a technical or social structure of a certain complexity. The network suggests notions of flow, heterogeneity, circulation and a non-strategic grid of connections, largely derived from French poststructuralist philosophy of such thinkers as Roland Barthes, Michel Serres, Gilles Deleuze and Félix Guattari – all being important figures for performance theory.[50] The French term for network is *reseau*, similar to the German *Netz*, a word, which is used in diverse contexts from fishing through to computer systems. The English translation would be either *net* or *network*, the former expressing the material aspect of tangled filaments and the latter suggesting an abstract technical or social system.

A more specific definition of networking can be derived, however, from the Actor-Network Theory as formulated by a research group led by Bruno Latour. Originally developed in science studies in the early 1980s, ANT equally encompasses social, economic and technical connections. The theory displays three main characteristics of the network: anti-hierarchy; no starting point or ending; and performed by an actor. Each will be outlined in turn.

Anti-hierarchy

ANT and poststructuralists theories alike have promoted the idea that thinking in terms of a network means to represent the technical and social connections as anti-hierarchical. In contrast essentialist theories promote as the starting point of philosophy either technology, nature or the world of objects (materialism) or the subject, language and thought (idealism). ANT, however, has no starting point. Unlike traditional hierarchies and action-reaction paradigms, a net allows for *equal access from every point*, it has no inside and outside or below and above. Calling into question the common relation of closeness and distance, Latour offers an insight into the perspective of Actor-Network theory:

> Elements which are close when disconnected may be infinitely remote when their connections are analysed; conversely, elements which would appear as infinitely distant may be close when their connections are brought back into the picture. I can be one meter away from someone in the next telephone booth and nevertheless be more closely connected to my mother 6000 miles away; an Alaskan reindeer might be ten meters away from another one and they might nevertheless be cut off by a pipeline of 800 miles that makes their mating for ever impossible; my son may sit at school with a young Arab of his age, but in spite of this close proximity in first grade they might drift apart in worlds that will become incommensurable later (Latour 1996, 371).

Latour's concept of network sheds light on the way different entities are related to each other. Mapping the world in relations of near and far thus appears to be only one of many possible patterns.

No Starting Point, No Ending

According to Latour, a network is not considered to be a built or communicated 'thing'; rather one has to think of a network as a conceptual perspective. This perspective implies, that any analysis of a network cannot be conducted from the outside, because the 'object' of observation, i.e. the actor-network, changes in the process of its analysis. It does so, because, among other influences, it reacts to the movement the beholder or observer causes in the process of his or her analysis, his or her moving around within the actor-network. That is to say, an actor network only exists when it is constructed through the process of reading. As Latour puts it, "No net exists independently of the very act of tracing it, and no tracing is done by an actor exterior to the net. A network is not a thing, but the recorded movement of a thing" (Latour 1997, 11).

Here, one point is key: within a network there is no hierarchy, just filaments and conjunctions. In science theory and physics, this inside/outside collision is known as the problem of feedback of observation. ANT would radically promote the idea that feedback-effects signify, not a failure of the planned observation of the 'real thing', but, in reverse, what an actor-network does or performs. It is the dynamics of change of actor-networks.

Performance of Actor-Network

One of the main features of ANT is to think of relations within a network as being performed by an actor. Already the double bind of the actor and the network is telling.[51] As Latour points out:

> [Actor-Network Theory] makes use of some of the simplest properties of nets and then adds to it an *actor* that does some *work*, the addition of such an onto-logical ingredient deeply modifies it. [...] A network in mathematics or in en-gineering is something that is traced or inscribed by some other entity – the mathematician, the engineer. An actor-network is an entity that *does* the tra-cing and the inscribing. It is an ontological definition and not a piece of inert matter in the hands of others, especially of human planners or designers. It was in order to point out this essential feature that the word "actor" was added to it (Latour 1997, 371f).

When talking about entity, Latour demarcates the difference to concepts of action as being intentionally pursued.

ANT refrains from concepts as 'intention' and 'subject' in the same way as Judith Butler's reading of Foucault led her to think of a gender performance as an act of citationality. A gendered body according to Butler is never something, an entity. It is not a thing, which we can intentionally decide to have or to alter. A gendered body rather is an *effect* of manifold relations, or an actor-network for that matter. The network maintains relation to other bodies, to role models, rules, norms, fashion, language and so on. We collectively and un-intentionally become gendered as we grow and learn to relate to other entities. The institutional segregation of the female and male in toilets possibly does more to establish gender hierarchies, than a subject's intention, which in the development of a gender identity only comes later.

A gender performance as well as an actor-network in this sense holds for the performance of an actor without necessarily thinking, that it is performed intentionally or even by a singular subject. Both approaches concur in the perception of action being performed collectively and both encompass physical action performed by subjects equally to actions performed by animals, inorganic matter, language or technology. Latour remarks that:

> An 'actor' in ANT is a semiotic definition – an actant – , that is something that acts or to which activity is granted by others. It implies *no* special motivation of *human individual* actors, nor of humans in general. An actant can literally be anything provided it is granted to be the source of an action (Latour 1997, 373).

In this sense "actant" refers to activities of subjects as well as things – an idea which is known within semiotics as "internal coding". In performance analysis the notion of an actant opens up the perspective towards the relation of different entities such as information, raw material, news, animals, and human beings. This does not mean, however, that entities can be thought of as randomly connected to each other. Relation is not to be mistaken for relativity. This is why the movements of actants are considered as performance. As Latour very precisely puts it, the "source of an action" is "granted" and this donation is given beforehand in choosing certain 'objects' and relations as subject of the investigation. Latour and Butler share the idea of a weak and circulating agency replacing a strong notion of the subject.

Another feature that ANT adds to performance theory is its close relation to science studies. ANT offers the advantage of opening up a perspective on the field of the technological, the world of matter and the economic field – and these are exactly the most predominant forces within contemporay networking of the YouTube kind. As a theory of long range, ANT fits to the contemporary interdisciplinary shift within performance studies aiming to enlarge the notion of cultural performance in looking at the technological and economic aspects of it as well. This is a project pursued by McKenzie (2001).

As McKenzie emphasises, performance always refers to processes of normal-isation and subversion. The interplay of both a norm and its subversion, however, is of different quality depending on the criteria that are chosen to evaluate the performance. Within the realm of the aesthetic it might be other criteria com-pared to, for example, the criteria for economic performance. A performance ana-lyst, for example, who evaluates operations within a financial institute, might ap-ply a different pattern to determine profit and loss than an audience would apply to a theatrical performance. The same holds true for institutional performances, for a university or a government department for instance, that primarily has to fulfill a social function (transfer of knowledge, providing financial aid). McKenzie charts three different qualities within the performance paradigm: *effectiveness, effi-ciency, efficacy. Effectiveness* refers to technical functioning, while *efficiency* describes processes within institutions and economical circuits. The most familiar quality is *efficacy* referring to the notion of resistance and affirmation within cultural perfor-mances. To conclude, according to McKenzie and Latour different types of per-formances of an actor-network can be analysed through a combination of ANT and performance theory that promises a possible perspective on the interplay be-tween action and affirmation, between technological and social interaction.

The Case of Christoph Schlingensief's *Ausländer Raus! Bitte Liebt Österreich!*

In Christoph Schlingensief's performance *Ausländer Raus! Bitte liebt Österreich!* (2000) passers-by in Vienna could participate in a game similar to the well-known TV performance *Big Brother*, which in itself cites a well-established agonistic game-structure of musical chairs. One player after the other is thrown out of the game, till the winner appears. The cynical and political denotation of this perfor-mance, however, is, that the game selects an asylum seeker from a group dwell-ing in a container on a main square across the Vienna opera house and expels him or her from the country. An aesthetic analysis reveals a common pattern of performance art in terms of appropriation: artists take a well-known TV format and remodel it in their performance into a provoking political statement, in this instance signalled by the slogan, "Ausländer raus!" ["Foreigners get out!"]. So far, this would follow conventional performance analysis. But, if we look at the performance as an actor-network, this perspective immediately affects the analy-sis at hand.

Consider the key characteristics: anti-hierarchy, no starting point and no end-ing, and the activity of an actor. According to ANT's demand to think anti-hier-archically, the starting point about the place of the performance is critical. The physical action of the performance is clearly centred in and around the container. Inside, the asylum seekers wait for their selection. Outside, the audience and pas-sers-by assemble, being encouraged by Schlingensief and other activists to par-ticipate in the game. A third and more important stage is the net-based community. Participation was on-line and thus, for organisational reasons, participants are located elsewhere, at home or in Internet cafes. While the real space of the performance is thus distributed all over town, it is dominated by a public sphere which encompasses the daily newspaper report on the event, local TV-broadcasts as well as national and international media coverage. The performance provoked media reports and journalists were keen to launch a hate campaign against it. These public spheres of the media are equally places of performance in that what has been written or broadcast altered the performance process and reciprocally. Without this polemic reaction, the performance could not have taken place on the terms in which it did. Anti-hierarchy thus calls for a critical rethinking of performance as defined by its space.

The second observation concerns the open beginning and ending of an actor-network. According to ANT, the performance "Ausländer Raus!" would not have ended yet. Nor did it actually start. The theatrical performance, of course, took place within a determined period of time on the Vienna opera square. But this is only the intentional part of it. A networking perspective fosters the idea of detecting a discourse against which Schlingensief's intervention merely reacts. Attention might be drawn to the xenophobic atmosphere in Austria fuelled by the governance of the right wing party (FPÖ) and the populist speeches of Jörg Haider. The excited announcements of the event in the boulevard newspapers (*Kronen-Zeitung*) before the actual opening might be noted. Equally important is the controversial TV format of *Big Brother* launched a year before by the Endemol-company, as it had already introduced the rules of a game about excluding certain persons from a social structure long before the actual Schlingensief event took place in Vienna. The xenophobic atmosphere and *Big Brother* both raise issues of social control and the rejection of the 'other', with accompanying public disputes that took place in different networks. If it makes sense to ask, when a discourse actually began, it might be maintained that the xenophobic shift in media and society since the early 1990s marks the beginning.

A third aspect might consider the actor within the network, beyond the predominant notion of subjectivity and intention. Who or what is granted agency in this network? Raising this question, leads us away from the notorious 'agent provocateur', Christoph Schlingensief, as the author and central figure of the performance. Rather we would differentiate between the well-known media figure called "Christoph Schlingensief" and the conceptual artist and performer of that name. Having made this distinction, another question comes immediately into play. How does "Schlingensief" become a brand name in the first place? How has he gained citationality? Our analysis will have to take into consideration preceding performances by Schlingensief, including his scandalous film-happenings, his open call to kill the German chancellor, his provocative appearance on TV, and the fake election campaign "Chance 2000. Vote for yourself!", which he launched for a "party of the unemployed". Analysis reveals that Schlingensief's reputation is closely related to the feedback of media coverage and media campaigning. Furthermore, his expertise relies greatly on his team's competence, an in-group of around forty buddies loosely connected to him. Ultimately, we will look at around two or three subsidised theatres and festivals, which provide an organisational backbone and financial sources to fuel his work. From here, we have to analyse, what the theatre institution adds to the performance in terms of reputation, agenda-setting and the level of attention they can draw. The same question then counts for the documentation of the performance: several news and documentary films, numerous photographs, a web-site and two book publications documenting the printing press around the event (Lilienthal 2001; Poet 2001) all came out of the performance. But what do we do with this material? It is almost impossible to analyse the performance without looking at the mediated material, but does this mean that these documents should be looked at as actively as one would examine, say, Schlingensief and his comrades themselves? Whether these documents are in fact passive representations of the event, or – which is more likely – whether they have added and still add to the performance, is indeed challenging to decide upon, because it cuts through the hierarchy of artwork and documentation. One can hardly decide upon such an issue without methodological reflection.

"It just happened to be this way", this is, how Bruno Latour describes the relational perspective of ANT. Does that mean that social forces or virtual communities perform without paying any regard to artistic intention and authorship? Does it mean that technological performance and inanimate matter takes over? Does this mark the rise of the posthuman (←PORTAL: POSTHUMANISM), cyborgian Actor? Surely not. However, the fact, that a cultural or artistic performance follows either a rigid intention or is based on a rather open concept equally of mind and matter, is no longer a question of alternatives but just one out of the many filaments in a network. A network perspective allows for a closer look at the performance without having to subscribe to a mind-matter distinction. As we hope to have demonstrated so far, the analysis according to ANT is to investigate the (artistic) performance as their result from within the network instead of applying a ready made concept of meaning to it.

In the case of Ausländer Raus!, then, we are less interested in the subjective perspectives of the participants in the container, of Schlingensief as creator/director or indeed of anyone who decides to participate in the piece by casting a vote. The event demonstrates 'efficacy' by virtue of the agency of all those involved – participants, event facilitators and designers, and the voting public. Such agency is not necessarily to common purpose. Instead, the outcome of the event might be thought 'un-intentional' in that it is the result of the accumulation of actions rather than a single shared drive. These actions, however, are those of a network of actors who (in Latour's terms) do some work. By way of such work, agency circulates.

Ausländer Raus! does not fully observe the anti-hierarchical character of a network. As indicated above, for instance, the piece itself has a beginning and an ending, and clearly the experiences and activities of the participants in the container are different from those of the public watching and voting. That said, you could say that the event connects with prior and subsequent activities. Individuals enter Austria seeking asylum; they leave it (or not) to continue their lives in altered circumstances. If this means that *Ausländer Raus!* is 'networked' to a past and a future by way of a larger time continuum, thematically and politically it demonstrates a larger characteristic of modern networks – their intertwining of social, economic and technological considerations. The event is both seriously and playfully to do with migration and asylum, national boundaries and geo-political territories, having and not-having, experience and its immediate mediatisation. And it is the latter – the mediation of *Ausländer Raus!* through broadcast technologies – that *produces* the event in the first place. As Latour says, "A network is not a thing, but the recorded movement of a thing" (1997, 11). To that end, the 'tracing' of Schlingensief's event in and through media creates and expands its networked characteristics.

As sketched out above the networking perspective for performance analysis is an attempt to take a modified idea of aesthetic acting into account and to integrate performative forms into the scope of an analysis that cannot come into play merely by focusing on intra-theatrical aesthetics or the intention of the author/creator. Thus the networking perspective promises new impulses for performance analysis.

transparency separation

experiencer deterritorialisation

glocalisation displacement telematic recursion

intertextuality hybridity

interrelations

interactivity connectivity

feedback loop presence

embodiment virtuality intimacy

materiality immersion

Node: Inter-relations

Connectivity. The term connectivity, initially growing out of digital media theory (Broeckmann 1998, Knowbotic Research 2000), is now used in the context of live theatre and its engagement with telematic (← TERM) technology, such as mobile phones, the Internet, and video-circuits. It assists in defining the aesthetics of long-distance transmissions of (digital) information within performance and media art when, for example, an unstable connection appears in performances such as an audio-guided walk or a pervasive game. In such instances, a participant walking through a city or a museum has to stay on track and must not take off the headset if he or she wants fully to follow the performance. The headset transmission is paradoxically a technical obstacle that creates connectivity in performance.

The ending '-ivity' further signifies potentiality, that is a perpetually unstable connection which needs to be continually maintained in order to function. Connectivity implies that any well-functioning connection is an exception to the rule of uncertainty and chaos. As such, the inherent instability (and exceptions) of connectivity challenges our conventional views of the world, instead of transforming those perspectives through new connections that simultaneously undermine conventional hierarchies of thinking, e.g. cause-effect, near-far, bottom-top. For example, a phone-call between different time zones may ironically produce an instance of intimacy (← TERM). In such an example of connectivity, intimacy is not taken for granted, as in a one-to-one conversation, but rather is heightened because of the awareness of the absence of physical proximity, the timing and costs of the call, and perhaps our longing actually to meet the other, while fully cognisant of its impossibility. The telephone line is thus either connected or disconnected, but its unstable emotional content reinforces the dynamic relations that connectivity allows between users and technology. (Wolf-Dieter Ernst)

Feedback Loop. The term feedback originated in the early 20th century to refer to the mechanical-electrical phenomenon produced when an output signal (from a loudspeaker) returns to affect its input signal (the sound into the microphone). The effect of the input signal tends to change or distort the original signal, causing the screech or hum associated with amplification. In everyday language, feedback refers to information in response to something produced, such as merchandise or a person's performance, which can be used as a basis for improvement. In theatre and performance, a system of feedback can be understood to take place between performers and spectators; a feedback loop is created when the audience reaction (output signal) returns to affect aspects of the performance (input signal). In theatrical history, new technologies have altered possible forms of feedback between performers and their audience. When gas lighting was first introduced to 19th-century European theatres, it became possible to light the stage in its entirety, eliminating the need for candelabras over spectator seating. The resulting darkened auditorium, however, eliminated the optic feedback loop that actors had previously enjoyed to gauge the audience's reaction and adjust their performances accordingly. Today, digital and wireless technologies are again expanding the potential for feedback between audiences and performers. (Michael Darroch)

Interactivity. The efficacy of intermedial performance often relies on interactivity, the perceived (if not actual) engagement of the viewer and a virtual, or simulated, environment. In many examples of intermedial performance, the viewer engages within the work from an immersive perspective. This change in interactive immersion is arguably the first major shift in visual representation since the development of position in two-dimensional media. As opposed to this two-dimensional perspective available to the viewer looking at an image in a drawing, painting, or a photograph, the interactive perspective enables the viewer to see from within the image controlling both one's own position in relation to the image, and the dimensions (even ontology) of the image itself. *How* one looks can largely determine the image that one sees and the experience of the virtual image. As Peter Weibel notes, in such context, "For the first time in history, the image is a dynamic system" (Rush 2001, 168). If the virtual is essentially a simulation in which the viewer becomes immersed within open-ended possibilities, then the viewer's perception and participation are essential components of **virtuality**. Expanding theatre's historical interactivity between audience and performance, virtuality deepens this relationship by relying on the viewer for the performance catalyst. (Sarah Bay-Cheng)

Hybridity. Derived from the Latin *hybrida*, or "mixed blood" (c. 1596), hybridity in biology refers to a crossing of species of different varieties. In a media context, Marshall McLuhan defined the hybrid as the "interpenetration of one medium by another" (McLuhan 1964, 2003, 76). Sound film, for example, results from the hybridisation of cinematography and radio (2003, 78). Bruno Latour argues in his *We Have Never Been Modern* that scientific inquiry is always a study of composites: quasi-objects/quasi-subjects (Latour 1999, 58-60). This leads Latour to the further conclusion that scientific knowledge is produced in networks across the previously discrete categories of art, culture, science, and politics. Bolter and Grusin, citing Latour, address the notion of hybrids as media composed of heterogeneous networks, such as digital photography, that likewise cross multiple fields as well as technologies (1999, 57-58).

Aesthetically, hybridity in the arts first appeared in the domain of music (Berlioz, Wagner and Rimsky-Korsakov) and is notable in contemporary principles of composition in which disparate creative elements are juxtaposed. Art also hybridises with science, culture and technology, as in digital art, which is intrinsically linked to information technology (cf. Poissant, 1997,165). In the context of intermediality, the effect of hybridisation mines the characteristics of different systems and places them in new configurations, either fused or remaining in tension. One of the paradigmatic figures of hybridity is the cyborg (← PORTAL: POSTHUMAN), a human who may have replaced one or more body parts with machines, or metaphorically extended to embrace a posthuman consciousness (cf. Harraway 1981 and McLuhan 1964). Lev Manovich's "cultural transcoding" similarly refers both to the blurring of human and computer interfaces and to the "cultural transfer" between humanist culture and the digital (Manovich, 2001,47). Amongst performing arts, Stelarc and Marcel.lí Antúnez Roca have been most prominent in exploring the cyborg (cf. Giannachi 2001; Parker-Starbuck 2006). (Izabella Pluta)

Intertextuality. In her influential essay on semiotics, Julia Kristeva coined the term intertextuality as the need to read any given text in light of its inherent references, allusions, and distinctions from prior texts. Synthesizing Saussure's semiotics with Bahktin's dialogism, Kristeva argued that "the notion of intertextuality replaces intersubjectivity", with the meaning of a given text heavily shaped by its allusions, references and connections to other texts (Kristeva 1967, 69). Consistent with much of postmodern critical theory, this perspective asserts the lack of a singular Ur-text and instead positions the text as inherently viewed within a network (← TERM) of other related and allusive texts.

More recently, theorists such as George Landow and Paul Delany consider intertextuality as the predecessor of hypertext – a text often experienced as a series of embedded computer links that enable a reader of electronic literature to move through a text in nonlinear and even recursive ways. As an accessible form of allusion in electronic writing, Landow and Delany describe hypertextuality as "an almost embarrassingly literal embodiment of intertextuality" (Delany and Landow 1990, 6). Within intermedial performance, intertextuality may refer not only to language and its expression in various forms of printed or electronic literature, but also to other readable forms of media, such as film texts, visual advertising, and non-verbal performances such as dance and music. In this context, intertextuality includes both a network of allusive printed texts and a larger universe of images, performances, and ideas within a particular performance. (Sarah Bay-Cheng)

Separation. Separation, meaning the state of being apart, suggests difference and diversity instead of similarity and unity. Separation is, therefore, a modernist concept, as opposed to a classical or traditional one, as it draws attention to aspects rather than totality. It may also relate to abstraction and negation, expressing doubt or even denial of conceptual totality. In aesthetic discourses on theatre, separation is usually considered to be antithetical to Richard Wagner's *Gesamtkunstwerk*, the paradigm of fusion in the sense of a (re)unification and (re)integration of the individual arts as in Wagner's own "music dramas". Separation aptly characterizes art works of the early 20th-century avant-garde. The dadaists and surrealists, in particular, separated all kinds of artistic procedures from their historically-determined stylistic norms and they declared the free availability of artistic means as an aesthetic principle, in particular with the artistic intention of shocking their audiences (Bürger 1974, 22-24).

Separation can also be considered a characteristic feature of respectively the epic and the postdramatic theatre (Hans-Thies Lehmann, 2006 [1999]). The "radical separation of elements" that Brecht (1964 [1930], 37-38) has in mind, is primarily related to an epical mode of representation, an argument-driven dramaturgy aimed at eliciting critical reflection. Characteristic of the postdramatic theatre is the non-hierarchical structure of its elements, arranged according to a spatial principle of next-to-each-other (in a relative independence from each other) rather than after-each-other (in a chain of cause and effect). Simultaneity, then, takes precedence over succession though the boundaries of elements arranged simultaneously are porous. Separation is inextricably linked with intermediality, since the intermedial is only conceivable if two or more inherently fused elements (media) are also seen to be separable from each other. (Chiel Kattenbelt)

Recursion. Recursion, from the Latin *recurrere* – to run back, or return – may well originate in human brain activity, as witnessed in descriptions of working memory and sleep, e.g., the ever-shortening cycles of dream-related Rapid Eye Movement sleep and non-REM sleep, essential for the brain's development and learning (Baddeley; Carlson 2004, 279 and 286-87). Recursion can also be found throughout history in fields as diverse as music (canon, fugue, ricercar; modulation), literature (framing and embedding), cinema (the reel's loop progressing the story), and mathematics (algorithms). More recently, recursion has been revalorised as an organizing principle of digital media (control and search procedures; computer games) and the postdramatic performing arts (Lehmann 2006 [1999]). From an historical perspective, then, recursion is the operating logic of remediation, the ongoing refunctioning of media (Bolter & Grusin 1999).

Generally speaking, recursion designates the repeated application of certain rules or operations to the same material (or to the product of the previous operations) until specific critical conditions are met. Intradisciplinary and intrageneric forms of recursion thus tend towards serial repetition and media transparency.

Disciplinary and intermedial crossings follow a recursive process which simultaneously systematizes the relationships between the material (physical or technical) support of the arts and media (old and new), and the cultural and disciplinary conventions with which these media and arts operate by working on that support. The resulting structures, then, reflexively "produce the rules that generate the structure itself" (Krauss 2000, 6-7), thus allowing the arts and media to arrive at their specificity. Intermedial recursion goes hand in hand with the postmodern or posthuman (← PORTAL: POSTHUMAN) subject's problematised presence, its unstable connectivity and telematic integration in the globalised information circuits the new media made possible. (Johan Callens)

Transcoding. In computing, to "transcode" refers to the conversion of data from one (digital) format into another. Facilitated by shared structural principles of data organisation and processing (such as numeric coding, modular organisation, and automation), it allows digital media to copy, convert, blend, store and reproduce any kind of contents and information, whether textual, visual, acoustic, or other. For media scholar Lev Manovich, transcoding points, moreover, to "the most substantial consequence of the computerization of media" (Manovich 2001, 45). He points to the fundamental cultural impact of the technological concept, as the digital principle refines the structural organisation of data as well as strategies of representation, fostering a "more general process of cultural reconceptualisation" (Manovich 2001, 47).

Where established conventions and concepts (aesthetic as well as everyday) are thus reconfigured along the logic of transcoding, the new composite notions disclose a typical "blend of human and computer meanings, of traditional ways in which human culture modelled the world and the computer's own means of representing it" (Manovich 2001, 46). Artistic practice broadly has long since reflected "cultural transcoding" but it is now particularly evident in the performing arts. In theatre and performance, it has been at the heart of the postdramatic move beyond the paradigms of mimetic representation, psychologic characterisation, and linear narration (cf. Lehmann 2006). Exemplary instances can be found in the processes of staging and directing a text which leave behind conventional notions of translation and adaptation, in the increasing interest in the practice of dramaturgy, or in the conceptions of bodies and corporeality as reflected in contemporary dance. Again, the deep, structural conversion of form within the medium itself, as well as the dialectic link between medium and culture, which are characteristic for digital transcoding, are reflected in these cases. (Peter M. Boenisch)

Instances

Instance: Robert Lepage and Ex Machina, *The Andersen Project* (2005)

Izabella Pluta

Contextual Outline

This instance involves an analysis of the impact of new media technologies on the theatrical performance of Canadian actor-director Robert Lepage in *The Andersen Project* (2005).[52] It explores the actor's function in relation to notions of hybridity (← TERM: HYBRIDITY) and proposes the concept of a "mediaphoric body". Lepage is a pioneer in the presentation of live performance that uses different sorts of technology. The integration of digital media into theatre brings about a complex transformation from the standpoint of the actor and his craft. Technological objects and devices become integral to the composition of the actor's performance. Various types of media interact with traditional components of the actor's repertoire, including his presence, his manner of expressing and reading emotions, and his connection to his role. Indeed, the impact upon the nature of characterisation in the staging as a whole has required a redefinition of the composition of acting through a postdramatic perspective (Pavis 2005, 91). Here, the actor appears as *operator* of the stage who ensures the aesthetic transitions between the theatrical and other technological media, both digital and analogue.

The Andersen Project is Lepage's fifth 'solo' show, and as usual in these pieces he is both actor and director and plays (almost) all of the protagonists, thus steering the creative process through multiple scenic perspectives.[53] Lepage developed the production text with Peder Bjurman and Marie Gignac through a process of scenic writing (l'écriture scénique) where, in contrast with dramatic writing (l'écriture dramatique), the story emerges through trials, rehearsals and discussions (see Pavis 2002, 112 and Ubersfeld 1996, 35). The plot consists of three threads woven together: a factually-based account of a journey to Paris made by the writer Hans Christian Andersen; two of Andersen's tales, The Dryad (written in 1868 on the occasion of the World Exposition in Paris) and The Shadow (1847); and a fictional story set in the present. The contemporary narrative is structured around two characters: Arnaud de la Guimbretière, the director of the Garnier Opera, and Frédéric Lapointe, a Canadian composer invited by the Garnier to write a libretto (ultimately never completed) based on Andersen's writings. Lepage weaves these different stories, periods and aesthetic reference points together in a characteristic narrative composition, one based on *transformation*, a key process in his work (cf. Hébert and Perelli-Contos 2001, 38; Charest 1995, 161). He juxtaposes the protagonists; finds analogies between them; and structures contrasts using theatrical solutions (from object theatre and Chinese shadow theatre, for example), as well as tools of cinematography (such as a succession of shots, editing and moving image technology). Andersen, for instance, always appears as a mute character and the Dryad as a marionette with his back to the audience. Lepage thus creates a hybrid aesthetic.

He has envisaged this hybridity for years and speaks of it by way of *métissage* (a mixing or crossbreeding), a term that he applies on both a cultural and aesthetic level. He articulated this idea in particular as curator of the exhibition *Métissages vus par Robert Lepage* (Musée de la civilisation, Quebec City, 2000-2001), describing the crossing of the languages of theatre and cinematography as "two forms of expression that will be merged together".[54] The division and superimposition of elements and the resulting reciprocal interrogation continuously feed the Lepagean *aesthetic of movement*.

The Mediaphoric Body

The contextual outline, above, frames a particular focus on the phenomenon resulting from the incorporation of the actor with particular media (here, theatre and cinema). The body is transformed and becomes host to a role through the configuration of multiple elements of the spectacle, a role *other* than that of the character. This role is born of the *coexistence* of different media. In this process, various techniques of acting are thrown into relief, and hybridity – or *métissage* with medial elements – brings about new forms of expression. This situation is usefully explored in terms of the "mediaphoric body", a notion that helps to articulate the intermediality of the actor rather than simply that of the media in play. From an etymological perspective, this concept incorporates three elements of a different order, both concrete and conceptual: the living, the media-related and the metaphorical. The actor in flesh and blood represents the first element. The media-related element is introduced on the stage (so might be thought extra-theatrical), and its components might range from the projected image to the device (such as the screen or camera). The third element, of a conceptual order, represents a semiological figure (the metaphor), and is linked to a semiological process (metaphorisation). Metaphorisation consists of a transformation from one sign to another, or, more precisely, of a "transfer by analogical substitution" (Kowzan 2005, 117, 120). Hence the fusion of the latter two terms, which become *mediaphoric* in this new understanding of the *mediaphoric body*, which takes shape within the process of hybridisation and is achieved by means of the metaphor. The connection with the technological device does not occur as it might in cyborg

MAPPING INTERMEDIALITY IN PERFORMANCE

theatre as envisaged, for instance, by Gabriella Giannachi (2004, 43). Here we have a *métissage* of intermediality and theatricality in which the actor becomes the *operator* of the stage. It is in this context that we situate the relationship between the actor's body and the device.

Fig. 1: The Andersen Project. *Performing the mediaphoric body*, © *photo Eric Labbé*

The initial scene of *The Andersen Project* serves to illustrate the mediaphoric body. The performance begins with a prologue in which we see the back of Frédéric Lapointe (the composer) (Fig. 1). As he explains why the performance for which he has been creating the libretto has been cancelled, a camera views his face which is projected in real time in close-up on a screen. The screen also has a fixed image of the auditorium of the Garnier Opera Hall as seen from the stage. The actor faces the projection of the auditorium, and he also sees his own projected image: he may act according to his effigy. However, he cannot see the audience. Here, Lepage as director achieves a nearly complete interpenetration of multiple universes: the virtual and the actual, the theatrical and the cinematic, the real and the imaginary. The mediaphoric body appears here as a composite figure: the image of the actor's face coexists with his body, present on the stage. The complex meanings of this hybrid appearance of the performer are constructed through a metaphorical process. The visual process constructs on the one hand the hybrid figure of the actor. On the other hand, we see this figure from a different angle, which elicits "a strange impression of...disparity (décalage)", to cite Lepage on his performance in Vinci (Hébert and Perelli-Contos 2001, 19). The complexity of this process and its significations are put to the test through the spectator's perceptual and interpretative process, in which habitual modes of perception are often transgressed.

In discussing the notions of the stage actor and the screen actor, Lepage emphasizes the importance of the cinematic effigy due to its effect on the actor's awareness of his body in the here and now of performance (Fouquet 1998, 326). For the actor is himself in the process of constructing and 'giving' body to this two-dimensional image while he is being filmed in real time. Once his image is projected, he performs through the interface of the screen. In the scene mentioned above, the actor appears not only in disjunction, but also on a different scale: the audience sees his entire silhouette as well as a close-up of his face, which in cinematographic language is powerful and significant. Even if we are watching the same actor onstage in the role of protagonist, this actor fixes the audience with another gaze, and his acting in this instance is defined through a cinematographic perspective. He generates the mediaphoric body that is situated between two aesthetic universes, theatrical and cinematographic, thus introducing the stage actor to the screen actor. Lepage thereby proposes a métissage of theatre acting and film acting, and generates a mise en abyme of the actor as defined by the dramatic stage.

Metaphorisation

Lepagean theatre as a whole is characterised by a strong tendency towards metaphor. In its Greek origins of the term, metaphor suggests a notion of transport, and Aristotle spoke of the process of metaphorisation in terms of movement and of transfer (Kowzan 2005, 115). In the semiology of theatre, the metaphor becomes even more complex, for it entails the interaction of different systems, the verbal and the visual in particular. The spectator's comprehension of the metaphor is stimulated by the intra-scenic context and is often oriented by the actor's body language and manner of applying it (Honzl 1971, 10). The actor is the generator of the metaphor – so there are powerful somatic and embodied aspects to metaphorisation. The actor's body thus enables a shift between the verbal and iconic spheres, between the theatrical here and now and symbolisation (Hébert and Perelli-Contos 2001, 109).

The Actor and the Screen

A performance with technological components adds a medial complexity to this metaphoric dimension. The mediaphoric body manifests itself in multiple forms – changeable, momentary and polymorphic. *The Andersen Project*, then, presents us with a mediaphoric body closely related spatially to the device, in this case the screen. The connection between body and device may evolve from a scenographic specificity or as a function of the acting. It can reveal shifts between the object and subject of the stage. The scenic space in this production was conceived by the scenographer Jean Lebourdais and image designers such as Jacques Collin, Véronique Couturier and David Leclerc. In this instance the stage is organised into several performance spaces: a shallow space forming a proscenium in front of the screen (often accompanied by a frontally projected fixed image of the Garnier Opera Hall); scenographic constructions with multifunctional and horizontal compartments (phone booths, peep-show booths); and mobile screens of different sizes rearranged in front of the audience, appearing in alternation.

One of the screens is concave, meaning that there is a space in front of it where the actor can remain standing. Such a screen allows for the transformation of the character in front of the spectators' eyes, for they see his passage from one protagonist to another through costume changes made before our eyes. This crossing-over is accentuated by the movement of entering into or exiting the screen. *The Andersen Project* features several scenic situations of this type: the opening scene, for instance, with the projection of the credits along with a tagger apparently creating graffiti live. Here we observe a passage from the theatrical (actual) to the cinematic (virtual): Frédéric entering into the on-screen Opera and climbing the stairs, represented by a projected image that reacts – moves – to the movement of the actor (an intermedial realisation where the present corporeal body and the projected image make a single visual figure); and the journey of Andersen, which is transformed into a metaphor of the passage of time.

In this latter example, Lepage as Andersen enters the space in front of the screen and sits down on the suitcases that have been placed there. He removes the costume of the historical figure (Andersen) and puts on the clothes of the contemporary protagonist (Frédéric the composer), who is also travelling.

The actor stays within the screen on which the changing landscapes of the journey are projected. Visually, this scene concerns a leap through time and space, calling attention to the process of the montage: we jump from one century to the next through the suggestion of the metaphoric transformation from steam train to TGV. Interestingly, the effect of visual immersion is achieved both digitally through the superimposed, computer-generated images, and through a theatrical, practically pantomimic, effect. The intermedial link between media undergoes a process of separation (← TERM: SEPARATION), which relates to Lepage's desire to show the mechanics of things to the audience (see Pluta 2006, 94-96 and Lepage 1996, 39-42). The mediaphoric body is composed of the living body of the actor and the construction of the device. The two together form an indivisible figure, located at the crossroads of the universes of theatre and technological screen media, in a space where the two are imbricated.

The screen thus becomes a close partner of the living actor and mediates a scenic subject. Conversely, in this process the actor may lose his status as subject and become a scenic object, a "sign of spatiality" (Honzl 1971, 12). The actor might then suggest space through his acting and become an 'actor-set', perhaps even an 'actor-prop'. The mediaphoric body is composed not only of this body in flesh and blood that transfigures a form of media, but also of the effect of this transformation. The *Andersen Project* integrates Hans Christian Andersen's tale, *The Shadow* (Fig. 2). The staging of this performance is heavily marked by diegetic elements, on a theatrical as much as a cinematographic level. Consider the scene in which Arnaud de la Guimbretière tells his daughter the tale in question: the story of a man whose shadow takes over and dominates him.

Fig. 2: The Andersen Project. *Performed by Yves Jacques,* © *photo Emmanuel Valette*

MAPPING INTERMEDIALITY IN PERFORMANCE

Lepage here uses the simple technique of projecting the eponymous shadow on a wall, which contrasts with the body of Arnaud, dressed in white and illuminated by a bedside lamp. Here, Lepage evokes the opposition between positive and negative as in the field of photography. Within the space of the stage, which is delimited downstage by a landing, we see the two protagonists of the tale along with the tale's narrator, all played by the same actor. By manipulating a small bedside lamp, Lepage alternately appears as a shadow (in negative) and as the character of the professor (as an illuminated silhouette, thus in positive). His body, in one moment a shadow and in the next illuminated, becomes the ground of the story being told. Through this process, Lepage synthesizes several roles: he tells a story, but at the same time he acts it out and his body becomes both materialised and dematerialised. He is both manipulator (of the light in this case) and manipulated, subject and object. He acquires a demiurgic role in creating the theatrical universe. The mediaphoric body here is a synthesis of the theatrical body and is a proto-cinematographic figure, given the play of shadow and light through the perspective of projection.

The Andersen Project presents the body of an actor who becomes the "pole of negotiation" between the forms of media with which he interacts (Hébert and Perelli-Contos 2001, 109). The living body is only part of the mediaphoric body whilst being both *close to* and *far from* the device, *with* and *within* the device. This requires a re-examination of the actor's methods, and an exploration of the process of the performer's adaptation to a new scenic environment, the hybridity of different orders of performance and a *métissage* of aesthetics.

Translated from the French by Ansley Evans

Instance: Frank Castorf and the Berlin Volksbühne, *The Humiliated and Insulted* (2001)

Peter M. Boenisch

This instance addresses the process of transcoding (← TERM) from a source novel to performance in Frank Castorf's stage production of Dostoevsky's *The Humiliated and Insulted* (*Erniedrigte und Beleidigte*) for the Berlin Volksbühne, the theatre of which Castorf is artistic director.[55] It outlines Castorf's dramaturgy of hybrid 'compositing' (← TERM: HYBRIDITY), which challenges hegemonic paradigms of representation and mediatised immediacy and enables a particular variety of reality effects.

Castorf commented on his attempt to realign theatrical dramaturgies and contemporary experiences while creating *The Humiliated and Insulted* in 2001:

> I am getting more and more estranged by the calculated modelling and closure of drama, and by its suggestion that reality can be conquered – where I can say: Ah, that's the story, ah, it's as easy as that in the world. This doesn't correspond to my experience of reality. I am fascinated by antagonisms and by what I cannot explain, by vague intuitions. [...] Novels offer more of the complexity I find in reality, and it's only logical that I can't even come close to masterworks like *The Possessed* (Castorf 2001, 22).[56]

Transcoding
This acknowledgement of an inherent failure is a first pointer towards Castorf's specific approach to transcoding. Linda Hutcheon mobilises the latter term as follows:

> In the move from telling to showing, a performance adaptation must dramatize: description, narration, and represented thoughts must be transcoded into speech, actions, sounds, and visual images (Hutcheon 2006, 40).

Castorf's intermedial dramaturgy, however, goes beyond such semiotic reformatting. He contests the very imperative to dramatize, evoking instead the mode of engagement Hutcheon describes as "interacting", which she, however, confines to computer-game adaptations of movies: they abandon the logic of linear narrative and draw on an experiential (rather than narratival) engagement with a virtual "heterocosm" (Hutcheon 2006, 50f.). Similarly, Castorf renounces a narrative-based logic in order to immerse the spectators in the unwieldy heterocosm that is our digital, global-capitalist reality.

Fig: Reality Gaps: Designer Bert Neumann's stage bungalow and the 'fifth wall' of the screen in Frank Castorf's production of Dostoevsky's Humiliated and Insulted (Volksbühne Berlin, 2001 © Iko Freese/drama-berlin.de

This approach already underpins the rehearsal process. As critic Robin Detje described, observing the creation of The Humiliated and Insulted:

> Castorf holds a pocket edition of the novel and plows through it chapter by chapter. There is no road map. He chooses the most difficult path, straight into the jungle, a path many would find impossible. [...] The only possible way to do the scenes has been found, and it will not be rehearsed again. It is dropped like a hot potato. Then everybody continues plowing through Dostoevsky's book. The monstrous task of recording what has been decided lies with the assistant director, who will diligently create something like a shooting script for the opening night: 7 percent of Dostoevsky, or maybe a little more, plus the blocking, the timing, and the actual lines. Synthesizing the scattered, forgotten work of long weeks of rehearsal is an effort of blood, sweat, and tears, of screaming and crying fits. Opening night performances often still contain unrehearsed material. Improvisation remains Castorf's fetish. It is needed to reach the 'authentic', 'the real'. The goal of rehearsals is to rechart the ocean of human behaviour, human drives, and human guilt. No maps are allowed (Detje 2005, 12, 15).

Castorf and his performers thus immerse themselves into the whole textual 'jungle'. As a result, their productions never merely *show* a fictional world on stage, clearly mapping characters and dramatic action. Instead, a full textual heterocosm is staged, which always remains imbued with the medial reality of the source but also that of the performers and the performance situation. This opens a far more complex field of transcoding: both the narrative and dramatic content as well as the textual form and materiality (← TERM: MATERIALITY) are rendered into a performance that breathes the openness and reality of improvisation.

Einbruch der Realität

Such a 'reality' should, however, be clearly distinguished from another recently popular urge for authenticity, in verbatim theatre or the use of untrained performers (← INSTANCE: RIMINI PROTOKOLL). It is more akin to Slavoj Žižek's Lacanian Real, which points to what escapes the symbolic realism created by medial representation, yet still forcefully pierces through its layers. This effect has been aptly captured in the ambiguous German title of the programme book accompanying Castorf's production of Bulgakov's *The Master and Margarita*, called *Einbruch der Realität* – the invasion, but equally the collapse, of reality. In the Real, hysteria, obsession, lust, perversion, depression and melancholy reign. Its logic of 'excess' is the third vital feature of Castorf's strategy; it manifests itself in visceral, emotional, atmospheric as well as semiotic excess. Dostoevsky's early novel assists such an approach in various ways.

The Humiliated and Insulted was written in 1861 for serial publication in a newspaper, driven equally by the author's necessity of earning money on his return from banishment to Siberia, and his desire for fame. As such, it shares many features with the offerings of contemporary television society: it is dramaturgically crude, shaped by the necessity of a 'cliff-hanger' at the end of each instalment, drawing on calculated stereotypes and excessive sensationalism, still lacking the philosophical *finesse* of Dostoevsky's later novels. Yet its narrative also interweaves business-driven intrigues in the wake of emerging capitalism with frustrated human desire in various love-triangles. For Castorf, this perfectly echoed both the ubiquitous narratives and the state of 'atomised individuals' in post-communist Russia, reunified Berlin and globalised capitalism at large: "The novel presents the social hierarchy and the division of human beings into winners and losers as natural. [...] Those who don't possess anything, can still enjoy their humiliation" (Volksbühne 2001).

The novel uses the device of a narrator, the failed writer Vanya, who on his deathbed remembers what is the central narrative of the book. Castorf capitalised on this peculiar double perspective right from the beginning of his production. In the first scene, Vanya, played by Martin Wuttke, tells the parents of his adored Natasha the story of an old man whose dog died as he warmed himself from the cold in a Petersburg café. At the same moment, an old man with a (living) dog crosses the stage and enters the living room, where Vanya and the couple are seated. Jens Roselt points to a typical, irritating experiential double-bind that implodes a conventional dramatic logic:

> This means that the production on the one hand follows the novel very closely, yet on the other hand, one is almost unable to grasp anything regarding its story. As linear narrative, the action does not make sense, as this story of the dead dog is being told while the very animal appears on stage alive and kicking. It remains unclear whether any knowledge of the novel is an advantage for spectating this production, or in fact an obstacle (Roselt 2005, 110f).

Elsewhere, Vanya meets an old school-friend. In his dialogue in the scene, as in the novel's retrospective account, he reminisces about the latter's future death from excessive alcohol abuse, in the presence of their encounter, of course. Again, the logic of representation, with its assumed linearity of dramatic time and immediate presence of the represented, is challenged. Throughout, Castorf's transcoding fosters the staging of discontinuous synchronous events that overlap and co-exist in the mode of the 'also-there' (← PORTAL: DIGITAL CULTURE), rather than promoting dramatic coherence, narrative transparency and linear progression of the plot. This central dramaturgic drive evokes the principle of 'compositing', which is central for digital media (Manovich 2001). Castorf generates an all-absorbing 'composite present', which reflects his analysis of our current world: equally complex and impenetrable, it permits nothing but affirmation.

The Fifth Wall

The same principle also structures the space, and is particularly amplified by Bert Neumann's set. For the Volksbühne's production of The Possessed (1999) Neumann had assembled a veritable building, including a small pool in front – itself a composite of the infamous dachas of Eastern Europe and the typical West German bungalows of the Wirtschaftswunder-era. Both the cast and the set of this production returned for The Humiliated and Insulted, yet the pool was now frozen over and smoke ascended from the chimney, all (assisted by the lighting design) metaphorically depicting an ice-cold society. In addition to the lush living space of Natasha's parents, the building also housed, further upstage, Vanya's (in the novel) rather distant dingy lodging, in which he gave shelter to the impoverished orphan-girl Nelly. Neumann's set thus invoked hyper-realism yet concurrently augmented the material reality of the performance. Situated at an odd angle stage-right, hardly visible from parts of the auditorium, it confronted the audience's gaze and perception rather than enabling fictional transparency. As Roselt suggested, Neumann "took Diderot's proposition of the fourth wall at his word" (Roselt 2005, 117), erecting four physical walls that made it impossible to look inside or behind. In fact, we were only ever able to catch glimpses of the living-room through the windows or the large French doors. We eavesdropped on the conversations by way of its transmission through the theatre's PA system. On the roof of the bungalow a huge screen broadcast images from inside – thus adding what Roselt termed "the fifth wall" (ibid., 122). Cameras and microphones were fixed on the walls and ceilings of the living room, reminiscent of the Reality TV series *Big Brother*. The scenes in Vanya's grimy quarters (whose small window was pasted up with newspaper) were captured by a handheld camera, visibly operated by the performers themselves. Even as the revolve started to turn and the audience's perspective on the bungalow changed, we only ever saw some fragments of the action directly, while other fragments appeared on the screen. Every now and then the projection additionally cut to images from the Berlin cityscape, a montage of German 1970s TV adverts, and graphic porn. This image-track also intervened in the narrative, for example when the entrances of Vanya's idolised love Natasha were cut against commercials for instant soup and toothpaste.

A Parallax View

Other composites included *intermezzi* typical of Castorf, here featuring pop-songs, quotations from Schiller, stage slapstick, and actors commenting about their performance or referring to their roles in the earlier *Possessed*. As a central interface for the audience, the complex dramaturgy extended the principle of fragmented, hybrid compositing to the audience's own experience, as it refused a unified and coherent reading, and a clear positioning of the spectator (← TERM: EXPERIENCER). Whether the screen showed the live-image from inside the bungalow-container or pre-recorded sequences, not to mention the presence of amplified sound and pop music, what we saw and heard no longer neatly 'added up'. Rather than maintaining a sole focus on the representation, the spectators' attention was always also drawn to the usually transparent reality of performing, all the more so because of the dimensions of the production itself, which at a running time of five hours mirrored the novel's abundance. The audience members were thus forced not only to deal with their own exhaustion but (even while seated in a traditional proscenium space) to adopt what Žižek termed a "parallax view" (Žižek 2006), sharing Lacan's favourite example of Holbein's painting *The Ambassadors*: looked at frontally, it contains an odd stain which – as one shifts one's position to look at it from an angle – reveals itself as a skull. It is, however, never possible to unify the two perspectives. Precisely this ever-incomplete non-totality, for Žižek, is the Real. Similarly, the composited heterocosm that results from Castorf's excessive transcoding refuses a complete, surveyable totality: it creates, rather, an intermedial space of overlaps and imbrications.

Expanding on the director's own distinction between realism, as prevalent in mediatised representation, and "the simple concept of Reality" (Castorf 2002, 75), Castorf's video designer Jan Speckenbach articulates the unique 'reality effect' emerging from the production's integration of live-images within theatre performance:

> This idea [of Reality] is correlated with the nature of the performer, not with the character they portray. Thus along with TV-technology, reality enters the theatre – yet not the exterior, the outside (which is present in some documentary images, which remain, however, mere citations of reality), but the inner reality of the stage itself. The heavy make-up and the colourful light contribute their part to stimulate a mood that is different from 'realism' (Speckenbach 2002, 82).

According to Speckenbach the "fifth wall" of the screen, especially with its close-ups captured by the cameras throughout the set, achieved the opposite of the 'talking heads' on TV and movie screens, with their suggestion of immediate presence. He draws selectively on film theorist André Bazin who at times sug-gested that the screen functions less as "window to the world" than as *cache*: a cover that principally shows what is being excluded rather than what is in the picture (Speckenbach 2002, 83). Equally, Castorf's production works as a *cache* which allows the Real to permeate the showing of the novel, by means of its composite, parallax perspectives, and its foregrounding of that "inner reality of the stage itself". Rather than *staging* the, in Detje's words, "ocean of human beha-viour, human drives, and human guilt", the production *pervades* the representation of the novel with the blood, sweat, tears and screaming fits of the performers and – not to forget – the spectators in this exhausting and exuberant production. The simultaneity of heterogenous, incompatible events, sounds and images, of con-cealing and disclosing, of theatrical realism and material reality of the perfor-mance, and of distance and proximity, creates an intermedial 'Reality gap' which disturbs the ideological construct of immediate, total representation. In the per-manent frustration of apparently missing out on the full picture (as some events happened out of our sight), far from preventing us from seeing the real thing, this missing out *is it*: from the irreconcilable parallax emerged an equally immediate yet dangerously open encounter with the excess of the Real. Rather than the en-joyment of consuming, it allows for a Lacanian *jouissance* of engagement with the realities of human beings, precisely in all their unenjoyable and unconsumable suffering, psychoses, and humanity. Castorf points accordingly to the possibilities of performing between the bungalow-enclosure, the magnifying fifth wall and the microphone transmission:

> I am able to work with very simple actions. I can pour a cup of tea. I know what it is. I sit there, and we for once start again to sit next to each other. People talk, and they listen. And they are in fact able to form and to articulate thoughts. That is something very special. That's what it's all about. At least for me (Castorf 2002, 78).

Instance: Gob Squad, *Room Service* (2003)

Wolf-Dieter Ernst

This instance looks at the performance *Room Service* (2003) by Gob Squad, to shed light on the ways in which the production demonstrates principles of connectivity (← TERM: CONNECTIVITY). The term points at the necessarily unstable and performative dimension of any connection within a network, and my analysis draws on an understanding of the network as paradigmatic to the show's structures and effects (← PORTAL: NETWORKING).

Gob Squad is a live art collective established in 1992. The company's name indicates the somewhat ironic attitude of the group towards theatre as entertainment and public service: Gob Squad, a squadron dedicated to talking your head off like a door-to-door salesman, people at whom you like to shout "Shut your gob!". The group gained recognition for site-specific pieces in urban environments such as offices, houses, shops, hotels and railway stations. For *Room Service*, it cooperated with the international Steigenberger Hotel Group to make a piece for a chain of hotels (I return to this later).

Room Service lasted from 10:00pm to 04:00am. The audience members were asked to make themselves comfortable on sofas and in sleeping bags in the hotel's lobby while the action took place in four hotel rooms several floors above them. The only way to see the show was to follow what was covered via surveillance cameras on four huge TV monitors set side by side. The audience was asked to call a particular room at moments indicated by subtitles, using the house-intercom system.

A partly improvised performance by nature, *Room Service* tends to switch the roles of audience and actor in terms of their activity. In fact, much of the performance was about "normal behavior in a hotel room". As the company indicates on its website:

> Each performer is in a separate hotel room, unable to see and hear the audience or each other. It's late at night, and none of them are sleeping, instead they kill time, sharing moments of hope, fear and boredom. Their only contact to the outside world is a phone line that puts them directly in contact with the audience. As the night progresses they call their voyeurs with increasingly absurd and desperate demands, in a plea to remain with them and help them make it through the night.[57]

The reference to the song-line "Help me make it through the night" is telling. Most of the time the four performers refused to entertain the audience and instead lay the burden of action ("Help them!") on the spectators. The audience members become cast as the hero whose task it is to save four possible victims (of boredom).

Room Service displays a double bind of distance and relatedness. The production relies on the well-established technologies of the house intercom and videophone. Gob Squad uses four channels where different performers display themselves to manifold users. The company adds to the media arrangement a plot (concerning boredom, loneliness, love and so on) that could also be told by conventional theatrical means. In its performance the group does not especially explore the media specificity of the connection but rather takes it for granted – there is a house intercom and videophone, the sorts of technology that people have grown used to over the last three decades.

The idea of agency and network can help us to reconsider traditional notions of connection and interaction. I will examine connectivity in relation to three different aspects of networking in *Room Service*: the media channel; the user/performer grouping; and the production's appropriation of existing communication networks.

The Media Channel
Connections between audience and performer in networked theatre can be remote and close at the same time, due to a layering of different media (telephone/video/theatre). Gob Squad makes specific use of this fact. The channel of address is kept within certain limits (TV monitor, intercom), and physical action and presence are reduced. An extra feature, however, is the semi-presence of the performers. They act in the same building several stories above the lobby but never appear in the lobby itself.

As the live contact of theatre is denied, the media transparency of the telephone and the TV screen are revealed and these devices gain a quasi-actor status. When Sean Patten, for example, after an hour of beating time in the hotel room, takes up the telephone and holds it to the camera, the apparatus itself suddenly takes control of the situation. It signifies what has been missing so far: that the audience should give some feedback to the performance. In a live performance, one would scarcely notice this feature. But here, we become aware of the constraints of the intercom network and its form of connectivity. It is of essential importance that the telephone channel is not open from the very beginning but, similarly to a plot point, comes into play to solve a certain conflict established beforehand. So the intercom relates to the video, to the observed situation of waiting, and it fuels the idea that the audience could indeed help the performers to make it through the night.

Fig. 1: *Sarah Thom in Mask with Hotel-Service Information in* Room Service, *photo © Gob Squad*

The User/Performer Grouping

Billed as a durational performance, *Room Service* asks the audience to stay the night in the hotel's lobby. Here, the problem arises: what will happen, what can possibly hold the audience's attention, let alone keep people entertained, over the entire duration of the event? It is all too evident that the audience takes on some responsibility for running the show. Each spectator is asked implicitly to decide whether she should remain passive, stay there at all, or even participate and, indeed, co-operate with the performers – a typical situation of double-contingency, where silence and absence become as telling as speaking and acting. It is worth looking at just one out of many audience-performer interactions that occur during the course of the performance, to explore the network of audience and performer. I quote this interaction at length to give some insight into the structure of this network, built up by the performer (Sean) and the user/spectator of the intercom (Kerstin).

> Sean   I have a telephone right here and I could give you a ring. I did say You. I said I could give you a ring. You people down there... [*points his indicating finger towards the camera*] I know you have a telephone as well. So, I could give you a ring. Uuh, I am really nervous ... slightly

MAPPING INTERMEDIALITY IN PERFORMANCE

... And we will see how it goes. I am absolutely serious ... generously, from the bottom of my heart. I am really excited to hear another human voice [*ring tone*] down there. I know it is ringing. So don't play the idiot.

[*A member of the audience picks up the phone*]

Kerstin   Hello.

Sean   Hello! Hello, who is that?

Kerstin   Kerstin.

Sean   Kerstin, nice to hear a human voice.

Kerstin   I can see that.

Sean   I can't see you though. What do you look like?

Kerstin   [*looks around her*] Like all the others.

Sean   Really, you all look the same? Anyway, Kerstin, look, do you like champagne [*he raises his glass*]?

Kerstin   Yes, sometimes.

Sean   Oh, what a shame because I nearly finished it. You can buy it in the bar. Well, look, Kerstin. Why don't we hover off together, I am going to get into a party mood [...] come with me [*takes her/the camera to a back closet*] and you can help me put on appropriate clothing.

The conversation can roughly be separated into two parts. Act One, we might say, is about getting into contact with the audience. Here, both parties are asymmetrically related to each other. It is the audience member's choice to leave her contemplative position on the pillow and take an active part in the performance. Patten repeatedly points out that he controls the situation ("I know, you have a telephone down there. ... I can hear it ringing."). But on the contrary, one rather gets the idea that he is highly dependent on both the audience's will to participate and the media control of telephone, camera and the technicians. Abstractly speaking, the first part of the excerpt is where the content of the conversation is about potential form – it is meta-communication.

Act Two deals with the interpersonal relation between performer and audience. Here, we see two different tendencies at work. One is Sean's strategy to entertain the spectators while not being able to see them (although they can see him). This is why *Room Service* is subtitled an "interactive film". The other is an attempt to keep Kerstin on the line and get something entertaining out of this conversation. This is partly achieved by being animated ("Look!" and "Come with me"), partly by making fun of her ("What a shame"). The necessity to maintain the conversation continues on a meta-conversational level ("I know you see me, I can't see you though").

Fig 2: *Sarah Thom from Room 121 on the line in Room Service, photo © Gob Squad*

The single interaction between Sean and Kerstin is in many ways related to other entities – the audience watching, the intercom channel, the habits of telephone talks – which over the last hundred years have supplied manifold tricks of meta-communication that allow us to come to terms with the absence of sight. Yet a network perspective would grant equal degrees of activity to all entities: the audience, the media channel, the mediatised 'reality' out there, the specific audience-performer community and the single participant represented by Kerstin. As the continuing meta-conversation indicates, the community needs constant reflection on the way in which the connection is established and maintained. Yet at no point within this network do we have a strong form of agency as, for example, a concept of the author would suggest. Instead the situation is characterised by a distributed and circulating agency. Sometimes the audience seems to have power; sometimes we are subjects of a strong concept of Gob Squad's. Sometimes decisions are taken by the performers but, above all, we as audience members are immersed within a technical network (← TERM: IMMERSION). For the duration of this performance there is neither a development on the content level, nor a change in form and this is why this piece is so much about a dynamic formation; in other words, about connectivity. Connectivity, here, means questioning the rules of a form of theatrical communication (and of social communities for that matter) that is usually self-evident and unnoticed.

MAPPING INTERMEDIALITY IN PERFORMANCE

Gob Squad allows the various actors to contribute equally to the conversation. Because no actor overrules another, the casting is painstakingly balanced. Sean, in the instance above, could take on the role of a single entertainer, making fun of Kerstin. This would bring him laughter in the short term, but he would very likely lose sympathy and Kerstin gain it in the long run. Kerstin, in return, might well decide not to play the game any longer. But then, why did she pick up the phone in the first place? She is as obliged to stay on the line, as is Sean. And this mutual responsibility is due to the constraints of technology. Even technology gains agency in as much as the telephone and intercom, which add up to an "interactive film", have potential for the miraculous of science fiction, because an interactive film, with actors reacting in real time, might be more supernatural than face-to-face communication. So if we follow the different connections, it becomes apparent that each affords connectivity in the way they relate actors and network to each other.

Appropriation of Existing Networks

This analysis of *Room Service* would not be complete without looking at the social network being appropriated by the group. The piece is designed for the Steigenberger Group's low-budget line Intercity Hotels, whose establishments are spread all over Germany, usually close to railway stations. In taking up the Deutsche Bahn's label for express trains, Intercity Express, the Intercity Hotel brand relates to the railway network and thus to mobility and progress. The ideal client for this kind of hotel is the modern sales representative. Accordingly, the design of the rooms and the service offered is highly standardised, to suit company budgets for field staff's travel expenses. Employees in the cultural industry – including Gob Squad's members touring diverse festivals – can be considered as part of this group of modern job-nomads. Networking thus is already a characteristic of the site where the performance happens.

Other considerations relate the piece to network theory and practice. Perhaps the most striking is that Gob Squad, like many other performance groups, is a collective without a designated director or leader. The group considers itself to be a social network built 'bottom up'. Moreover, the company often makes durational or street performances that demand much more participation and patience from the audience (and passers-by) than would traditional black-box theatre. In this respect, connectivity is not merely an aesthetic effect. Rather, it suggests the amount of risk, chance and vulnerability a production process can allow. It implies the risk not to come up with a clear, formulated aesthetic object (a prescribed show), but rather to merge social action with theatre and performance. It demands that the process of production, as well as the performance itself, is left open to the audience and other entities. And it asks all participants really to get in touch with their vulnerabilities rather than sticking to strong expectations, rules of power and overwhelming aesthetic or technical effects.

Instance: Anne-Marie Boisvert, *Identité dénudée: regard sous le maquillage de Sherman*; Manon Oligny, *Pouliches: autour de l'oeuvre de Cindy Sherman*; Thomas Israël, *Looking for Cindy* (2006)[58]

Johan Callens

This instance explores the nature of recursion (← TERM: RECURSION) as evidenced by a compound work consisting of two live choreographies and a short filmed one, which cannot be isolated from their shared subject, the photography of Cindy Sherman.

The occasion for the works under discussion dates back to the Sherman retrospective which ran at the Jeu de Paume in Paris, from May 16 to September 3, 2006. Sherman is famous for disguising and staging herself in more or less obvious fictive situations, deriving immense pleasure from putting photography, a medium with a potential for high verisimilitude, in the service of theatre, a medium often forced to exploit its low verisimilitude. That she develops her subjects in series is related to the self-generating character of the feminine stereotypes she exposes, what Barry J. Mauer has called the obsessive re-enactment of mediatised scenes of a normative identity instruction and construction. At the same time, these series reflect upon the serial reproducibility of photographic images and of art in the postmodern era.

Realizing the opportunity offered by the Sherman retrospective, the Centre National de la Danse in Paris commissioned a work from the Canadian choreographer Manon Oligny, who called upon fellow-Canadian dancer Anne-Marie Boisvert and Belgian multimedia artist, filmmaker, actor, and stage director Thomas Israël.[59] During workshops in Paris and Montréal, they then elaborated their different views, refracting them through the prism of Boisvert's bodily character, the only dancer featured. The kaleidoscopic 'middle-look' resulting from this collective research consisted of (1) the dancer's self-directed preparatory study, *Identité dénudée: regard sous le maquillage de Sherman* [Bared identity: a look beneath the make-up of Sherman] (20 minutes), developed within her own company ZélénaGora; (2) Oligny's choreography, *Pouliches: autour de l'oeuvre de Cindy Sherman* [Fillies: around the work of Sherman] (30 to 40 minutes); and (3) Israël's filmic impression, *Looking for Cindy* (3 minutes 42 seconds) (in the Paris version still called *Looking for C*). Together these works and their titles can be considered exemplary for the intermedial artists' predominant concern with perception and the perceptual field, displacing the perceptual modes associated with the singular art object. Ultimately, the recursion of Oligny's approach allows for a systematisation of the relationships between the material (physical or technical) support of the arts and media, and the conventions with which these media and arts operate by working (on) that support.

Identité dénudée

The conceptual nature of Identité dénudée paradoxically concretised this systematic self-conscious confrontation with Boisvert's choreographic medium and Sherman's photographs. Taking her cue from the exhibit at the Jeu de Paume, allowing the visitors freely to circulate among the two-dimensional pictures attached to the walls, Boisvert presented herself as a physical installation or living sculpture, closely scrutinised in three stations. The spectators were invited onto the dance floor by a guide ironically meant to reassure them that no further participation would be required (Boisvert in Corbeil), as if such participation entailed a threatening non-differentiation between the self and the other, the proper and the improper. A crucial difference with the circumstances in the museum was indeed that the doors of the performing space were closed during the choreography. This added to the intimacy and urgency of the experience a heightened sense of the performance's time-based character. As in the camera's and dark room's black boxes, with which the space invited comparison, temporality materialised as length of exposure when the lighting consecutively framed and brought to life three different zones for Boisvert to perform in. From one area to the next, transparent tights, knee protectors, bandages and silky top were shed, thus heightening her vulnerability during the spectators' ever closer look at the dancer's body: its muscular tensions, visible exertion and almost palpable skin.

In combination with her title, Boisvert's divestment of clothes and attendant power seemed to betray the essentialist dream of certain performance artists, contrary to Sherman's belief in the superficiality of a constructed identity, implied by her obsession with masks and personae, the proliferation of make-up, wigs, and costumes. The dancer in her preparatory study nevertheless adopted some of the photographic medium's constraints (flatness, framing, viewpoint,...) and (sub) generic givens (portrait, landscape, still life,...) as parameters to work with. Starting from Sherman's mostly seated position and truncated appearance in the History Portraits, also known as the Old Masters (1988-90), a kneeled or crouched Boisvert in the first section initially allowed herself only the limited freedom of her upper body and the occasional stretched leg. Though she did not want to emphasize the feminine side (Corbeil), the echoes of belly dancing in her undulating and rotating arm movements potentially gendered her lowly and limited position. By arching her back, and using the articulations of knees, elbows, and shoulders, she then probed her corporeal reach and extensibility on all fours, raising herself ever so tentatively until she reached an upright position.

Sherman's History Portraits criticize high art's pretensions and the conventions of the classic painterly tradition. By contrast, the Rear Screen Projections (1980), which served Boisvert during her second movement enacted against a wall, involve a more obvious photographic look into notions such as depth-of-field and the split between the figure and background from which it seems (unable) to detach itself. Departing from the conspicuous layering of these pictures as an impetus towards three-dimensionality, Boisvert echoed classic choreographic notions and gestures (demi-pointe, elevation, arabesque), as well as tested and transposed dance's primary gravitational force into photography's normative verticality, through her strenuous struggle with the wall. It was as if the spotlight had activated a magnetic field that held her captive until she collapsed in exhaustion.

The third movement began in total darkness, undifferentiated space, disrupted three times by a massive flashlight, hardly long enough for the surprised spectators to regain their vantagepoint by spotting the semi-naked dancer elsewhere on the floor. In four excruciating minutes Boisvert gradually assumes three positions from The Centerfolds, also known as Horizontals (1981), on account of the camera's objectifying high-angle close-up, common in the double-page spreads of fashion and so-called adult magazines (Krauss, 2006, 114, 117-118). As the guide with a handheld torchlight zoomed in on disconnected planes and curves, (vainly?) trying to expose the sinews, tendons and veins of her straining body, Boisvert in slow-motion moved from one position to the next, three more flashlights marking the results and demonstrating the ease with which performance artists and women of flesh and blood are remediated, in this case into an aestheticizing nude photography tending toward the abstract, as borne out by the stills Valérie Boulet and Mélanie-C. Bazinet took during the final run-through and Boisvert posted on her website.

Pouliches

The recursive frame-breaking or level-jumping evident in the migration of Boisvert's snapshots from the performative space to cyberspace was anticipated when her already recursive preparatory study, consisting of three stations, was embedded in Manon Oligny's choreography. The formal rigour of Identité dénudée felt loosened in Pouliches, whose general set-up was more frontal and confrontational, as if the perspectival approaches evident in the subtitles of Boisvert's and Oligny's choreographies had been further complicated to confuse the viewers – certainly in the Paris version which integrated Israël's visual images, though the screen at times went dark to give Boisvert the necessary attention. The different movements from Identité dénudée could still be recognised, though the wall section now was doubled or mirrored by sequences left and right, just as Boisvert was now accompanied on the dance floor by Anne Gouraud playing the acoustic bass (Laurent Aglat on the electric bass in Brussels), and by Mona Somm, a classically trained singer intoning fragments from Bach's Agnus Dei, which paced the choreography. If the singing's high art connotations (aided by the classical chair on which Somm was seated but countered by the consumerist Coke can) reprised the history portraits, they also comprised Sherman's breaches of decorum through Somm's provocative dress with frontal slit and immodest seating poses distracting the spectators, whose gaze at times already was divided between the choreography and projections. By 'casting' Somm in a more complex part – having her move around, interact with Boisvert and imitate some of her leg spasms while she is singing and pursued by the dancer – Oligny already criticised the performative, melodramatic aspect of some of Sherman's photographs, her presenting "des pouliches boîteuses, blessées et *performeuses*" ["limping fillies, hurt and playing up the hurt"], that is, victimised women, in tears, battered (Oligny quoted in Corbeil, original emphasis).

In Montreal and Brussels Boisvert started out as a long-haired vamp on high heels, wearing a silky print dress and staring down her public's gaze, before assuming a slightly-off movie-star or pin-up pose. She even mounted a pedestal and further advertised her exploitative sublimation as fetishised commodity through the 'forgotten' price-tag of her dress. Like the poses, the few props are rich in connotations. Long before the heels are taken off and followed by an animalistic groan, as if in gratitude for the tack removed after hard labor, the woman's false braid comes into its own by intertwining different semantic strands: being rope to restrain horse and woman alike, sado-masochistic gear, and fe/male 'tail' dangling from the front of Boisvert's pants in a travesty of the female belly-dance insinuated at the start of *Identité dénudée*. In the Paris version Somm at this point had her legs spread wide to drive home the pun and her singing briefly descended into the male register, accompanied by a mannish military salute. Like Sherman donning moustache and beard in some of the *History Portraits*, Boisvert and Oligny thereby expose the performative nature of gender identity, depending on fetishes, surfaces, and appearances, or on subject and object positions, whose absolutism the sado-masochistic overtones had already undone.

Even if the third station in Boisvert's study took its inspiration from the *Centerfolds*, its implications are only followed through in *Pouliches*. For the *Centerfolds*' downward look from above accentuates the base horizontality or desublimation of the subject. Thus exposed it is relegated once more to the animal level, deprived of man's upright position, allowing for the empowering frontal visuality supposedly necessary for an aestheticised formal view, as argued by Gestalt psychologists and Freud in *Three Essays on the Theory of Sexuality* (1905) and *Civilization and Its Discontents* (1930) (Krauss, 2006, 117, 139n34). *Pouliches*, then, recursively replicates the descent from the failed actresses of the *Film Stills* (1977-80) to the desublimated figures of the *Sex Pictures* (1992), *Horror and Surrealist Pictures* (1994-96), and *Broken Dolls* (1999), obscene assemblages of bodily fragments, strongly reminiscent of Hans Bellmer (1902-1975), even more disturbing for being recomposed and reanimated by Boisvert: arms and legs twisted and contorted; trunk flush with the floor and legs split; screwing one leg into the socket of her pelvis; in handstand upturned against the wall, skirt hiding her head, legs akimbo to form a bull's head; squirming and writhing like an animal an all fours, skin itching, pawing herself and the dance floor.

Looking for Cindy

Bellmer's doll photographs, eighteen of which were published under the title "Variations sur le montage d'une mineure articulée" in the surrealist journal *Minotaure* 6 (Winter 1934-35), form historical parallels for the recursive operations in Sherman's, Boisvert's, and Oligny's iconography. They evince a relentless oscillation between, on the one hand, the compulsive attraction and multiplication of fetishised visions of women and, on the other hand, the attendant repulsion on account of the castration fear these fetishes generate, next to the threat but also desire of the self's abject dissolution (Foster 2004, 230-38). This oscillation constitutes a traumatic version of recursion seized upon by Thomas Israël. In *Looking for Cindy* the recursion of Oligny's compound intermedial work is therefore rendered as the re-enactment of a traumatic incident, a symptomatic resi(gh)ting of the repressed Real. By dissolving the borders between inside and outside Israël stages an obscene 'scene of instruction' which screens the battered yet resilient feminine unconscious. That is, he exposes it in a veiled way, allowing it to seep through, like the light escaping around the edges of the black canvas covering the screen-sized window in the performing space where the film was shot. During the live footage of the Paris version of *Pouliches* (lacking in Montreal and Brussels) abject visual compositions of hairy substances, further degrading the fetishistic braid, fleetingly lit up the screen in-between more stylised black-and-white images resonating with Sherman's black-and-white *Broken Dolls*. A racking cough, nailing Boisvert to the floor on hands and knees, segued into gleaming organic stuff, the innards she might have vomited up merging instantly with the decomposed, distorted image of her bruised face, whose multiple dephased contours stretched the skin and skull to bursting. Somewhat later, an inviting smile slowly opened up a gaping orifice, edged by a row of glistening teeth. By the time the yawning hole had closed up again in a cutely pursed mouth adorned with lipstick, no spectator could rest assured that the dancer's bodily container would not unexpectedly spill its guts, tearing the pleasing façade and discrete identity it is meant to uphold. Even the projection screen itself became uncannily permeable when the speeded up, jumbled series of Boisvert's prerecorded impersonations – laughing, crying, with lush blonde locks, brown eyebrow bangs, or patient's plastic cap over a sickly face with lolling tongue – was suddenly infiltrated by images of the live dancer and singer circling the floor.

In Paris the final sequence of *Pouliches* was accompanied once more by Israël's live images of Boisvert as if replicated by a distorting mirror that gave her bodily reflections oily shapes and contours, seeming closer to the iconography of Francis Bacon (1909-1992) than Cindy Sherman. And yet, the work of the homosexual Dublin-born painter of British parents equally asserts the hybridity and fluidity of the self. Bacon's paintings – often on recycled canvases for lack of money and incorporating the dirt of his famously chaotic studio – expressively convey on-slaughts on the human body, whose surface is scratched and wiped off the can-vas, its painterly flesh liquefying, leaking and draining. This made the apparent drippings on the richly textured brown wall in the Cité européenne des Récollets, Paris, where a DVD of *Pouliches* was recorded on June 20, 2007, so highly appro-priate. The material, visual, and thematic echoes from Bacon should be consid-ered evidence of the manner in which strongly recursive intermedial performance works supply and develop analytical (inter)disciplinary and intermedial tools, in this case an art historical context from which to assess the work evolving in front of the spectators' very eyes.

Coda

In Montreal Oligny compensated for the absence of the Sherman exhibit by let-ting the spectators of *Pouliches* consult the catalogue (Durand *et al*.) before and after the show. For the Brussels run she forgot to bring along the catalogue and therefore plucked a selection of images from the internet and presented them in the lobby of the Théâtre de la Balsamine on an obsolete cathode-ray tube televi-sion set, apparently the only piece of equipment the technicians could fall back on. Depending on the time at her disposal, her selection was more or less deter-mined by what Google's algorithmic or recursive search procedures and the lar-ger Internet community have interactively made available. That Oligny's final se-lection was shown in a loop on an improperly used, closed-circuit TV, without aerial or cable connection and turned into an outdated slide projector, can be considered remediation with a vengeance, as if the solidification of Sherman's cultural stereotypes no longer warranted the liveness of television. Meanwhile, on the box-office counter sat a slick flatscreen monitor and keyboard for the benefit of the theatre patrons. On its screen was displayed the default webpage of the Balsamine, an outside view of the theatre in the former Dailly barracks of the national guard, magnificently renovated, or perhaps we should say remediated, by Francis Metzger and Associates (Ma²). That webpage either mocked the Inter-net's capacity to break the theatre frame by providing a window onto the world virtualised or else it vaunted performance's capacity to do things differently, that is, intermedially.

Portal: Pedagogic Praxis

This portal affords a view of the impact of intermediality in performance from an educational perspective. In different ways, both contributions foreground the implications of the coming together of actual bodies as experiencers (← TERM: EXPERIENCERS) with new media technologies.

In the first piece, Groot Nibbelink and Merx articulate a flexible method of analysis in response to the demands of fresh perceptions mobilised by new configurations of body, time and space in digital culture. They argue that new circumstances in theatre and performance require new discourses, seeking a method of analysis and a vocabulary to address "presence" and "perception" as "highly dynamic and performative phenomena". Closely relating principles of composition to the effects experienced, they draw upon Rancière's *Politics of aesthetics* to frame a fresh formulation of radical potential. They draw upon two performance pieces, Ivana Müller's *While we were holding it together* and Blast Theory's *Rider Spoke* by way of "laboratory" examples of their proposed critical approach.

In the second piece, Havens utilises a Deleuzian model of "de-territorialisation" and "lines of flight" to recount a transitional process from the training of actors to the preparation of performers, impelled by the impact of new technologies and intermedial practices. Indeed, he proclaims that "theatre is unthinkable anymore without technology and intermediality". With specific reference to the experience of the prestigious Maastricht Theatre Academy, he demonstrates the need for would-be professional performers to pay attention to the diverse needs of today's cultural industries, and for theatre schools to adapt their programmes to meet those needs. Referencing the innovative practices of Guy Cassiers and Peter Missotten, he also illustrates his account with examples of student projects.

Presence and Perception: Analysing Intermediality in Performance

Liesbeth Groot Nibbelink and Sigrid Merx

To perceive is to render oneself present [to something] through the body, according to Maurice Merleau-Ponty, one of the most influential philosophers in the field of phenomenology (Garner 1994, 27). But when this body is met by what Steve Dixon terms a "digital double" (2007), perception is complicated by a continuous interplay and interconnectedness of modern media (←INTRODUCTION). Presence becomes both virtual and actual simultaneously. In intermedial performance, body, time, space and perception reveal themselves as multifaceted and dynamic phenomena. This complexity in turn invites a reciprocally flexible method for describing and analysing the phenomena. This portal affords access to an initial map of such a method, by exploring some of its tools and vocabularies.

We will focus in particular on the concepts of presence and perception – still major points of reference when approaching theatre and performance – coupled with two related concepts: the live performance and spectatorship. The use of digital media in performance, set against the background of the intermedial turn of society, reveals presence (← TERM: PRESENCE) and perception as highly dynamic and transformative phenomena. Studying perception immediately raises questions of experiencing (← TERM: EXPERIENCER), as does the concept of presence with regard to theatre as a live event.[60] We will argue that in intermedial performances spectatorship in itself becomes a self-reflective act and in this process of becoming, is able to entail a politics of spectating. In our view, perception processes are reshaped most radically in the interaction between, and simultaneous presence of, the live and the virtual. However much the ontology and the experience of the live may be provoked or problematised by digital intermediality, we believe it is exactly the live performance that enables such a provocation.

Following Chiel Kattenbelt, we define intermediality as performance and performative practices in which media not only exist next to each other, but through their interplay result in both a redefinition of media and resensibilisation of the senses (2008, 25).[61] This process of redefinition entails amongst others a fundamental refiguring of spatial and temporal relationships, it questions concepts related to the body and transfers media characteristics from one medium to another.

The redefinition of media has a huge impact on the way we perceive intermedial performances. Intermediality often addresses various sensory modalities at once, and typically the senses contradict each other. The process of redefinition of media thus is intrinsically linked with a resensibilisation of the senses.

To apprehend new circumstances, we need tools and vocabularies that describe both the interplay of media and intermedial relationships as well as the experience and self-reflexivity of the corporeal spectator. The transformability and self-reflexivity of presence and perception in intermedial performance call for a mode of performance analysis that not only explicitly addresses and embodies the transformational nature of these phenomena, but also sheds a light on the digital culture in which this practice is inscribed. In order to do so we propose a mode of analysis that uses *concepts* as its main analytical tools. In *Travelling concepts in the humanities* (2002) Mieke Bal argues that concepts can travel from one discourse or context to another, exceeding disciplinary or medial barriers. Concepts are able to carry across their particular histories but at the same time they are in a state of disentanglement or deterritorialisation, thus providing new ways of thinking within their newly found territory.

Each performance calls for or generates its own concepts. Performances can be considered as "instances of thought embodied in the artistic discourse of theatre" (Bleeker 2002, 17), inviting a particular way of reading. This is what turns a performance, according to Bal, into a theoretical object. Analysing intermedial performance involves a continuous dialogical negotiation between a performance as a theoretical object, and a concept that is generated to analyse the performance. In the explorations below, we follow how these concepts come into existence, and how, through this process of negotiation, they may be useful for analysing digital intermediality.

The Intermedial Experience

When analysing the digital in performance it is important to pay close attention to the perception of the interplay between different media as an embodied *intermedial experience*. Intermedial experience provides a key for understanding what intermedial performances communicate. With regard to this experience, different modalities can be distinguished. The intermedial performance often plays with or even explicitly deconstructs perceptual expectations and produces sensations ranging from subtle experiences of surprise or confusion, to more uncanny experiences of dislocation, displacement or alienation. The clash between digitally influenced perceptions and embodied presence manifests itself particularly as a *disturbance of the senses* and results in a *blurring of realities*. Theatre makers often deploy digital media in the live performance in order to disturb clear-cut perceptual distinctions between fictional and real, physical and virtual, live and pre-recorded and so on. Although such moments of *perceptive dislocation* (Barton 2005) by no means necessarily involve digital media, it is clear that digital technology and its capacity for image and sound manipulation are significantly extended the potential to *disorient* the spectator.

We believe it to be precisely these moments of disturbance and confusion that function as *gateways* into the performance that can help both to relate to and form an understanding of the performance. At first glance intermedial experience seems to entail a *not knowing*; the spectator does not know what she sees, what she hears, what she feels, where she is or what is what. She is only very much aware of the fact that she *is* seeing, hearing and, feeling; that she is *present*. One might want to characterize this not knowing as being overwhelmed and confused by an excess of conflicting signifiers and sensations. Some would consider it to be the cultural condition of our time: the endurance of the chaos that surrounds us. What we notice in intermedial performances however is that they invite the spectator to work through these unstable sensual experiences to become aware of precisely this instability of the reality we live in and to *deal* with the fact that we don't know.[62] From this perspective intermedial experience manifests itself as a specific kind of knowing. 'Knowing', as distinct from 'knowledge' indicates that the perception of intermedial affects ignites reflection on perception itself.

Intermediality in the live performance calls for an active attitude on the part of the spectator that Lehmann describes as "evenly hovering attention" (2006, 87). The spectator has to negotiate the perceptual experiences evoked by the various, simultaneous media relationships. Not only does the intermedial experience entail a perceptual awareness of the simultaneous presence of multiple sensual and cognitive impressions, it also makes the spectator aware of the experience of *simultaneity* itself. To experience intermediality therefore is an active embodied process of negotiating and shifting between different and conflicting medial realities, moving in and out of perceptual worlds, relating different impressions and signs, looking for a point of connection that might integrate the confusing and disturbing sensations in a meaningful whole, however unstable and ephemeral this whole may be.

Locating Intermedial Relationships in the Live Performance

We have argued that the intermedial is located in the body of the spectator. But the intermedial is to be found as much in the structuring of the performance itself, where it manifests itself not as an experience, but as the interplay between different media. Therefore understanding intermediality also calls for a careful consideration of media relationships. Locating the intermedial both in the body and in the performance requires a perceptual as well as a cognitive awareness. To approach intermedial moments of disturbance and dislocation as gateways into the performance is a way to start recognising how digital media in the live performance contribute to and optimise an experience of intermediality.

Different modalities of media interaction can be distinguished. Staging video cameras, screens, and images in the live performance for example, entails an interaction between two institutionalised forms of media: theatre and video. Using digital technologies to connect these video visuals with sound samples results in an interaction between different sign systems such as image, sound and touch. But also body, time and space can be considered as media in this context and, in contemporary performance, the body often interacts with digital media. Not only is the actor supposed to relate to digital performers; she is increasingly

MAPPING INTERMEDIALITY IN PERFORMANCE

surrounded by and wired with all kinds of technology such as microphones, cameras, and other sorts of sensors. The same goes for the spectator who finds herself armed with I-pods, mobile phones or video goggles. In addition digital technology interferes in the here and now of the live performance. In the interaction between digital media and live performance space and time are often radically reconfigured, though some media interactions are conjunctive, primarily affirming, rather than interrogating, the signification of other elements (digitally-projected scenery, for example). But even when a medium is not materially present, perceptual conventions connected with a specific medium can be so apparent that the intermedial can be established by only referring to media (Rajewski 2005, 53). A performance might qualify for example as *televisual*, *cinematographic* or *digital* without actually staging the respective technologies in the performance.

Intermedial relationships can be located on different levels in the performance. Many performances play with and deconstruct established cultural connotations normally assigned to either live or mediatised performances. Clear-cut distinctions between *unmediated/mediated*, *presence/absence*, *life/death*, *real/virtual*, *present/past*, *visible/invisible*, *subject/object*, *private/public* become blurred. Therefore we prefer to see these word-pairs not as oppositions, but as constituting and constructing each other, operating as an 'axis'. It is at these axes that media relationships are established. Moreover in intermedial performance different axes are present at the same time, crossing each other, creating temporary 'knots', and thereby intensifying the experience of dislocation or the perception of disjunctive media relationships.

Strategies to relate media are manifold. Looking closely at how media interact, the performance itself provides us with a conceptual network of terms and enables a more dramaturgical understanding of intermediality. For example: The digital *merging* of sound and image expresses the state of *amnesia* the character is in and 'performs' on the *present-past* axe. The performer *extended* with technology *mutates* in a kind of *cyborg*, raising questions about the boundaries between *subject* and *object*. The *staging* of security cameras transforms the theatrical space into a *panopticon*, opening up a discussion of the *private* and the *public*. It is this process of displacing binary oppositions that distinguishes intermedial praxis. The dislocations and relocations involved invite consideration of the effects and affects of intermedial experience. In what follows, we investigate how a moment of disturbance can function as an analytical gateway into the performance and how strategies of medial interaction generate concepts that enable understanding how intermediality shapes both experience and meaning.

Laboratory I: Ivana Müller – While we were holding it together (2006)

Five performers on a bare stage strike a fixed pose in a seemingly simple tableau. In the following hour they try to hold the tableau together as well as they can. Meanwhile they comment on their configuration with lines that all start with "I imagine". For example: "I imagine we are enjoying a picnic" or "I imagine we are a collection of 21st-century human beings in a museum in the 23rd century" or "I imagine we are a rock band". In themselves all these lines correspond in a way with what we see. But at the same time every new line conjures up a different image that replaces the previous one, resulting in a montage of disjunctive images. Text is used to refigure the perception of what is there to be seen. These bodies, although not actually moving, are constantly being redefined and therefore displaced by the text, and what they communicate is in a process of continuous transformation.

Fig. 1: While We Were Holding It Together, *photo* © *Ivana Müller*

One of the most disturbing moments of dislocation occurs when the sound of one dancer's voice is displaced, being transported to a body of one of the other dancers, through the invisible use of digital voice recording and microphones. We consider this moment to be an important gateway into the performance because here in particular the intermedial most forcefully ignites an awareness of one's own perception: it is utterly uncanny to look at a thin woman, speaking with the voluminous voice of a much larger man, a man who is in fact present in the same room, speaking with the soft voice of an androgynous male dancer, and so on. One knows that voice and body don't match, what one sees does not correspond any longer with what one hears, but still the voices appear to be embodied.

MAPPING INTERMEDIALITY IN PERFORMANCE

As a result the bodies become 'other', disturbing notions of the body, subjectivity, corporeality, and presence (← PORTAL: CORPOREAL LITERACY).

Working back and forth from this moment we can see how different strategies of displacement are used throughout the performance; and how displacement (← TERM: DISPLACEMENT) manifests itself as a productive concept to analyse the intermedial. The strategy of displacement contributes to the spectator's awareness both of her own haptic experience and of her attempt to assign meaning to what she sees. The specific interaction between different media – text, image, and body – provokes constant shifts in thinking and perceiving. In this sense not only are the bodies of the performers displaced, but also the perceptions of the spectators.

The intermedial manifests itself in this performance as a dynamic interplay between location and dislocation, placement and displacement. Whenever a new line is uttered and therefore a new suggestion made of what is there to be seen, it is up to the spectator to relocate in his perception these performing bodies in such a way that they fit the image that is expressed in the text. The spectators' attempt to relocate what was dislocated is severely hampered when not just the text displaces the bodies on stage but also the digitally amplified voice that speaks the text. Now different questions are being raised. Do you really see what you expect to see? What do you actually expect to see? And what do you want to see?

Displacement is a concept generated in and through the performance that promotes understanding of how the intermedial functions in this performance both as a specific interaction of media and as an experience. It can do so precisely because displacement is a relational concept, apt to point to medial relationships, since something is always displaced in relation to something else. Thus, one emerges in a new state of knowing, though not perhaps with the certainty of knowledge.

The Dramaturgy of Intermediality

Intermediality in the live performance has given way to new dramaturgical strategies and investigating them affords another way of analysing the intermedial in performance. In this section we consider two different but closely connected kinds of dramaturgical strategies.

Firstly, intermediality allows for particular ways of structuring the stage, employing aesthetic strategies such as *montage* (spatial, simultaneous) and *collage, doubling, difference, framing* or *interactivity*. As indicated above, these strategies, which unfold both in space, as well as in time, could be conceived of as concepts, giving way to a more dramaturgical understanding of intermediality. A second aspect is related to the dramaturgy of spectatorial address: the structuring of the encounter between the stage and the spectator. Both principles organize the performance as a process, and in doing so, certain themes emerge by which intermedial performance – as a theoretical object – reflects on its position within a digital culture.

For example, with regard to the process of structuring the stage, it is remarkable how in many contemporary intermedial performances the theme of the *retrieving of, and negotiating with, the past* emerges. This may be realised by putting the act of remembering centre-stage, or the use of the archive or database as a model for a performance.[63] The focus on negotiating with past and storage might refer directly to the main icon of the digital, namely the computer, and its primary function of (re)storing information. But this fascination could perhaps better be explained by digital culture itself. According to Sean Cubitt (cited in Nelson, 2007), the ontology of the digital culture in general lies in ephemerality, the opportunity to erase and start again being present as constant options. Exploring memory-related issues thus can be understood as a way of dealing with an incorporation of the past in the present in this aspect of digital culture.

Secondly, dramaturgy involves spectatorial address. In *Visuality in the Theatre* (2008), Maaike Bleeker distinguishes between three (subject) positions in the interaction between performance and spectator: the one seeing as subject, the subject seen and the subject of vision (10). Bleeker compares this subject of vision with the point-of-view in a perspective drawing. It is a painter's technique to imply the viewer's position. The subject of vision is thus a strategy of positioning the spectator, negotiating between the one seeing as subject and the subject seen.

We have described the intermedial experience as a process of continuous repositioning, or negotiating different positions. The intermedial experience thus seems to foreground the subject of vision, the act of being addressed, in it self. The exploration of perception as a process, and the spectator's involvement become meaningful components of performance. This again can be related to the performance's position within digital culture (← PORTAL: DIGITAL CULTURE), which is to a large extent a participatory culture. The Internet afforded the coming into existence of online communities, chat rooms, discussion forums, Twitter, and so on: forms of communication that thrive on participation and interactivity. Being part of this culture, it is no surprise that intermedial performance incorporates and investigates these forms. As we shall see in our second laboratory, on Blast Theory's *Rider Spoke*, participation often explores issues of commitment and the building of communities.

Self-reflexivity, Performativity and Theatricality

Up to now we have looked mainly at how intermedial relationships function within the performance. But intermediality in performance can also be positioned in a broader social, political, aesthetical context. Analysing intermedial relationships in performance may allow for a more general critical interrogation of media and spectatorship as themes in their own right and for a questioning of media and their role in today's society of the spectacle. In this light the subjects of self-reflexivity, performativity, theatricality, and the questions they raise, deserve some attention.

With regard to performativity and intermediality it is important to emphasize that theatre is able not only to represent but also to *stage* other media. Theatre offers a *hypermedium* (Kattenbelt 2006, 32), a platform for other media to perform on. Media therefore become visible as media, as means of communication, each with their own materialities, medialities and conventions of perception. Moreover intermediality in performance often refers explicitly to the media themselves. This entails both references to concrete media objects staged within the live performance, as the remediation of specific medial aspects such as framing strategies, spectatorial address, cultural codes and so on. In the staging of media, conventions are often played with, whether the goal is to tease the spectator or to show the construction of (the effects of) media. Self-referentiality typically encourages distanciation, which in turn promotes self-reflexivity in the process of negotiating the intermedial. Staging and play, self-referentiality and self-reflexivity: these aspects refer to the basic qualities of intermedial performance and we understand this as the performativity of intermediality.

Next to performativity we posit theatricality. Following Michael Fried's study of Diderot, Maaike Bleeker distinguishes between absorption and theatricality (2002; 2008). Where absorption is used to describe the kind of performance in which the spectator automatically adopts the spectatorial address implied by the performance (and as a result, communication between stage and spectator seems almost unmediated), theatricality refers to performances in which:

> a certain distance makes itself felt between what is presented on stage as object of vision and the seer as subject. The perspective presented by the performance becomes visible as sign and loses its power to evoke absorption. It becomes *theatrical* [italics by the author] (Bleeker 2002, 82).

In becoming visible as a sign, while at the same time representing,[64] a performance increases the spectator's awareness of employed strategies. Media become visible *as* media, as a result of their being staged: we can now see that performativity and theatricality are closely related.

Re-visiting Ivana Müller's *While we were holding it together*, we evaluate this performance as both performative and theatrical. Using displacement as its strategy it stages text, image, and bodies *as* media through which we understand reality. Equally important the performance demonstrates in a self-reflexive way how these media interact and redefine each other. It makes visible how text not only describes (the text as image) but also inscribes bodies (the body as text); how images have actually more to do with what we *think* we see, than with what is there before our eyes (the image as imagination). The performance makes us aware of how we, by looking at bodies, classify people at first sight, displacing them in fact, as such-and-so a human being. Revealing the material body and the discursive body simultaneously, this aesthetic research into media and perception surpasses its own boundaries and truly functions as a theoretical object.

The Radical Potential of Intermedial Performance

> Intermediality manages to stimulate exceptional, disturbing and potentially radical observations, rather than merely communicating or transporting them as messages (Boenisch 2006, 115).

In this section we investigate the radical potential of intermediality in relation to the questioning of the position of the spectator, and the self-reflexivity of media. In its ultimate form the interplay of media in the live performance takes shape as a pure clash or collision. To our view, the clash can be understood as a specific radical aesthetic strategy, which can be related to, but at the same time differs from Eisenstein's "montage of attractions" or Brecht's "Trennung der Elemente" (← TERM: SEPARATION).

We agree with Nelson (2007) and other critical reviewers of the 'shock' that the radical nowadays doesn't involve a change of society or power relations within that society. Post-Brechtian theatre has not made the world a better place by distributing economic wealth more equitably. Indeed, on the level of experiencing shock, it is a question whether human beings in today's society, as mentioned previously, would experience the collision of different media as shock. The qualifications named above are all more of the gentle kind, though perhaps no less disturbing. They are not about seeking confrontations with the audience, but about seeking a critical awareness of the process of perception. Therefore we stress the aesthetic in the radical, referring to the Greek *aesthesis*, meaning perception.

Dutch artist Lotte van den Berg, who often explores perception processes in her performances, asks:

> What is looking, and what does it mean to see something? (...) You can look at something without changing anything, and still be involved. (...) The way you relate to the world doesn't only concern the things you do, but also the way you are present in that world. One actualizes this presence through the act of perception and the close survey of this perception (Groot Nibbelink translation).[65]

From a more theoretical, but related standpoint, Jacques Rancière's notion of "politics of perception" is relevant. A crucial argument in Rancière's The Politics of Aesthetics (2004) concerns the distribution of the sensible, the survey of strategies and power relations that determine what is to be seen in the world, and what is made imperceptible. Distribution of the sensible not only establishes what is visible, or audible, but extends itself as well to what can be said, thought, made or done; it refers both to forms of inclusion and exclusion.

Although Rancière explores the large-scale politics of aesthetics, this main argument is similarly present in the effects and affects of intermediality. We have grown so accustomed to living in a digital culture that we rarely notice how media bombard and manipulate the senses. The fact that our reality is constantly mediated has become invisible. Producing colliding sensual impressions in performance can mobilize a process of knowing by making these acts of mediation once again perceptible. Intermediality invites a new perception and realignment of the body; one perceives what was not seen before, or one remembers what was forgotten or had been taken for granted. This is a politics of perception that can be qualified as radical, implying a thorough commitment to, and involvement in, the world we inhabit. In a second laboratory, we explore a potential politics of perception in Blast Theory's *Rider Spoke*, addressing as well issues of dramaturgy and media's self-reflexivity.

Laboratory 2 – Blast Theory's *Rider Spoke*

In *Rider Spoke* (2007) the British performance group Blast Theory sends the participant out into the streets on a bike with a handheld computer mounted on the handlebars. At night, alone, the biker is asked to look for a hiding place, exploring and traversing the city in a manner that exceeds the daily routine. Meanwhile the computer functions as a positioning system, signalling any hiding place nearby. Having entered the hiding place, the device's screen delivers a personal question. The participant records an answer onto the device. Now the biker can continue his journey and look for hiding places of other participants. Entering such a place the recordings and stories of other participants are revealed. To share secrets with one another, in spite of not being present in the same room and not sharing the same timeframe, is an experience of intimacy. In this ambulant performance the body of the biker, the bike, as well as the handheld computer, function as media caught up in a playful interaction, creating hybrid social spaces in which the interplay of the private and the public again disrupts common understandings of intimacy. Therefore we choose the concept of *intimacy* as our gateway into analysing this performance. Intimacy, like the concept of displacement used previously, is a relational concept that can be employed to focus on media relationships.

The process of structuring the 'stage' develops through a dramaturgy of intimacy. The initial state of being alone, cycling without a clearly-defined direction, separated from the usual routine, is an encounter with an 'other' self. One answers questions with an increased awareness of the self. Simultaneously, and developing gradually, this is an encounter with an 'other' city, a re-acquaintance with an environment that was thought of as well-known. The state of intimacy is gradually enlarged to an intimacy with other bikers. The more stories one records, the more other stories a participant is able to find. Each recording is connected to a particular place; they are only available in the place where they were recorded. Slowly, the city is staged as a depository of voices; an *archive* of identities coinciding with spaces; intimacy enlarges its territory. Thematically, intimacy may refer to another characteristic of digital culture: the intertwinement of the private and the public. There is joy in confessing secrets to strangers and increased emotional awareness in receiving confessions from others. Through the use of digital media intimate behaviour is made public, while at the same time the public is transformed into a one-on-one relationship.

Fig. 2: Rider Spoke, *photo © Blast Theory*

Being alone, disorientated, personally interrogated and 'touched' by invisible others; these are all ingredients of spectatorial address. The participant is (inter) actively engaged in this performance. Screen, microphone and headset mediate between participant and the city, and between the participant and others. Increasingly, the city itself appears both as medium and concept; this self-referential aspect points to the city as being constituted by and dependent on the actions of its inhabitants. The participant is positioned as part of a particular present/absent community, and as co-producer of the city. This kind of address increases the experiencer's awareness of presence, while at the same time she is surrounded by, and feels intimately connected to, the stories of others. Herein lies the radical

MAPPING INTERMEDIALITY IN PERFORMANCE

potential of *Rider Spoke*; it invites a rethinking of the notion of intimacy. No longer a property of one's own social sphere of friends and family, intimacy is linked into the awareness of being a part of a larger, open-ended, mobile network of people. Owing to its politics of perception, the performance distributes intimacy onto a larger scale, inducing an engagement with the world we live in.

The Open-ended Territory of Concepts

Exploring a method of performance analysis that lacks pre-fixed categories is in many ways similar to travelling without knowing where you will arrive. Taking up such a journey is exciting however; it is an invitation to be creative and to be responsive to what is met on the road. Dispersed through this account we have marked concepts that hint at directions in analysing intermediality. We'd like to stress however that these should be conceived of as a preliminary mapping of *performance of analysis*, not as a final and fixed map. Each intermedial performance gives rise to particular experiences, media relationships, and concepts. It is a matter for the spectators and participants to explore the meaningful and pleasurable potentialities that arise from them.

The Intermedial Performer Prepares

Henk Havens

Introduction

Theatre is unthinkable anymore without technology and intermediality. Nobody can be trained as a theatre professional, without at least being aware of the image languages of cinema, television and the digital media. In theatre and performance practice, video equipment, digital tools, and high-tech sound-systems are increasingly significant. Gradually a wide spectrum is being formed by the assembly of more diverse performative domains, and the dramaturgical surplus value of digital aspects such as live streaming demands increasing recognition. Guy Cassiers, for example, has shown with his widely-acclaimed *Proust cycle* (2003-05) that the intensive use of microphones and cameras on stage, interactive with live acting, intensifies and deepens performance instead of impoverishing it, as has often been assumed.[66] This fast-developing context has implications for the training of performers, which this contribution considers, specifically in respect of experience at *Maastricht Theatre Academy* (MTA), but with broader implications.[67]

The Dutch Theatre System in Transition

If we review the Dutch theatre system of the last sixty years in a Deleuzian manner from 1950 until 1970 it could be seen as 'tree-structured', with deep taproots. The hierarchy in the theatreworld was inescapable, and the MTA was set up in 1950, as one of the new theatre academies to be part of this clearly arranged theatre order. The number of postwar Dutch theatre companies and well-respected stage directors was limited. There was a need for young actors and actresses to populate the companies, and they slipped seamlessly into the manners of the Dutch literary dramatic tradition. In the mid fifties, however, television marked the beginning of new circumstances. What for some was cultural anathema, was for others a new and privileged reality. In Deleuzian terms, this was a *signifying rupture*, without closure in the traditional sense of ending some kind of a connection, because Deleuze and Guattari consider these breaks to be intrinsic parts of a certain domain or process. After such a break, however, they envisage *territorialisation*[68] and, indeed, the theatreworld of that time saw more and more actors, stage-directors, dramaturges, theatre designers and others, finding work in the new medium of television. Television was being *territorialized* by the emergent culture of the time. In consequence, the importance of the official canonic theatreworld gradually declined as the medium of television gained ascendance. Deleuze calls this a *flight*, a way of leaving a domain temporarily or for good.

In the decades after the 1950s, most people came to agree that the theatre could be very well served by media-attention, generated in a lot of different ways. By means of other new media sources (television and, nowadays, the internet), vital channels could be explored to generate bigger and new audiences. The theatre influenced other performative practices and, in turn, these other practices are of considerable influence on the theatre. The degree of ascendancy of the line of flight depends on the time, place, and conventions in force. Areas of meaning may be territorialised, de-territorialised, and even re-territorialised. According to Deleuze and Guattari, it is important to realize that in every sequence of time powerful expressiveness is not set along fixed demarcation lines or confined to any canon. In their rhizomatic universe there are always non-fixed and meandering connections with a broad outside world of different "plateaus". The connections between one plateau and one or more other plateaus they call lines of flight.

The Maastricht Theatre Academy in Transition

The transitions of MTA serve as a specific example of this process. Where, formerly, young people were trained almost exclusively for the tree-structured world of Dutch and Flemish state-funded theatre, in current artistic practice the collection of performative domains increasingly resembles a Deleuzian rhizome: a performative spectrum of highways and little paths, not limited by geographical or linguistic borders. Following the Bologna accords of 1999, institutes of higher education are destined increasingly to embrace the conservatories and the result will include Masters programmes and research degrees. There will be more structured professional networks of cognate art disciplines, practice-based research, links with the sciences and even with domains of commerce. For Dutch theatre academies this change from a nearly exclusively 'training isolation' to prepare students for a traditional profession in Dutch theatre practice, towards an international arena of higher art faculties for training and artistic and scientific research, can be seen as a quantum leap.

Investing in well-equipped digital audio and video studios for the purpose of expanding the curriculum in a post-Bologna context,[69] MTA additionally appointed in 2003 the Flemish film and stage director and scenographer, Peter Missotten, as a member of staff, and in 2002 theatre and media scholar, Chiel Kattenbelt, on a programme researching New Theatricality.[70] MTA chose also to adapt and extend the established curriculum. It began to integrate technological applications into the learning programme of the existing traditional vocational theatre training. Now, no specialist islands of discrete training courses remain, but rather a few former specialist emphases 'interfere' with each other under one roof. In Deleuzian terms, classic literary dramatic territory, with its attendant acting skills, is being territorialised by new practices of devised and mediatised theatre and performance and, conversely, new media artists are undoubtedly influenced by classic dramaturgy.

A feature of the new structure of the MTA curriculum is four *intermedial* projects. In these projects undergraduate theatre students work intensively together, grouped in non-subject-specific blocks.[71] In the first three weeks of their entire program, first-year students work in small groups, full-time and independently, on the *Shakespeare Project*, involving production of a show and a short film trailer referring. Any type of interpretation and design is allowed. Secondly, in the project *Theatrical Column*, each first year student performs a solo for an audience of a 150 people, but the personal commitment and the process of artistic research are the most important criteria. All students are being confronted with equipment and sources, less obvious for theatre people, such as discourses and practices from fine art, photography, cinema and new media. In the project, *Making Television*, all first year students have to solve problems working in small mixed-subject groups with joint responsibilities as producer, camera-operator, light- and sound-technician, and location manager in making items for local broadcasting company TV *Maastricht* over six weeks. In the project *Technolab*, upgrading skills in their second year of study, small subject-mixed groups of students have at their disposal a working set: one or more powerful laptops with specific software; cameras and beamers; a rehearsal room and professional editing facilities. In recent years, students have worked with the software program, *Isadora*.[72] Very quickly in the above processes, all students discover how manipulated image, computer, beamer, camera and microphone deliver surplus value in combination with their own performances. They learn to construct series of images which bring them far beyond the boundaries of the classical theatrical *and* cinematographic dramaturgy. In this last project particularly, students and tutors are searching for answers to questions such as: what does the use of this technological equipment mean for the physical context of the live performer?

Furthermore, these contemporary practices are being recursively re-territorialised by classic dramaturgy. By anticipating the future and exploring the boundaries of classic acting, by inviting guest professors from the new and hybrid artistic practices to work alongside established stage directors, and by stimulating reflective support by cooperative philosophers and dramaturges, the preparation of intermedial performers has aimed to draw on tradition whilst calling it in question. The result is now firmly anchored, in MTA policy and curriculum. In December 2008, the executive team of NQA (Netherlands Quality Agency) wrote the following:

> The Maastricht Theatre Academy takes its role as a performing art school expressly as a connecting function, a link between tradition and renewal in the performing arts. MTA profiles itself as a training course in which the classic verse drama as well as inter- and multimedial performance projects are common practice. By doing this, MTA is a link in the chain of passing on stories and traditions, and in researching new directions for these stories. [73]

MAPPING INTERMEDIALITY IN PERFORMANCE

As a result MTA was granted by NQA the distinguishing mark of *intermediality* to denote its 'both-and' approach.

Correspondingly, a growing number of stages have emerged for self-produced images, films, photo series, video clips, and other digital repertoire of pictures, beside the live performances. All these new picture stages have their own very specific, artistic hybrid, cultural and public dynamics, as well as functioning as Deleuzian *assemblages* within existing stage practices. An explosion of types of performance, species of staging, is extending the spectrum of what constitutes intermedial performance. Where film and television were often experienced by many theatre professionals just as just work one does alongside a 'real' career on the state-funded performing arts circuit, nowadays it is common practice to be professionally operative in a range of theatrical practices as well as in film, television, advertisement or other media.

Indeed, armed with cameras and recording equipment, more and more untrained people produce audiovisual material. Many of them are able to operate new technologies from a very early age as equipment becomes more readily available and cheaper. Theatre students, as future performance specialists, play their part in the process of transition of current artistic practices. They too film, edit and write scenarios in the new artistic arenas. Indeed, the boundary between creatives and users both amongst formally educated students of performance and in culture more broadly, is increasingly becoming blurred. As Bianca Stigter writes:

> On the web the difference between creators and users, between producers and consumers, between artists and audiences fades, but not in such a degree that those borders can be discarded. But the means to create art have been democratised. Maybe film is going to look more and more like music in this point of view, where at home people no longer just listen to it. Music is being played, criticised, performed. Maybe film scenarios one day will become something like written music. [74]

But becoming familiar with the equipment does not simply turn somebody into a good director, performing artist, journalist, or documentary-maker.[75] The fact that Internet surfers globally deposit twenty hours worth of 'stuff' on the internet every minute, draws attention to the need to edit and shape material.[76] It recursively demands reflection on what kind of education and training are appropriate for the intermedial performer, where 'performance' embraces creative practice involving a number of related and interactive technologies. A selection of examples of the outcomes of MTA's new curriculum serves to illustrate the range of practices in which fully-prepared practitioners might be engaged, and something of the rigour of the praxis in new encounters.

Some Examples

In the spring of 2008 Peter Missotten coached students at MTA in a project called *Congo Blue*. It was a strongly expressive performance about religious right wing sentiments in the USA and the connection with official foreign policy of the US by the Bush government. The entire script was assembled by the four actors from unedited fragments of text taken from existing websites of extreme religious groups in the US. The performance culminated in a strongly shaped image of a realistically represented *waterboarding*, directly connected with the Christian ritual of baptism – Americans 'baptize' their enemies to grant them the true image of the world. The performance has many inventive technological highlights, for instance an intriguing use of a laser and a surprisingly effective old-fashioned surveillance camera including a small screen.

Fig. 1: Congo Blue, MTA 2008, photo © Peter Missotten

Another example of a luminal artistic area is illustrated by a collaboration with commercial communication bureau, KesselsKramer.[77] Founded by Erik Kessels and Johan Kramer, this worldwide organisation, centred in Amsterdam, has been commissioned by major brands, such as Nike, Audi, Levi's, Heineken and Diesel. Creative director, Kessels, has won prestigious international prizes in advertise-

MAPPING INTERMEDIALITY IN PERFORMANCE

ment but he has also published several books on art and photography.[78] In his work the dividing lines between autonomous artworks and applied commercial works of designers and advertisers are fading into a hybrid art area. In January 2007, Kessels gave a lecture at MTA, inspiring students with his thesis that in working in the cultural industries, no concessions were made to artistic freedom. The idea that MTA students might deliver surplus value to creative processes at a bureau like KesselsKramer inspired the MTA staff to initiate a cooperative process. The first collaboration was not entirely satisfactory, but it was very informative. On analysis the problem seemed to be diametrically different visions of how to produce the film material. The professional film crew, hired by KesselsKramer, intended to use the MTA students as actors or 'experience trainees', whereas the students and staff of the MTA performance course as outlined above had other expectations. There were misunderstandings based on badly functioning interferences between the resonant cultural system of the new curriculum of MTA with that of the hired film production crew. The traditionally thinking film professionals did not recognize the different capacities of the 'rookies' from Maastricht. The film professionals weren't ready to be territorialised in an open way, their field was still too closed at that moment.[79]

Fig. 2: TNO-project, MTA 2008, photo © Henk Havens

A final example of changing repertoire is a student workshop with TNO.[80] TNO is interested in a connection between the artistic and creative world. In 2008 a working group of the *Zuid-Limburgse SIA/RAAK project*, assembled in Maastricht to research possibilities for innovations on crossing borders in performing arts, vocational training courses, science and the world of innovative technology and new media. Two engineers of TNO demonstrated a so-called *trilvest*, developed at TNO to give helicopter pilots and vehicle drivers a better (tactile) experience to determine their direction in difficult situations. Performance students engaged immediately, asking which applications might be thinkable in a situation of performers and their audience. They questioned whether it is possible to let someone choreograph simultaneously a number of people equipped with a *trilvest* and to improvise with it. This is a typical example of innovative "practice as research" in which MTA has become involved over the past decade.

Though much remains to be achieved, domains which might be called *exploding theatre* and *expanding theatre*, parallel with the established *exploding* and *expanding cinema*, might be envisaged as a result of new approaches to performer education at Maastricht and elsewhere, for example Giessen, Hildesheim and Oslo.[81] Theatre academies have to map an intermedial territory through practice-based and academic research. MTA aims to mix these multiple ways of treating new performative material and established repertoire. Theatre academies do have to prepare for a near future with a rich performative spectrum, dynamic, growing, and without rigid values. They will have to deal with an international 'performers Diaspora'. It is inescapable that future performance specialists will be less guided by *gated communities* of literary dramatic traditions of language and nation bound theatre cultures. They will make the quality and media critical differences within several more and more rhizomatic connected artistic practices and hybrid (←TERM: HYBRIDITY) performative domains. Theatre academies will no longer have to nourish exclusively classic dramatic repertoire, but also have to map hybrid and new intermedial repertoire by practice based and academic research. The art faculties of Zuyd University are researching the possibilities of creating a new kind of higher art education which they are calling *integrated arts*. MTA director Leo Swinkels and his colleague director of the Music Conservatory Harry van den Elsen put it this way: "We are going to mix up two kinds of 'blood groups' the coming decennium, academic students with vocational training art students of the different art disciplines. Not instead of, but beside existing courses in fine arts, theatre, architecture, music and the university faculty of cultural and social sciences."[82] It is not difficult foreseeing all kinds of 'alloys', like Deleuzian assemblages, under this one roof of the planned future integrated art faculty in Maastricht.

MAPPING INTERMEDIALITY IN PERFORMANCE

Retrospection: The Pre- and Proto-digital

The aim of this two-part **retrospection** is to set this book's characterisation of intermediality in digital culture within a broader context of 20th-century developments in the arts. As remarked in the introduction: Prospective Mapping, colleagues have sought to identify the impacts of digital culture on theatre and performance at the intermedial turn in the spirit of Benjamin's address of "The Work of Art in the Age of Mechanical Reproduction". However, different contributions acknowledge continuities as well as discontinuities and, accordingly, this retrospection aims to sketch aspects of the pre-digital and proto-digital.

Tim Hopkin's instance *Give me your blessings for I go to a foreign land* stands in multiple relations to the book overall. As a two-dimensional rendering in words and images of a studio production of a lyric theatre performance in process, it is an example of transcoding. Since the lyric theatre piece is concerned with shifting inter-relationships of various arts and media technologies through modernism into postmodernism, it stands also as a praxical retrospection. Furthermore, in affording access to a recording of the live performance through a website, it constructs an interface between the old technology of a book and the new digital space for publication.

The first section of Klemens Gruber's essay "Early Intermediality: Archaeological Glimpses" marks the emergence of such factors as the separation of the elements and semiotic fundamentalism as precursors to relationality and new sets of inter-relations. It notes new compositional principles and new experiences afforded by new technologies and new applications of those technologies in the arts. The second section addresses the distinctive features of interruption, navigation and exhibition which have been extended and accelerated in digital culture but were nascent in aspects of the proto-digital.

Instance: *Give me your blessing for I go to a foreign land*

Tim Hopkins

The rituals of peasant life it depicted were once a source of consolation, at the heart of a folk heritage eagerly exploited by an artistic elite since Pushkin and Glinka in the 1830s. Now, as if pulled through barbed wire, the tradition was torn from the past into a fiery present, in an aesthetic that for its authors was informed by the technological transformation of their world.

Our new piece is a meditation on the ambivalent experience of transitional change, then and now, and how different versions of 'then' and 'now' are evoked by the artefacts of technology itself.

In Stravinsky's world people and objects could become separated from what gave them meaning, as mass production and communication favoured the portable, the repeatable, the disposable. Mobility was often accompanied by loss of context.

In our world digital media permit a hyper-portability of information, usually presented as a beneficial phenomenon, particularly in terms of the emancipation of the individual voice. **Give me your blessing . . .** alights on this idea of portability in terms of migration across time and space, of dissolving emotional geography, of the adrenalin of a journey and the alienation of arrival. It invites its audience to reflect on the eutopian excitements of new technology and critical perspective about what may be lost.

Give me your blessing, for I go to a foreign land . . .

This is an instance in visual form of an Intermedial Opera, a work-in-process by Tim Hopkins and Elena Langer. These words are sung (in Russian) by a young girl on the eve of her wedding, in Stravinsky's modernist lyric theatre masterpiece, *Les Noces* (1923.) Our work is inspired by this historic context, concerned with its echoes in the technological transformation of our contemporary world. This transition is made possible by the economics of digital signal processing, and the 'digital media' it has introduced.

Les Noces used traditional texts and melodies in a devastating new sound world. It represented the ancient rituals of transition associated with Russian peasant weddings as violently energetic processes, emotionally indifferent to the individual feelings of the bride and groom. It was visualised in explosive, folk-referenced mechanistic choreography (Nijinska,) and pared-down scenic design (Goncharova.) It extended the 400-year multi-media tradition of Opera by reconfiguring its key expressive elements – sung text, dance, musical accompaniment, scenography – diverging their relationships, devolving song into an invisible chorus in the orchestra pit, creating an orchestra from four pianos and percussion, and delivering narrative visually through a large company of dancers who were forbidden facial expression.

CLORE STUDIO UPSTAIRS

It is February 2009. At the Clore Ballet Studio, The Royal Opera House, London, performers from Moscow's Pokrovsky ensemble become human vessels for the migration of pre-Stravinsky folk materials across time and space. Arks of authenticity, they come from Russia, past the technological triumphalism of the Eiffel Tower, to imperial, Edwardian Covent Garden. Then on, to modern Covent Garden, where we are performing. . .

Their route is marked by encounters with historic and contemporary media technologies, often in temporary relationships involving more than one machine or historic register. The media play various roles in the totality of the experience — one may dominate, only to give way to the intimidating effectiveness of the next generation. But they all leave their traces, and most deliver something in a way that is unique to their design:

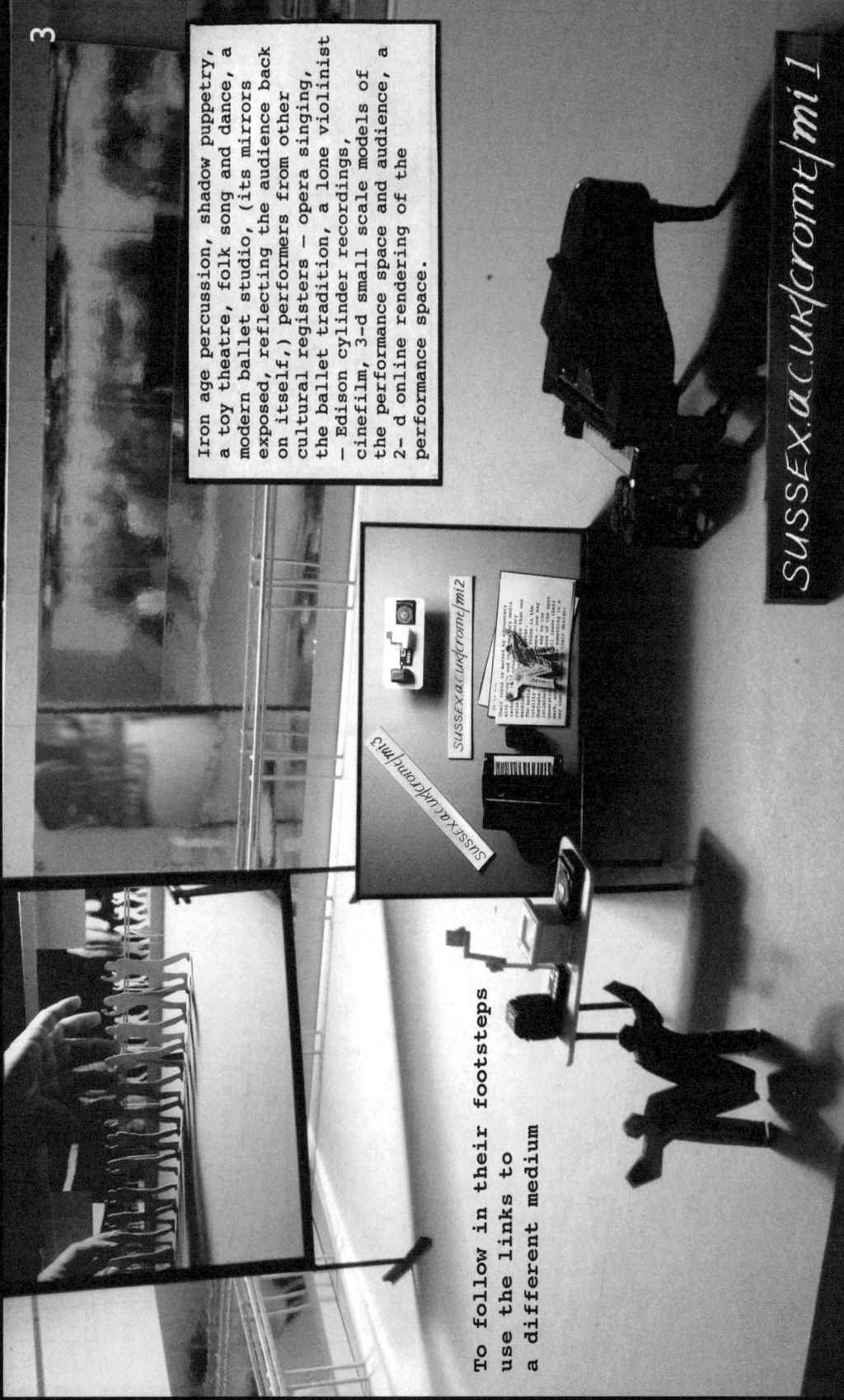

Iron age percussion, shadow puppetry, a toy theatre, folk song and dance, a modern ballet studio, (its mirrors exposed, reflecting the audience back on itself,) performers from other cultural registers – opera singing, the ballet tradition, a lone violinist – Edison cylinder recordings, cinefilm, 3-d small scale models of the performance space and audience, a 2- d online rendering of the performance space.

sussex.a.c.uk/cromt/mi1

sussex.a.c.uk/cromt/mi2

sussex.a.c.uk/cromt/mi3

To follow in their footsteps use the links to a different medium

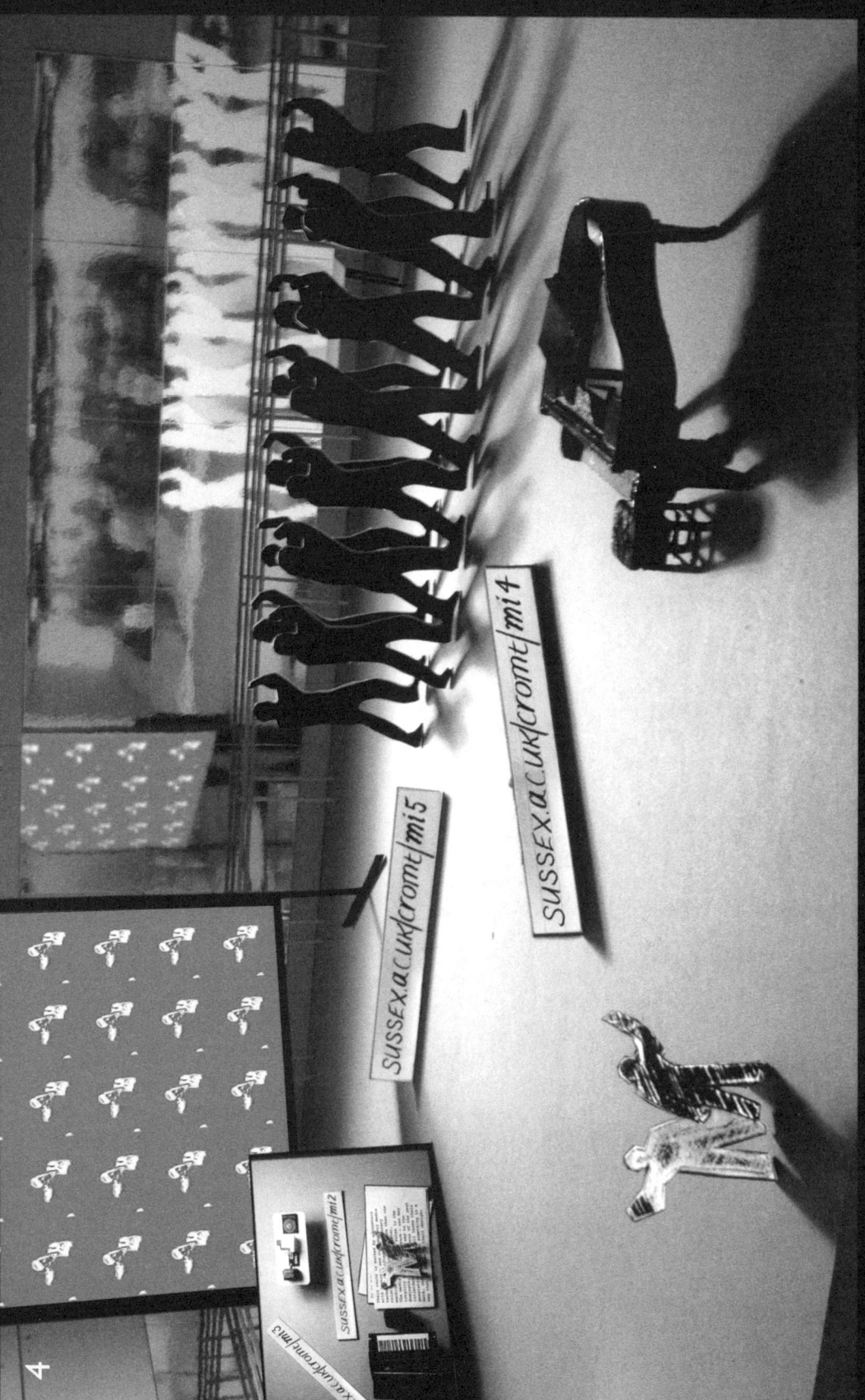

sussex.ac.uk/cromt/mi5

sussex.ac.uk/cromt/mi4

sussex.ac.uk/cromt/mi2

SUSSEX.ac.uk/cromt/mi3

4

SUSSEX.ac.uk/cromt/mi6

SUSSEX.ac.uk/cromt/mi2

SUSSEX.ac.uk/cromt/mi3

SUSSEX.ac.uk/cromt/mi8

SUSSEX.ac.uk/cromt/mi7

SUSSEX.ac.uk/cromt/mi9

SUSSEX.ac.uk/cromt/mi10

5

Early Intermediality: Archaeological Glimpses

Klemens Gruber

Intermediality was a mode of experimentation in the arts and media even when medium was a term used mainly with reference to spiritist séances. To explore the terrain of such experiments and historically to unpack the concept of intermediality with a view to the various inter-relationships between media, three contextualising frames are offered in this retrospection: "semiotic fundamentalism", "aesthetic misuse" and "epistemological euphoria". Following the exposition of the historical contexts, a 'tiger's leap' through time will be made to demonstrate the crucial role the avant-garde played in constructing what we call intermediality today.

Semiotic Fundamentalism

The art of the early 20th century left behind the naturalist landscapes of the 19th century and the grandly appointed interiors of the fin de siècle. New work was created in the context of the fundamental exploration of modern mass media. Photography had caused painting to break with all forms of imitation and to move on to abstraction. Art as mere likeness, painted from nature, had lost its meaning and artists were forced to work "from their ideas", as Marcel Duchamp put it. And they depicted the world under the aspect of its changeability.

Today, intermediality has become the dominant cultural reality. In the century of blurred genres, mixed media and fuzzy codes, the conjunction of art and technology has created entirely new forms of expression that can no longer be described in terms of conventional concepts of artistic creativity. However, the elements of change were there from the beginning, in the technological inventions that formed the basis of many transformations, and in the wilful efforts to subvert all aesthetic traditions that characterised the early decades of the 20th century. What seemed like an arbitrary, radical break with all artistic conventions was rather an encounter with the new conditions of the production of signs, with the industrialisation of the production and distribution of signs. Thus, intermediality in performance in digital culture might be seen as an extension – into an encounter with the digitisation of signs – of a process begun in the early twentieth century.

The analytical approaches of the historical avant-garde resulted from the fundamental crisis in art. This crisis, originally caused by the proliferation of photographs with their power of verisimilitude, could not fail to affect the status of works of art, the role of artists and the perspective of observers. When faced, for example, with Malevich's "Black Square" (first exhibited in 1915 but designed two years previously for the scenography of the futurist opera "Victory over the Sun"), observers were forced to ask, "Who am I, seeing this black square, and how and where do I stand in relation to it?"

Fig. 1: *Kasimir Malevich*, Black Square, 1915

The resensibilisation of the senses proposed in this book as an effect of dislocating experiences in digital culture patently has its precursors in earlier encounters.

As Jakobson recalled, "Malevich's visits and our talks in the years 1913/1914 were dedicated to what we called 'releasing the energy' in painting and poetry: non-mimetic painting and non-referential poetry, those were the slogans with which we wanted to set out for Paris" (1976, 293). Roman Jakobson, the celebrated linguist and companion of the Russian futurists, thus outlines the aesthetic programme of the early avant-garde, its break with conventions of representation that had reached their historical end-point in naturalism. Indeed, the rejection of everything narrative and representational in all realms of the arts led to new aggregate states: to constellations of colour, texture and space never before seen in painting; to a systematic exposure of language as material in literature; to the rise of tonal music and noise art against programmatic music; to the abandonment of the stage illusion in a theatre which became increasingly liberated from the dominance of literature by exploring space, bodies in movement and staged voices. Digital culture, as contributors to this book have recounted,

MAPPING INTERMEDIALITY IN PERFORMANCE

extends corporeal, temporal and spatial possibilities in performance, but the anti-illusionist and anti-narrative disposition was mobilised in earlier times.

Indeed, the former primacy of all things narrative, illustrative and figurative was replaced by a sort of "semiotic fundamentalism" (Hansen-Löve 1992, 34), a strategy of "presenting the medial, semiotic structure of art forms and genres in unblended form in each case, so as to ascertain the rules of each specific system of symbols in this way" (Hansen-Löve 1992, 40). Everywhere, the energy of each art form was released, and the aesthetic raw materials were systematically exposed. In 1913, for instance, "The Word As Such" was one of the Russian avant-garde's most famous manifestos advocating "the self-sufficient word", a pared-down definition of poetry and its artistic devices (Chlebnikov and Kruchenykh 1971, 115). Malevich's Black Square does not represent a square in nature, but instead is intended to exist as a perceptual event, as pure excitement, as such.

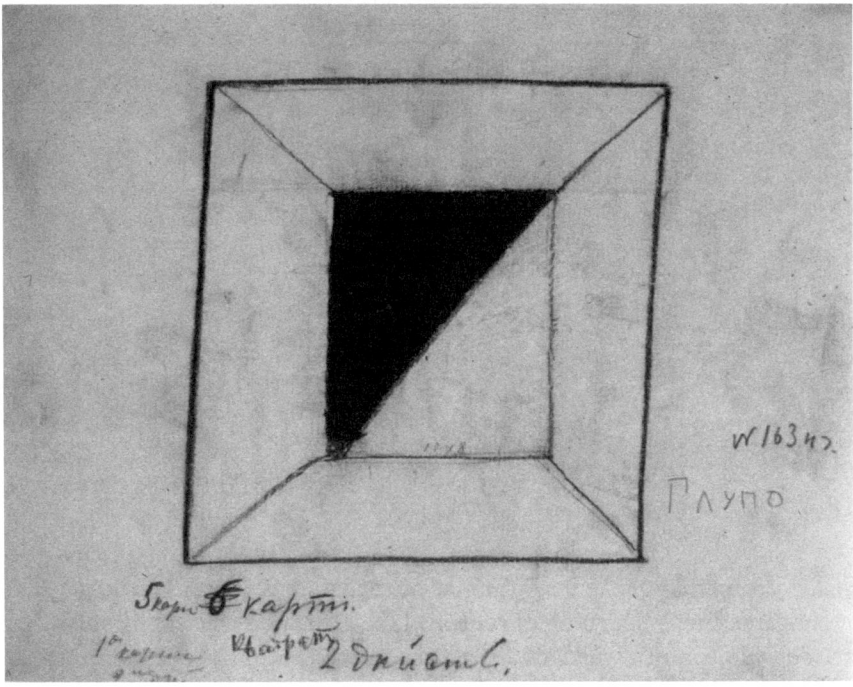

Fig. 2: Kasimir Malevich, Design for Victory over the Sun, 1913

Similarly, when Brecht demanded the "separation of the elements" (← TERM: SEPARATION) word, tone and image for epic theatre, he also insisted on the elementary energy of each art form (Brecht and Suhrkamp 1991, 79f).

Returning to the fundamentals of the art form in question meant not only reflecting on its specific means, but also exploring its new tasks: in painting, it meant depicting movement by the unmoving, static medium of the picture, mobile perspective and ultimately non-representational painting; in literature, it meant working on a poetic language, the words of which would cast off their worn-out meanings – as in Chlebnikov's invention of the language "zaum", which he saw as going "beyond reason"; and in theatre, it meant turning away from decorated literary texts, and instead telling stories through – and ultimately involving the audience in – the staging of space, light and construction.

Fig. 3: Dziga Vertov, Kino-pravda no. 16, 1923, photo: Bernhard Riff

Again pre-figuring the refunctioning of perception traced in this book, the early avant-garde's redefinition of art contained the seeds of a redetermination of the relationship between works of art and their observers. Signs and constructions brought into play the observers' awareness of their position as spectators replacing a comfortable relationship to familiar naturalistic illusions. Requiring a mobile gaze and employing multiple perspectives, painting had been working on different forms of interactivity between the image and the observer and, in theatre, the forestage's status as an insurmountable barrier was questioned. However, it was competition from the mass media that led to a first general reflection on the cultural needs of a new audience, the new urban masses because, as Viktor

MAPPING INTERMEDIALITY IN PERFORMANCE

Shklovsky put it, "for the new spectator, old art was something unfamiliar" (Shklovsky 1986, 122).

Aesthetic Misuse

The fundamentalist exploration recounted above was enhanced by the technological development of modern media. Technology was now able to isolate each sensory perception purely in itself: telegraphs rendered only writing, telephones only voices, gramophones only sounds (Moebius 2000, 151). Despite the 'semiotic fundamentalism' of the individual arts, which foregrounded their specific systems of signs, there were nonetheless intense processes of exchange between them. Indeed, the works and biographies of avant-garde artists bear ample witness to intermedial formations. However, this is only an apparent contradiction. The investigation of its exclusive defining elements by each individual art form by no means led to the arts' isolation from each other. In contrast to their amalgamation as a *Gesamtkunstwerk* under the auspices of opera, moreover, the arts were now able confidently to generate a range of combinations while simultaneously sustaining their independence.

In the process, the international avant-garde developed a strong awareness of boundaries and began to mark breaks, moments of transition and exchange. "The reflection of preconditions specific to the media and genres" enabled avant-garde artists to develop analytical procedures for structural transgressions of boundaries. For instance borders were crossed between: writing and images; stage and film; painting and photography; practical and poetic language; and between art and everyday life (Hansen-Löve 1992, 35). These procedures most generally involved an element of 'making strange' with the aim of rendering perception less automatic. The device was to achieve worldwide fame as 'defamiliarisation', that stance of illuminating distance, and the most expansive of these procedures involved 'laying bare the device', showing as such how the trick is done by opening up the laboratory (Jakobson 1988, 43).

The historical boundary of modernism – of its radicalism in the formal sense – consisted in the crisis of relating to the new mass audience (Buchloh 1984, 86ff). At that point, the withdrawal to the elementary energy of each art form, the minimalism of pure form and pure energy, was superseded by different strategies based on in-depth research on relations between the various media, that is to say intermedial strategies which resonate with this volume's conception of 'intermediality in performance': strategies that envisaged interactions with observers; an abandonment of self-sufficient art and involvement of the entire terrain of mass media; the exploration of a new aggregate state of art influenced by the urban masses and their cultural demands.

Fig. 4: Dziga Vertov, Kino-pravda no. 16, 1923, photo: Bernhard Riff

To take an example of an early intermedial encounter, in Dziga Vertov's "Kino-pravda no. 16" we see people in Moscow on 01 May 1923 cheerfully wave to the camera, and finally a young man who cheerily but respectfully doffs his hat to the apparatus.

Intermedial forms in potential were favoured by the fact that the avant-garde took on the challenge of the modern mass media, which ironically would banish it ultimately from the presumed paradise of the fine arts. The avant-garde sought to appropriate technological media, to abstract them to aesthetic ends and, of course, also to exploit them politically.

"When does technology generate aesthetic values?" the artists of the avant-garde asked (V. Markov, as quoted in Hansen-Löve 1989, 213). They explored how artistic functions emerged from the technological means, as well as the deficits and constraints of the medium. Their radical experimentation started with film tears and the option of letting images that were not proximate in reality collide by the simple expedient of taping the strips of film together. Ultimately the procedure developed into the art of montage, juxtaposing images, and later also sounds, in a context that had never existed before, in a manner that no one had ever experienced before. At a very early point, the film camera was understood as a device that could "do far more than just create the effect of an illusion" (Schulte 2006, 106).

The use of materials foreign to art and the artistic appropriation of technological media led from cutting to montage, from the darkness of the cinema to a new way of seeing, from the dream factory to an engine of enlightenment. These innovations became hallmarks of the historical avant-garde and have remained so. Indeed, though the ecounters with new media in digital cultures have led to distinctive intermedial engagements, they might be seen as an extension of the critical avant-garde trajectory. It is certainly the case that the avant-garde never hesitated to combine, assemble and let the new mass media of the time collide with each other and with the traditional arts, drawing no firm distinctions between images and words, theatre and film, architecture and broadcasting, typography and exhibitions. The potential for crossovers, even bastardisation, was infinite.

Epistemological Euphoria

An entire generation of artists and intellectuals was imbued with what Annette Michelson has called a "generalized epistemological euphoria" (Michelson 1990, 21f). The new technological means – film first and foremost – promised an entirely fresh approach to a more complete, precise and concrete understanding of new realites than any medium had permitted before. To the generation after the First World War – Michelson names Dziga Vertov, Jean Epstein and Walter Benjamin – the film camera was a device to refine our way of seeing. Not only could this device call forth images that would forever have remained invisible to the human eye, thus causing an expansion of our perception, it also promised a more comprehensive understanding of reality, "a way of penetrating as it were to the underside, the farther side, the darker side of reality". Herbert Molderings has described as "enlightened opticism" (Molderings 1996, 8) this determination to ascribe to optics a role in cognition until then reserved for reason by modern philosophy. And to that generation, an analytical understanding of reality was inextricably linked to the project of changing that reality, even more, of changing the world, the human condition as a whole.

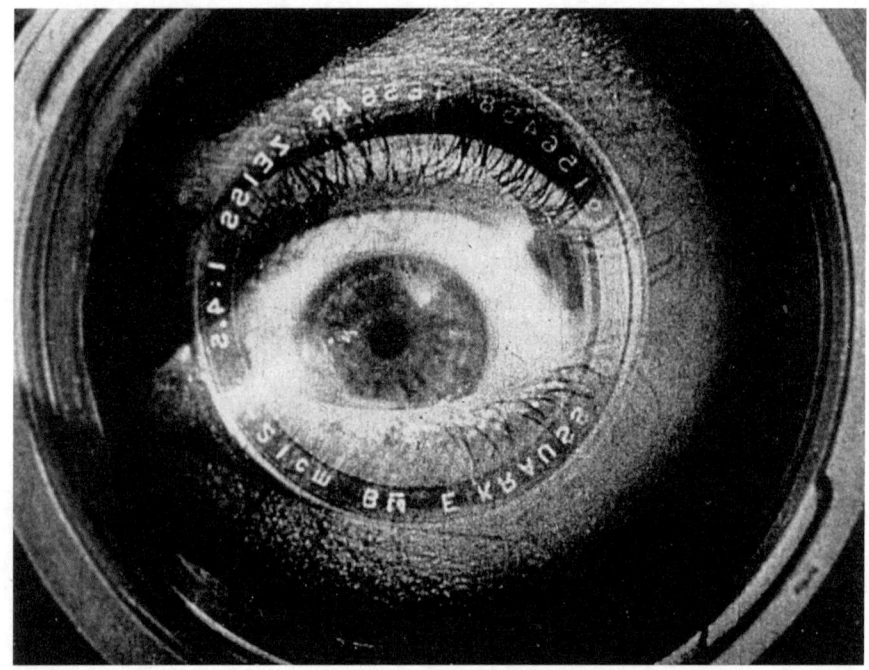

Fig. 5: *Dziga Vertov*, Man with a Movie Camera, 1929

Semiotic fundamentalism and aesthetic alienation of the media thus corresponded to an analytical instinct, an analytical enthusiasm that the Russian formalists encapsulated in the simple question of how a work of art is constructed, of "How is it made?" (Eichenbaum 1965, 119-142). With the same curiosity, playful enjoyment and determination that lead children to take apart their toys, the formalists set out to lay bare the structures of works of art, the rules that governed their workings and devices. Moreover, the device as such became the "only hero", as Roman Jakobson put it (Jakobson 1972, 33); not humans or mythical creatures as in the past, but the artistic, aesthetic devices as such became the protagonists of modern art.

The 'Tiger's Leap': Interruption, Navigation, Exhibition
Three key aesthetic procedures, interruption, navigation and exhibition, make the avant-garde artists our contemporaries, though in an inverse sense. Today's digital code attributes the wealth, liveliness and incompleteness of the world to discrete units that can be numerically depicted, calculated and thus made operational. To call the avant-garde a precursor of the digital age renews the epistemological tension of its artistic experiments with their hymnic and analytic qualities.

Being one of the main aesthetic procedures of modernity, interruption is closely related to the advent of mass media, and especially linked to film. Film cuts through the continuum of reality, mounting even single frames. As a kind of proto-digital behaviour, film converted the analogue continuum into abstract signs, tiny units – still by artisanal means – only to reassemble the individual frames in different styles of montage, from classical parallel editing to frenetic montage. That gesture of generalised interruption, which operates on the very smallest units of film-making, deconstructed reality itself. What we might call an early digital gesture transcended the historical habits of perception, and heralded a new way of thinking.

Fig. 6: *Dziga Vertov*, Man with a Movie Camera, 1929

Radio, too, has changed the reception habits of listeners who have developed the ability to tune in anywhere, anytime and, in consequence, interruption was able to play a major role, in epic theatre. As Walter Benjamin pointed out in "What Is Epic Theatre?" (1931/1939), the more interruptions the spectators are exposed to, the more easily they become aware of the conditions of modern life. The general principle is interruption: the desire to interrupt the progression of the plot and bring other possibilities of the story into play corresponds to the political conception of epic theatre as a platform aimed at changing the course of history. Some decades and barbarisms later, interruption would find its technical device *par excellence* in television's remote control, which serves both as a distraction machine and an editing table in the living room. Furthermore, the widespread need for multi-tasking today has become a form of generalised interruptive behaviour.

Besides interruption, another precedent can be detected. By its construction, avant-garde art instantly creates the impression that we can navigate within the artwork as such. Especially within film, going back and forth by intensifications and digressions produces the most stunning experiences of contrasts, which today are characteristic of digital consumption. In the avant-garde, the facility to navigate in this way constituted a pure innovation: as El Lissitzky pointed out as early as 1930, "we are on the threshold of organised consumerism".

Moreover, the avant-garde artists also supplied the schematics, making the construction principles of a work of art apparent. Right there in the painting, in the theatrical performance, the photography, the architecture, the film, structure was rendered transparent by means of what the theoreticians of Russian formalism called "laying bare the device". Evidence of the process survives in the artists' blueprints – all those diagrams, shot-lists and tables, preserved in part as wonderful autographs in the collections of many museums and galleries. If it is true that "all real beauty is analytic," as Edgar Alan Poe noted, the various schemata of that era depict the complementary beauty of an analytic production process of art.

Nowadays the 'making of' supplements of various kinds pretend to deliver such insights. However, the avant-garde 'making of' was not an appendix, not an explanatory, anecdotal narrative off-scene, but an integral element of the artwork: it was the artwork itself, exposing its aesthetic procedures in a playful staging of signs. Staging the devices was already an initiation into intermediality: the confrontation of different representational modes destroyed the illusion of the immediacy of the situation by reflection on its constructed characteristics – scenes were made transparent as an artificial construction.

The exhibition of the medium, its mise en scène, is a further step in that direction: the staging of media shows them in their relational functionality and epistemological dimension. Thus, the reflection on media becomes the artwork's second nature. Exposing the media themselves in their multiple intermedial practices, their transgressive aesthetics and their analytic exuberance produces media self-reflexivity: a playful staging of media.

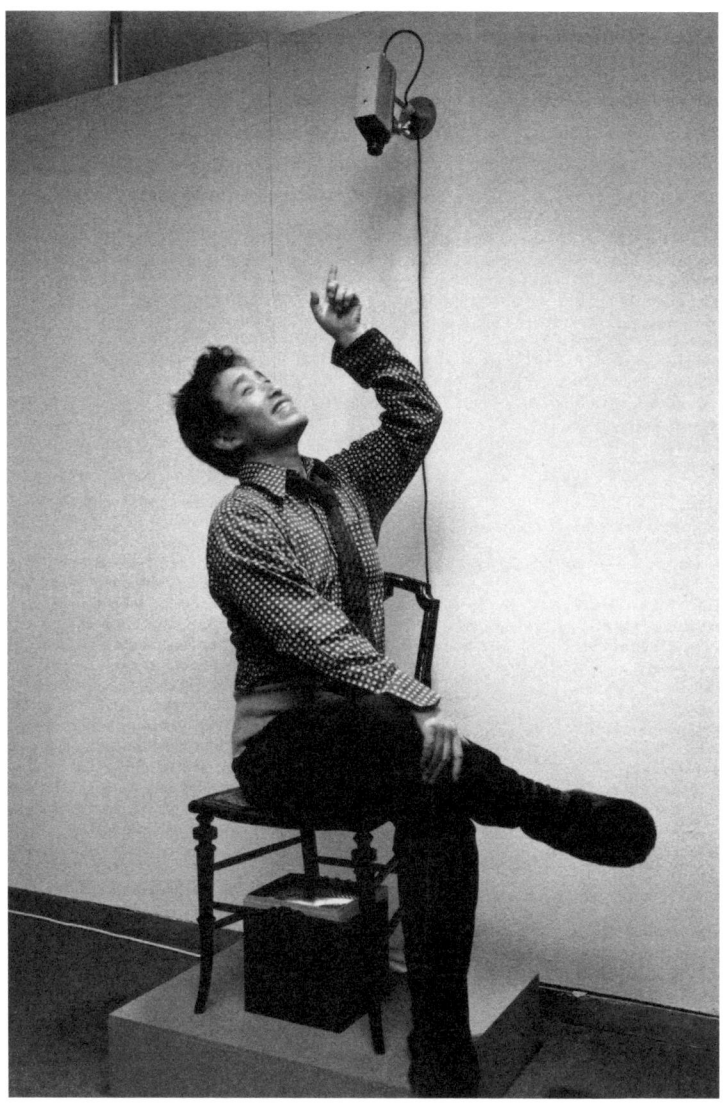

Fig. 7: "Nam June Paik on his TV-chair", 1976, photo: Friedrich Rosenstiel

Notes

1. Additional contributions have been made upon the invitation of IFTR group associates.
2. Since our book was mostly written before Elleström (2010) was published, we have been able to respond only provisionally to what is a productively nuanced model.
3. Elleström suggests that theatre is "a qualified medium that is very much multimodal and also, in a way, very much intermedial since it combines and integrates a range of basic and qualified media" (2010, 29).
4. The three other modalities in Elleström's model are: sensorial, spatiotemporal, and semiotic.
5. In anthropology, the notions of the liminal and liminoid were developed by Victor Turner drawing on Van Gennep. In a media context, the notion of the in-between was introduced in 1996 by Samuel Weber (1996, 2-3).
6. Aceti's observation was made in a presentation to the Screen conference, University of Glasgow, 4 July 2009.
7. For a discussion of the posthuman condition, see Hayles 1999.
8. For a summary discussion of Stelarc's ideas and practices, see Dixon 2007, 312-321.
9. In Dutch, I would use the word '*gebeurtenis*' (in German '*Ereignis*') for 'event'. This word is etymologically related to words like '*baren*' (giving birth), '*geboorte*' (birth), '*gebeuren*' (taking place, happen, happening) and '*gebaar*' (gesture). All of these words have the same stem ('*baar*') which refers to 'bringing into existence' and that is exactly what happens in the case of a performance or presentation.
10. She refers, for instance, to John Cage's so-called *Events* and *Pieces* in the early 1950s, to action painting and body art in the 1960s, and then the light sculptures and video installations, to artists presenting themselves to an audience or exhibition visitors who become part of a performance, to labyrinthine novels that offer the reader material that she could arbitrarily combine and to authors reading from their work or actors reading from literary texts to an audience, and to performances since the 1960s in which the relationship between the actors and spectators is newly determined by emphasising what is actually happening in their interaction in the physical co-presence of the here and now (Fischer-Lichte 2004, 22-30).
11. In Dutch, I would use the expression '*voor hetzelfde geld*', which means literally translated 'for the same (amount of) money'.
12. Being involved in and directed to corresponds with the phenomenological term 'intentionality' as used by Charles Sanders Peirce, Martin Heidegger, Maurice Merleau-Ponty and Hans-Georg Gadamer.

13. I share this view with Georg Lukács (1913). What I definitely don't share with him is his almost hostile attitude toward technology, particularly regarding the effect that technology has on the arts. I use the concept of theatre as a collective term for all live performing arts.

14. My production was presented as part of the 2006 Adelaide Fringe Festival at the Hartley Playhouse, University of South Australia, March 6-11.

15. The 'liveness' debate, which began in the 1990s, has featured prominent theoreticians such as Phillip Auslander, Peggy Phelan and Patrice Pavis. More recently a number of academics have further responded to this theme including Hans-Thies Lehmann, Steve Dixon and Chiel Kattenbelt.

16. I draw here on Chantal Pontbriand's differentiation between 'classical presence' and 'post-modern presence' in the early 1980s (See Pontbriand 1982: 155)

17. US-based international theatre designer George Tsypin commented recently that:
    Projections are important but ultimately play a secondary role. We go to the theatre to see real people in space [...] The problem is that I've never seen an emotional connection between the person and the projection on the screen. There is something alienating about the medium. However as an additional texture, as part of something more dimensional it can be a great device [...] it's the emotional impact that is important. (2006, 7)

18. All of the quotes by the artists who worked on *The Lost Babylon* are from interviews conducted by the author after the 2006 production.

19. The Japanese media portrayed a series of violent crimes committed by schoolboys in Japan in the 1990s as being caused partly by the boys' 'inability to discern reality from the video games and gangster movies they consumed' (Jansen in Kawamura 1999, 65).

20. The psychologist and the schoolboy are known simply within the play as 'Middle-aged Woman' and 'Boy' respectively.

21. We are referring to Fredric Jameson's account of schizophrenia as "a breakdown in the signifying chain": the author uses Lacan's proposition to describe the supposedly postmodern inability "to unify the past, present, and future of our own biographical experience or psychic life. Thus, with the breakdown of the signifying chain, the schizophrenic is reduced to an experience of pure material signifiers, or, in other words, a series of pure and unrelated presents in time" (Jameson 1999, 27). This conceptual description comes close to the aesthetic experience of the immersant in CREW, who, not unlike a contemporary incarnation of *La Jetée* (Chris Marker, released 1994), is cut out of a time-space continuum.

22. This new immersive surround video-system was developed by the Expertise Centre for Digital Media (EDM) at the University of Hasselt (Belgium), of which the initial concept was conceived by the artist Eric Joris and the project manager of EDM Philippe Bekaert.

23. The effect can be seen to subsume what we today know as augmented reality (AR), an environment that includes and mutually enhances both factual and virtual reality. But AR and VR are computer-generated worlds, whereas ODV is video-based, mingling prerecorded with real-time filmed images, creating a transitional world between different levels of reality. What is the real real? We believe what we see and we see what we believe.

24. Technology embodies the very contact between the subject and the imaginary on which societal forms are themselves constructed, thus giving way to what Walter Benjamin in a re-reading of Georg Lukács termed "second nature" … Or, more pragmatically, in the words of David Bartlett, the former chief of operations at the Defense Modeling and Simulation Office, a high-level office within the Defense Department and the focal point for computer-generated training at the Pentagon: "The technology in games has facilitated a revolution in the art of warfare … When the time came for him [meaning Sgt. Swales, a young American combat engineer in Iraq] to fire his weapon, he was ready to do that. And capable of doing that. His experience leading up to that time, through on-the-ground training and playing 'Halo' and whatever else, enabled him to execute. His situation awareness was up. He knew what he had to do. He had done it before – or something like it up to that point." *Washington Post*, "Virtual Reality Prepares Soldiers for Real War" (Jose Antonio Vargas, *Washington Post*, Tuesday, February 14, 2006).

25. The seductive appeal in academic and artistic scenes throughout the 1980s and 1990s of the theory of the simulacrum, the abolition of the relationship between reality and appearence, has been most succinctly parodied (and reproduced) by the influential Flemish artist Jan Vercruysse in his work *Baudrillards are Dollars* (1990).

26. "And then I left my body", thus the first sentence of the article in the leading newspaper *De Standaard*, that concludes with the Rimbaudian cry "Je est un autre". (Sels 2004).

27. We borrow the term from Johan Huizinga, his famous passage in *Homo Ludens: A Study of the Play-Element in Culture* (1955, 10): "The arena, the card-table, the magic circle, the temple, the stage, the screen, the tennis court, the court of justice, etc., are all in form and function play-grounds, i.e., forbidden spots, isolated, hedged round, hallowed, within special rules obtain. All are temporary worlds within the ordinary world, dedicated to the performance of an act apart." Liminality and the model of performance as social drama are still a central motive in performance studies (see Schechner and Appel 1990).

28. Shortly before, the company had tried to integrate both perspectives in a more radical way by implementing the immersive experiments on a classic stage. In *O_Rex* (2007-2008) the mythological figure of Oedipus embodies modern man and his tragic fate. Chosen by the audience and crowned with a HMD, the ignorant immersant – O_Rex – is blind when she can see and she only starts to see when she becomes blind. Her personal tragedy is that she never succeeds in obtaining a central – external – perspective on the world.

29. 20203D Media is a large-scale European Research Consortium consisting of 16 partners, which includes academic institutes, some of Europe's most prominent manufacturers of digital technologies and CREW. The main goal is the production of new creative forms of interactive, immersive and high-quality media (such as 3D, virtual and augmented reality). See http://www.20203dmedia.eu/ and http://crewlab.wordpress.com/.

30. All translations from the German are by Kara McKechnie.

31. See also Benkler 2006 for a discussion of the paradigm shift effected by the "networked information economy" (3).

32. See Mosco 2005, 2-3, for a more sceptical account of the notion of 'Ages', where the technologies and the habits they produce "entered the realm of the commonplace and the banal" (2). Dixon makes the salutary observation that the computer console is a feature of post-industrial countries and reaches "no more than 5 percent of the world's population" (2007, 158).

33. The first use is attributed to literary critic Ihab Hassan in 1977. See his "Prometheus as Performer: Toward a Posthumanist Culture? A University Masque in Five Scenes." *The Georgia Review* 31 (1977): 830-850.

34. For a video trailer of the performance go to www.falk-huebner.de/ThespianPlay.html

35. For a detailed discussion of the technique of using live video to create effects of doubling to express difference see: Sigrid Merx (2006b). For a discussion of interactive live electronics in combination with dance see the papers by Todd Winkler at http://www.brown.edu/Departments/Music/sites/winkler/research/ (accessed June 4, 2010).

36. As part of what I call the cause-and-effect-chain of making music – sound is an effect of a specific movement, with the two elements usually not separable from each other in a traditional musical performance.

37. By intermodality of rhythms I understand that rhythms as temporal events can be experienced by more than one sense. Visual rhythms, for example, can be set against musical or textual rhythms. For a more detailed description on intermodality see Brüstle/Ghattas/Risi/Schouten 2005, 16-18.

38. In my experience of this piece, this does not produce arbitrariness but on the contrary gives more orientation to the spectator, as the sound is not related to the instrument (which is absent), but the finger movement. As every finger has a specific sound assigned to it, it is in fact much easier to follow what is happening. Actually the relationship between movement and sound would become much more arbitrary if the 'real' sounds resulting from the different finger settings had been used.

39. These aspects apply especially for this specific performance within this specific setting. In my next performance *almost equal / meistens gleich* for conductor and percussion player (2010), I will use solely the movement of the two performers as choreographic material, completely independent from sound, even in stillness. Here visual rhythms will become much more important for the performers than in *Thespian Play*.

40. There are passages in the piece that are so polyphonic and complex in sound that they cannot be completely doubled by one player. Still, in these passages the performer doubles at least one of the audible voices, and also switches between different voices.

41. For a more detailed discussion of task performance, in particular in respect of the work of Heiner Goebbels, see: Siegmund 2002.

42. *Super Vision* toured extensively across the USA, Europe and Australasia between 2005 and 2007.

43. My forthcoming PhD contains a much longer chapter that deals with *Virtuoso (working title)* in terms of the pixel and cognitive science.

44. The cameras are connected to the televisions via a video-switcher that controls which images is sent to which screen.

45. We had wanted to construct a raised stage that more closely mimicked the Crewdson images, more explicitly echoing the television studio, but the costs of constructing and the logistics of touring a large set proved prohibitive.

46. Maysles's, documentary concerns the cousin and aunt (both named Edie) of Jacqueline Kennedy shot in their dilapidated estate on Long Island. In *Grey Gardens* a young handyman, whom the younger Edie (Little Edie) calls the Marble Faun, styles his hair in a mass of curls that is mimicked in the wig that Mark wears.

47. Among the sounds sampled by the composers, [zygote], are a washing machine, dishes clanking, dishwasher, and a refrigerator.

48. Foreman filmed part of his newest film project in Buffalo, NY in March 2009 in conjunction with Elliot Caplan and the Center for the Moving Image at the University at Buffalo.

49. Compare recent figures on media access in Hüser and Grauer 2005.

50. See e.g. the concept *hyphos* (= spider net, texture) in Barthes 1973; the concept of *fissure* in Serres, 1985; the notion of *rhizome* in Deleuze and Guattari 1987.

51. "Actor" is the English translation of the French semiotic term "actant", which is common within narratology (see Greimas 1972).

52. *The Andersen Project*, mise-en-scène Robert Lepage; première: 2005 in Quebec City. Performed by Robert Lepage and later by Yves Jacques.

53. In his 'one-man' shows Lepage sometimes works with an actor who 'doubles' him in some scenes, whilst *The Andersen Project* featured another actor who played an Arab character in a short cameo appearance.

54. http://lacaserne.net/index2.php/other_projects/metissages/. (accessed October 15, 2009).

55. Previews were shown at the Vienna Festwochen festival from 28 May 2001, the Berlin première then took place on 12 October 2001.

56. All translations from the German are my own.

57. www.gobsquad.com/archivesubpage.php?id_project=6. (accessed January 18, 2010).

58. For a longer version of this article, see Johan Callens, "Anne-Marie Boisvert, Manon Oligny, and Thomas Israël: Three Artists in Search of Cindy Sherman." *The Drama Review* 54.1 (T205) (Winter 2010): 39-58.

59. In my notes on Oligny, Boisvert and Israël, I have drawn on their personal websites at http://www.manonfaitdeladanse.com, http://annemarieboisvert.hautetfort.com and http://www.thomasIsraël.be/ (accessed October 12, 2009). Excerpts from *Identité dénudée* and *Pouliches* are available through YouTube.com, and *Looking for Cindy* can be found at http://www.dailymotion.com (accessed October 12, 2009). The Paris version of *Pouliches* is available on DVD, in Europe through Anouk Peytavin (anouk_peytavin@yahoo.fr) and in Canada, through Manon Laflamme (manon@laflamme.ws).

60. The importance of spectatorial address is met as well by Hans-Thies Lehmann. In *Postdramatic Theatre* (2006) he observes a shift in focus from the events on stage towards communication between stage and audience, placing the process of perception at the core of theatrical communication. One of the means to achieve this is the fragmentary, disjunctive and disruptive way of organizing theatrical means and media, replacing a coherent, teleological mode of representation with a much more flexible, open-ended, 'landscape' way of structuring performance. Intermediality in performance exactly tunes in into these disjunctive, disrupting practices, and can therefore be understood as a subset of postdramatic theatre.

61. Kattenbelt distinguishes between *multimediality*, *transmediality* and *intermediality*, employing the concept of intermediality exclusively to denote the interplay between media within a performance that results in a *redefinition of media* and *resensibilisation of the senses* (2008).

62. With regard to new media and technologies Susan Buck-Morrs argues in her article "Aesthetics and Anaesthetics: Walter Benjamin's Artwork Essay Reconsidered" (1992) that these technologies can help "to undo the alienation of the corporeal sensorium". (5) Buck-Morrs believes that under the influence of the industrial conditions of modernity the cognitive system of synaesthesia has turned into a condition of *anaesthesia* whose goal is no longer to be bodily receptive to external stimuli but to "numb the organism, to deaden the senses, to repress memory". She argues that "(i)n this situation of "crisis in perception", it is no longer a question of educating the crude ear to hear music, but of giving back hearing. It is no longer a question of training the eye to see beauty, but of restoring: perceptibility". (11) We believe that intermedial performances might have such a restorative potential.

63. An example of staging the process of remembering is Guy Cassiers' *Proust-series*, which is organized through the juxtaposition and interplay of different time layers, exploring relationships between memory, remembrance and identity. See also Merx (2006). An example of a performance playing with the concept of the archive is Blast Theory's *Rider Spoke*. Edit Kaldor is a Hungarian performance artist using the database as a structuring principle in her work. See for instance *Or press escape* (2003) and *Point blank* (2008).

64. According to Peter M Boenisch, intermediality in performance consists of three semiotic layers, in which a media-object on stage is simultaneously present, presented and representational. (Boenisch 2006, 114).

65. Interview (in Dutch) with Lotte van den Berg (2007).

66. In 2003, 2004, 2005, *the ro-theater* from Rotterdam produced an impressive cycle of 4 multimedial theatre performances based on the novel cycle *A la Recherche du Temps Perdu* by Marcel Proust, directed by Guy Cassiers. The titles were: *Proust I, II, III en IV* (see also Merx 2009).

67. MTA = (in Dutch) Toneelacademie Maastricht.

68. "A *rhizome may be broken, shattered at a given spot, but it will start up again on one of its old lines, or on new lines.*" (Deleuze and Guattari 2007, 9)

69. These investments were made possible by the Dutch Ministry of Education and the very cooperative policy of the board of Zuyd University, willing to invest in upgrading higher education in European perspective. In 1999 all 29 European ministers of education signed the 'Bologna accords' to create one European higher education area by making academic degrees more compatible throughout Europe (the BaMa-system).

70. The research project was reshaped during 2006/2007 and is now called *Autonomy and public space in the Arts*. The project is led now by Chiel Kattenbelt's successor, Peter Peters, Assistant Professor at the Philosophy Department of University Maastricht.

71. At MTA there are 6 subjects (study courses): Acting, Performer (devised theatre), Direction, Theatre teaching, Costume design, and Theatre design.

72. It is conceivable that in the course of time one get to use different software besides or instead of *Isadora*. On the software marked appear innumerable programmes which

can be interesting to use on stage. On academies like MTA there will be always innovative assessments in combination with user-friendliness of software in higher education and research.

73. Accreditation report NQA Maastricht Theatre Academy / Zuyd University (2008). The NVAO (Nederlands Vlaamse Accreditatie Organisatie = Dutch Flemish Accreditation Organization) awarded a distinguishing mark for "intermediality" in the final accreditation report, published in The Hague in December 2009 (59).

74. Stigter, Bianca "Surrealisme van de straat" ("Surrealism on the streets") in NRC Handelsblad. Cultural Supplement is the weekly cultural quire of the Dutch newspaper NRC Handelsblad.

75. It must be acknowledged that there are examples of "uneducated" providers of quality. One of them is the film Hunger (2008) by British fine artist, Steve McQueen, based on the hunger strike of IRA members in the Maze prison of Northern Ireland in 1981. The first line of a review in an important Dutch newspaper asks: "Do fine artists (do theatre people...HH) make a different kind of film than regular film directors?" This example defines exactly why questions like: Is this a film? is this a performance? Is this science? Is this an installation, art or cinema? should be asked more frequently.

76. Managing director EU-business Simon Hampton from Google about Internet in the European Parliament on Tuesday 3 February 2009.

77. www.kesselskramer.nl

78. The most well known of Kessels' books, perhaps are: The Instant Men, Useful Photography and Almost Every Picture.

79. Interview on the 16th of June 2008, with two involved performance students, Mustafa Duygulu and Emile Zeldenrust.

80. TNO = A major Dutch organization of Applied Scientific Research (Toegepast Natuurwetenschappelijk Onderzoek).

81. In the digital magazine E-View, Joost Raessens writes:

> The exploding Cinema program of the International Film Festival of Rotterdam more or less experiments with the 'cinema-effect'(Metz), which is characterizing for the classic film. Under the influence of the process of digitalization, these experiments respectively resulted in shaping 'expanded' and 'exploding' cinema.

82. MTA director Swinkels and Head of Maastricht Art Faculties Harrie van den Elsen, interviewed in: "Quartier des Arts, Ambitions of Maastricht Art Faculties towards European summit" Editie Zuyd (June 2009). Published in Maastricht.

Cited Works

Abramović, Marina. 1998. Interview with Edward Scheer on March 8.

Adams, Andrew A., and Rachel J. McCrindle. 2008. *Social and Professional Issues of the Information Age*. Chichester: Wiley.

Adorno, Theodor Wiesengrund. 1963. Prolog zum Fernsehen. In *Eingriffe: Neun kritische Modelle*, 69-80. Edition Suhrkamp, 10. Frankfurt am Main: Suhrkamp.

Althusser, Louis, and Etienne Balibar. 1971. *Reading Capital*. New York: Pantheon Books.

Aristotle. 1970. *Poetics*. Ann Arbor: University of Michigan Press.

Ascott, Roy, and Edward A. Shanken. 2003. *Telematic Embrace: Visionary Theories of Art, Technology, and Consciousness*. Berkeley: University of California Press.

Auerbach, Erich. 2003a [1953]. Farinata and cavalcante. In *Dante: The Critical Complex*, vol. 6 *Dante and Critical Theory*, ed. Richard Lansing. New York and London: Routledge [first published in *Mimesis: The Representation of Reality in Western Literature*. Princeton: Princeton University Press].

Auerbach, Erich. 2003b [1959]. Figura. In *Dante: The Critical Complex*, vol. 4 *Dante and Theology: The Biblical Tradition and Christian Allegory*, ed. Richard Lansing. New York and London: Routledge [first published in *Scenes from the Drama of European Literature; Six Essays*. New York: Meridian Books].

Auslander, Philip. 1999. *Liveness: Performance in a Mediatized Culture*. New York and London: Routledge.

Auslander, Philip. 2002. "Life from Cyberspace or, I was sitting at my computer this guy appeared he thought I was a bot." *PAJ: Performing Arts Journal* 70 (1): 16-21.

Auslander, Philip ed. 2003. *Performance: Critical Concepts in Literary and Cultural Studies* (4 volumes). New York and London: Routledge.

Baddeley, A.D. 2001. "Is Working Memory Still Working?" *American Psychologist* 56: 851-64.

Bal, Mieke. 2002. *Travelling Concepts in the Humanities: A Rough Guide*. Toronto: University of Toronto Press.

Balme, Christopher B. 2008. *The Cambridge Introduction to Theatre Studies*. Cambridge Introductions to Literature. Cambridge, UK: Cambridge University Press.

Barthes, Roland. 1973. *Le plaisir du texte*. Paris: Éditions du Seuil.

Barton, Bruce. 2005. "Navigating Turbulence: The Dramaturg in Physical Theatre". *Theatre Topics*. 15 (1): 103-119.

Baudrillard, Jean. 1985. *De fatale strategieën*. Amsterdam: Duizend & Een.

Baudrillard, Jean. 1986. *In de schaduw van de zwijgende meerderheden*. Amsterdam: SUA.

Baudrillard, Jean. 1994. *Simulacra and Simulations*. Ann Arbor: University of Michigan Press.

Beacham, Richard C. 1993. *Adolphe Appia: Texts on Theatre*. London and New York: Routledge.

Benjamin, Walter, and Siegfried Unseld. 1972. *Zur Aktualität Walter Benjamins aus Anlass des 80. Geburtstags von Walter Benjamin*. Frankfurt am Main: Suhrkamp.

Benjamin, Walter. 1985 [1928]. Surrealism: The Last Snapshot of the European Intelligentsia. In *One-way Street and Other Writings*. London: Verso.

Benjamin, Walter. 1977a [1936]. *Das Kunstwerk im Zeitalter seiner technischen Reproduzierbarkeit.* Frankfurt am Main: Suhrkamp.

Benjamin, Walter. 1977b. *Illuminationen: Ausgewählte Schriften.* Selected by Siegfried Unseld. Frankfurt am Main: Suhrkamp.

Benkler, Yochai. 2006. *The Wealth of Networks: How Social Production Transforms Markets and Freedom.* New Haven, CT: Yale University Press.

Bequer, Marcos and José Gatti. 2005. Elements of Vogue. In *The Subcultures Reader*, 445-453. Ed. Gelder, Ken, 2nd edition. London: Routledge.

Bergson, Henri. 1911a. *Creative Evolution.* New York: Henry Holt and Company.

Bergson, Henri. 1911b. *Matter and Memory.* London: George Allen & Unwin.

Birringer, Johannes. 2006. "Digital performance". *Performance Research* 11 (3): 42-45.

Bleeker, Maaike. 2002. *The Locus of Looking: Dissecting Visuality in the Theatre.* Ph.D. diss., University of Amsterdam.

Bleeker, Maaike, Lucia van Heteren, Chiel Kattenbelt, Kees Vuyk, ed. 2006. *De theatermaker als onderzoeker.* Amsterdam: Amsterdam University Press.

Bleeker, Maaike. 2008. *Visuality in the Theatre: the Locus of Looking. Performance Interventions.* Houndmills, Basingstoke and Hampton: Palgrave Macmillan.

Boal, Augusto. 1998. *Legislative Theatre.* London: Routledge.

Boenisch, Peter M. 2003. "coMEDIA electrONica: Performing Intermediality in Contemporary Theatre". *Theatre Research International* 28 (1): 34-45.

Boenisch, Peter M. 2006. Aesthetic Art to Aisthetic Act: Theatre, Media, Intermedial Performance. In *Intermediality in Theatre and Performance*, ed. Freda Chapple and Chiel Kattenbelt, 103-116. Amsterdam and New York: Rodopi.

Bogatyrev, Petr. 1971 [1938]. "Les Signes du Théâtre". *Poétique* 8: 517-530.

Bogue, Ronald. 1997. "Art and Territory." *The South Atlantic Quarterly* 96 (3): 465-482.

Bolter, J. David, and Richard A. Grusin. 2000. *Remediation: Understanding New Media.* Cambridge, Mass: MIT Press.

Braidotti, Rosi. 2009. Meta(l)flesh. In *The Future of Flesh: A Cultural Survey of the Body.*, ed. Zoe Detsi-Diamanti, Katerina Kitsi-Mitakou and Effie Yiannopoulou, 241-261. New York: Palgrave Macmillan.

Brandstetter, Gabriele, and Birgit Wiens (ed.). 2010 (in print). *Theater ohne Fluchtpunkt | Theatre without Vanishing Points. Das Erbe Adolphe Appias | The Heritage of Adolphe Appia: Szenographie und Choreographie im zeitgenössischen Theater | Scenography and Choreography in Contemporary Theatre.* Berlin: Alexander Verlag.

Brecht, Bertolt, and Peter Suhrkamp. 1991. Anmerkungen zur Oper Aufstieg und Fall der Stadt Mahagony. In *Bertolt Brecht Werke. Große kommentierte Berliner und Frankfurter Ausgabe*, vol. 24. Berlin and Weimar/Frankfurt am Main: Aufbau/Suhrkamp.

Brecht, Bertolt. 1964. *Brecht on Theatre : The Development of an Aesthetic.* New York and London: Farrar, Straus and Giroux.

Broadhurst, Susan, and Josephine Machon. 2006. *Performance and Technology: Practices of Virtual Embodiment and Interactivity.* Houndmills, Basingstoke and Hampton: Palgrave Macmillan.

MAPPING INTERMEDIALITY IN PERFORMANCE

Broadhurst, Susan. 2007. *Digital Practices: Aesthetic and Neuroesthetic Approaches to Performance and Technology*. Houndmills, Basingstoke and Hampton: Palgrave Macmillan.

Bröckers, Mathias, and Carl Hegemann. 2002. *Einbruch der Realität: Politik und Verbrechen*. Berlin: Alexander-Verlag.

Broeckmann, Andreas. 2000. Wirksamkeit und konnektives Handeln. In *Heute ist Morgen, Über die Zukunft von Erfahrung und Konstruktion* [published on the occasion of the exhibition "Heute ist Morgen, über die Zukunft von Erfahrung und Konstruktion" from June 30, 2000 till January 7, 2001 in der Kunst- und Ausstellungshalle der Bundesrepublik Deutschland in Bonn]. Ostfildern: Cantz Press.

Bromfield, David. 1991. *Identities: A Critical Study of the Work of Mike Parr, 1970-1990*. Nedlands, WA: University of Western Australia Press.

Brook, Peter. 1968. *The Empty Space*. Harmondsworth: Penguin.

Brouwer, Joke, and Arjen Mulder. 2000. *Machine Times*. Rotterdam: NAi Publishers and V2-Organization.

Brüstle, Christa, Nadia Ghattas, Clemens Risi, and Sabine Schouten, ed. 2005. *Aus dem Takt – Rhythmus in Kunst, Kultur und Natur*. Bielefeld: transcript.

Buchloh, Benjamin H.D. 1984. "From Faktura to Factography". *October* 30: 82-119.

Bürger, Peter. 1990 [1974]. *Theorie der Avantgarde: mit einem Nachwort zur 2. Aufl*. Frankfurt am Main: Suhrkamp.

Butler, Judith. 1990. *Gender trouble: feminism and the subversion of identity. Thinking gender*. New York: Routledge.

Butler, Judith. 1993. *Bodies that matter: on the discursive limits of "sex"*. New York: Routledge.

Cage, John. 1981. *For the Birds: Conversations with Daniel Charles*. Boston and London: Marion Boyars.

Carlson, Marvin A. 1996. *Performance: a critical introduction*. London: Routledge.

Carlson, Marvin A. 1989. *Places of Performance. The Semiotics of Theatre Architecture*. Ithaca, NY: Cornell University Press.

Carlson, Neil R. 2004. *Physiology of behavior*. Boston: Pearson A & B.

Castells, Manuel. 2004. *The network society: a cross-cultural perspective*. Cheltenham, UK, and Northampton MA: Edward Elgar Pub.

Castorf, Frank. 2001. "Ich bin ein Querulant": Interview – Der Regisseur Frank Castorf über Größenwahn, langweiliges Theater, "Big Brother" und seine neue Arbeit für die Wiener Festwochen. *Profil* 22, 28 May, 130-131.

Castorf, Frank. 2002. Nicht Realismus, sondern Realität: Frank Castorf spricht über seine Arbeit. In *Politik und Verbrechen: Einbruch der Realität*, ed. Carl Hegemann, 71-79. Berlin: Alexander.

Catts, Oron, and Ionat Zurr. 2006. The Tissue Culture and Art Project: The Semi-living as Agents of Irony. In *Performance and Technology: Practices of Virtual Embodiment and Interactivity*, ed. Susan Broadhurst and Josephine Machon, 153-168. New York: Palgrave Macmillan.

Causey, Matthew. 1999. "The Screen Test of the Double: The Uncanny Performer in the Space of Technology". *Theatre Journal* 51 (4): 383.

Causey, Matthew. 2006. *Theatre and Performance in Digital Culture: From Simulation to Embeddedness*. Routledge Advances in Theatre and Performance Studies (5). London: Routledge.

Certeau, Michel de. 1984 [1980]. *The Practice of Everyday Life*. Berkely: University of California Press.

Chapple, Freda, and Chiel Kattenbelt. 2006. Key Issues in Intermediality in Theatre and Performance. In *Intermediality in Theatre and Performance*, ed. Chapple, Freda and Chiel Kattenbelt, 11-25. Amsterdam and New York: Rodopi.

Chapple, Freda, and Chiel Kattenbelt (eds.). 2006. *Intermediality in Theatre and Performance*. Amsterdam and New York: Rodopi.

Charest, Rémy. 1995. *Robert Lepage*: quelques zones de liberté. Québec: L'Instant même.

Chocano, Carina. 2006. In Lynch's 'Velvet' the Real is Unreal. *Los Angeles Times*, July 14, 2006 (online: http://articles.latimes.com/2006/jul/14/entertainment/et-blue14 (accessed April 15, 2010).

Corbeil, Marie-Eve. 2007. 'Physiques.' *Ici*, 18-24 October: 56.

Couchot, Edmond. 1998. *La technologie dans l'art: de la photographie à la réalité virtuelle*. Rayon photo. Nîmes: Jacqueline Chambon.

Crang, Mike, and N. J. Thrift. 2000. *Thinking Space*. Critical Geographies, 9. London: Routledge.

Crewdson, Gregory, Katy Siegel, Martin Hochleitner, and Stephan Berg. 2007. *Gregory Crewdson 1985-2005*. Ostfildern: Hatje Cantz.

Crewdson, Gregory. 1998-02. *Twilight*. New York: Luhring Augustine.

Crewdson, Gregory. 2003-05. *Beneath the Roses*. New York: Luhring Augustine.

Crimp, Martin. 1997. *Attempts on her life*. London: Faber and Faber.

Cubitt, Sean. 2000. 'Cybertime: Ontologies of Digital Perception', paper for the Society for Cinema Studies, Chicago, March 2000, published online at http://repository.unimelb.edu.au/10187/1862 (accessed April 15, 2010.

Davy, Kate. 1976. *Richard Foreman: Plays and Manifestos*. New York: New York University Press.

Debord, Guy, and Jaap Kloosterman. 1976. *De spektakelmaatschappij*. Baarn: Het Wereldvenster.

Debord, Guy. 2001 [1967]. *De spektakelmaatschappij*. Amsterdam: Uitgeverij de Dolle Hond.

Delany, Paul. 1990. *Hypermedia and Literary Studies*. Cambridge Mass.: MIT Press.

Deleuze, Gilles and Félix Guattari. 1972. *L'Anti-Oedipe: capitalisme et schizophrénie*. Paris: Les Editions de Minuit.

Deleuze, Gilles, and Félix Guattari. 1987/2003/2007. *A Thousand Plateaus: Capitalism and Schizophrenia*. Minneapolis: University of Minnesota Press.

Deleuze, Gilles. 1992. "Postscript on the Societies of Control". In *October* 59: 3-7 (also available online: http://www.n5m.org/n5m2/media/texts/deleuze.htm (accessed May 09, 2010).

Deleuze, Gilles, Félix Guattari. 2004. *Rizoom: een inleiding*. Utrecht: Spreeuw, libertaire uitgeverij.

Detje, Robin. 2005. "Remembering Never-Ever Land: How Frank Castorf Renconjured Berlin's Volksbühne". *Theater* 35 (2): 5-17.

Diedrichsen, Diedrich. 2007. Betroffene, Exemplifizierende und Human Interfaces. In *Experten des Alltags: Das Theater von Rimini Protokoll*, ed. Miriam Dreysse and Florian Malzacher, 158-163. Berlin: Alexander Verlag.

Dixon, Steve, with contributions by Barry Smith. 2007. *Digital Performance: A History of New Media in Theater, Dance, Performance Art, and Installation*. Cambridge, MA: MIT Press.

Donsbach, Wolfgang, ed. 2008.*The International Encyclopedia of Communication*. Oxford: Blackwell Publishing. Blackwell Reference Online (accessed June 8, 2009).

Dreysse, Miriam, and Florian Malzacher. 2007. Foreword. In *Experten des Alltags: Das Theater von Rimini Protokoll*, ed. Miriam Dreysse and Florian Malzacher, 8-11. Berlin: Alexander Verlag.

Durand, Régis, Jean-Pierre Criqui, and Laura Mulvey. 2006. *Cindy Sherman*. Paris: Flammarion.

Eco, Umberto. 1977. "Semiotics of Theatrical Performance". *The Drama Review: TDR*. 21 (1): 107-117.

Eco, Umberto. 1986. *De alledaagse onwerkelijkheid: essays*. Amsterdam: Bakker.

Eichenbaum, Boris Mikhailovich. 1965. Wie Gogols Mantel gemacht ist. In *Aufsätze zur Theorie und Geschichte der Literatur*, by Boris Eichenbaum, 119-142. Frankfurt am Main: Suhrkamp.

Elden, Stuart. 2006. The State of Territory under Globalization, Empire and the Politics of Reterritorialization. In *Metaphoricity and the Politics of Mobility*, ed. Margarita Margaroni and Effie Yiannopoulou, 47-66. Thamyris/Intersecting: Place, Sex and Race 12. Amsterdam and New York: Rodopi.

Elleström, Lars. The Modalities of Media: A Model for Understanding Intermedial Relations. In *Media Borders, Multimodality and Intermediality*, ed. Lars Elleström, 11-48. Houndmills, Basingstoke and Hampshire: Palgrave MacMillan.

Ernst, Wolf-Dieter. 2006. Kartografien des Interface. Zum Widerstand des Lesens und Schreibens bei Duchamp, O.U.L.I.P.O., Jodi und Knowbotic Research". In *"System ohne General": Schreibzenen im digitaler Zeitalter*, ed. Davide Giuriato, Martin Stingelin and Sandro Zanetti, 101-130. Munich: Fink.

Erstić, Marijana, Gregor Schuhen, and Tanja Schwan. 2005. *Avantgarde, Medien, Performativität: Inszenierungs- und Wahrnehmungsmuster zu Beginn des 20. Jahrhunderts*. Medienumbrüche, 7. Bielefeld: transcript.

Falkheimer, Jesper, and André Jansson. 2006. *Geographies of Communication: The Spatial Turn in Media Studies*. Göteborg: Nordicom.

Faulkner, Michael and D-Fuse, ed. 2006. *VJ: Audio-visual Art and VJ Culture*. London: Laurence King Publishing Ltd.

Fell, John L. 1970. "Dissolves by Gaslight: Antecedents to the Motion Picture in Nineteenth-Century Melodrama". *Film Quarterly* 23 (3): 22-34.

Fischer-Lichte, Erika, Doris Kolesch, and Matthias Warstat. 2005. *Metzler Lexikon Theatertheorie*. Stuttgart: J. B. Metzler.

Fischer-Lichte, Erika. 2005. *Ästhetik des Performativen*. Edition Suhrkamp, 2373. Frankfurt am Main: Suhrkamp.

Fischer-Lichte, Erika. 2008. *The Transformative Power of Performance: A New Aesthetics*. London: Routledge.

Flaker, Aleksandar. 1989. *Glossarium der russischen Avantgarde*. Graz: Droschl.

Foreman, Richard. 1976a. Ontological-Hysteric: Manifesto II. In *Richard Foreman: Plays and Manifestos*, ed. Kate Davy. New York: New York University Press.

Foreman, Richard. 1976b. Ontological-Hysteric: Manifesto I. In *Richard Foreman: Plays and Manifestos*, 67-79.

Foreman, Richard. 1992. Visual Composition, Mostly. In *Unbalancing Acts: Foundations for a Theater*, 54-66. New York: Theatre Communications Group.

Foreman, Richard, and Ken Jordan. 1992. *Unbalancing Acts: Foundations for a Theater*. New York: Pantheon Books.

Foreman, Richard. 2005. "The Gods are Pounding My Head!: (aka Lumberjack Messiah)". *American Theatre*. 22: 37-45.

Foreman, Richard. 2008. Production Notes to Deep Trance Behavior In Potatoland. *Ontological-Hysteric Theatre: Richard Foreman*. January http://www.ontological.com/RF/rfproductionfiles/2008DeepTrance/index.html (accessed April 15, 2010).

Foster, Hal. 1993. *Compulsive Beauty*. Cambridge, MA: MIT Press.

Foster, Hal. 2004. *Prosthetic Gods*. Cambridge, MA: MIT Press. http://www.netlibrary.com/urlapi.asp?action=summary&v=1&bookid=126018 (accessed April 15, 2010).

Foucault, Michel. 1986 [1984/1967]. "Of Other Spaces" (1967), *Diacritics* 16 (Spring): 22-27. http://foucault.info/documents/heteroTopia/foucault.heteroTopia.en.html (accessed April, 15 2010).

Fouquet, Ludovic. 1998. "Du théâtre d'ombres aux technologies contemporaines" (Entretien avec Robert Lepage). In *Les écrans sur la scène: tentations et résistances de la scène face aux images. Etudes et témoignages*, ed. Béatrice Picon-Vallin, 325-333. Lausanne: L'Age d'Homme.

Fouquet, Ludovic. 2005. *Robert Lepage, l'horizon en images: essai*. Québec: L'Instant même.

Fried, Michael. 1998. *Art and objecthood: essays and reviews*. Chicago: University of Chicago Press.

Früchtl, Josef, and Jörg Zimmermann. 2001. *Ästhetik der Inszenierung: Dimensionen eines künstlerischen, kulturellen und gesellschaftlichen Phänomens*. Frankfurt am Main: Suhrkamp.

Fuchs, Elinor, and Una Chaudhuri. 2002. *Land/Scape/Theater*. Ann Arbor: University of Michigan Press.

Fuegi, John. 1972. *The Essential Brecht*. Los Angeles: Hennessey & Ingalls.

Gallasch, Keith, and Virginia Baxter. 2002. "Part 1: Smoothing the Visceral/Virtual Mix" in *Real Time* Oct-Nov. no 51: 22.

Garner, Stanton B. 1994. *Bodied Spaces: Phenomenology and Performance in Contemporary Drama*. Ithaca and London: Cornell University Press.

Gere, Charlie. 2002. *Digital Culture*. London: Reaktion Books.

Giannachi, Gabriella. 2004. *Virtual Theatres: An Introduction*. London: Routledge.

Gibson, James Jerome. 1966. *The Senses Considered as Perceptual Systems*. Boston: Houghton Mifflin.

Gibson, William. 1984. *Neuromancer*. New York: Ace.

Giuriato, Davide, Martin Stingelin, and Sandro Zanetti. 2006. *"System ohne General": Schreibzenen im digitaler Zeitalter*. Munich: W. Fink.

Glotz, Peter, and Stefan Bertschi, Chris Locke, ed. 2005. *Thumb Culture: The meaning of Mobile Phones for Society*. Bielefeld: transcript.

Goffman, Erving. 1959. *The Presentation of Self in Everyday Life*. Garden City, NY: Doubleday.

Goggin, Gerard. 2006. *Cell Phone Culture: Mobile Technology in Everyday Life*. London: Routledge.

Grau, Oliver. 2003. *Virtual Art: From Illusion to Immersion. Revised and Expanded.* Cambridge, MA: MIT Press.

Greimas, Algirdas Julien. 1972. Die Struktur der Erzählaktanten. Versuch eines generativen Ansatzes. In *Literaturwissenschaft und Linguistik. Ergebnisse und Perspektiven,* vol. 3, ed. Jens Ihwe, 218-238. Frankfurt am Main: Athenäum.

Groot Nibbelink, Liesbeth. 2007. "De regen valt niet voor ons. In gesprek met Lotte van den Berg. *Theaterdramaturgie. Bank.* http://ltd.library.uu.nl/doc/723/interview.htm (accessed January 8, 2010).

Gumbrecht, Hans. 2004. *Production of Presence: What Meaning Cannot Convey.* Stanford: Stanford University Press.

Habermas, Jürgen. 1972. Bewußtmachende oder rettende Kritik – die Aktualität Walter Benjamins. In *Zur Aktualität Walter Benjamins,* ed. S. Unseld, 173-223. Frankfurt am Main: Suhrkamp.

Habermas, Jürgen. 1985 [1981]. *Theorie des kommunikativen Handelns. Band 1: Handlungsrationalität und gesellschaftliche Rationalisierung. Band 2: Zur Kritik der funktionalistischen Vernunft.* Frankfurt am Main: Suhrkamp.

Habermas, Jürgen. 1988. *Nachmetaphysisches Denken: philosophische Aufsätze.* Frankfurt am Main: Suhrkamp.

Habermas, Jürgen. 1988. *Il pensiero post-metafisico.* Bari: Editori Laterza.

Habermas, Jürgen. 1990. *Posuto keijijogaku no shiso.* Tokyo: Miraisha.

Habermas, Jürgen. 1993. *La Pensée postmétaphysique: essais philosophiques.* Paris: Armand Colin.

Habermas, Jürgen. 1995. *Postmetaphysical Thinking: Philosophical Essays.* Cambridge: Polity Press.

Habermas, Jürgen. 1996. *Postmetaphysical Thinking: Philosophical Essays.* Cambridge, MA: MIT Press.

Halberstam, Judith, and Ira Livingston. 1995. *Posthuman Bodies. Unnatural Acts.* Bloomington: Indiana University Press.

Hansen-Löve, Aage. 1989. "Faktur, Gemachtheit". In *Glossarium der russischen Avantgarde,* ed. Aleksandar Flaker. Graz: Droschl.

Hansen-Löve, Aage. 1992. "Wörter und/oder Bilder. Probleme der Intermedialität mit Beispielen aus der russischen Avantgarde". *Eikon* 4: 32-41.

Hansen, Mark B.N. 2004. *New Philosophy for New Media.* Cambridge, MA: MIT Press.

Hansen, Mark B.N. 2006. *Bodies in Code: Interfaces with Digital Media.* New York: Routledge.

Haraway, Donna J. 1991. *Simians, Cyborgs and Women: The Reinvention of Nature.* London: Free Association Books Ltd.

Haraway, Donna. 1991. A Cyborg Manifesto. In *Simians, Cyborgs and Women: The Reinvention of Nature,* 149-181. New York: Routledge.

Harris, Jan L., and Paul A. Taylor. 2005. *Digital Matters: Theory and Culture of the Matrix.* London: Routledge.

Harris, Samela. 2006. "Guns, Guns and more Guns [Review of The Lost Babylon dir. Russell Fewster]". In *The Advertiser* 8 March: 10.

Harvey, David. 1989. *The Condition of Postmodernity: An Enquiry into the Origins of Cultural Change.* Oxford: Blackwell.

Hassan, Ihab. 1977. "Prometheus as Performer: Towards a Posthumanist Culture? A University Masque in Five Scenes". *The Georgia Review* 31 : 830-850.

Hassard, John and John Law, ed. 1999. *Actor Network Theory and After*, Oxford and Malden, MA: Blackwell/Sociological Review.

Havens, Henk, Chiel Kattenbelt, Eric de Ruijter and Kees Vuyk (eds.). 2006. *Theater & technologie*. Amsterdam: Theater Instituut Nederland.

Hayles, N. Katherine. 1999. *How We Became Posthuman: Virtual Bodies in Cybernetics, Literature, and Informatics*. Chicago: University of Chicago Press.

Hayles, N. Katherine. 2000. The Condition of Virtuality. In *The Digital Dialectic: New Essays for New Media*, ed. Peter Lunenfeld, 68-96. Cambridge and London: MIT Press.

Hébert, Chantal, and Irène Perelli-Contos. 2001. *"La face cachée" du théâtre de l'image*. Paris: Harmattan.

Hegemann, Carl Georg, and Mathias Bröckers. 2002. *Einbruch der Realität. Politik und Verbrechen*, [1]. Berlin: Volksbühne am Rosa-Luxemburg-Platz.

Honzl, Jindrich. 1971. "La mobilité du signe théâtral". *Travail théâtral* 4: 5-20.

Huizinga, Johan. 1955. *Homo Ludens: A Study of the Play-Element in Culture*. Boston: Beacon Press.

Hüser, Gisela, and Manfred Grauer. 2005. Zur Verbreitung des Internets und des Mobiltelefons in der Netzwerkgesellschaft. In *Wissensprozesse in der Netzwerkgesellschaft, ed.* Peter Gendolla and Jörgen Schäfer, 83-115. Bielefeld: transcript.

Hutcheon, Linda. 2006. *A Theory of Adaptation*. Abingdon and New York: Routledge.

Jacoff, Rachel. 1993. *The Cambridge Companion to Dante*. New York: Cambridge University Press.

Jacoff, Rachel. 2003 [2000]. "Our Bodies, Our Selves": The Body in the Commedia. In *Dante: The Critical Complex, vol. 3: Dante and Philosophy: Nature, the Cosmos, and the Ethical Imperative*, ed. Richard Lansing. (New York and London: Routledge [first published in *Sparks and Seeds: Medieval Literature and its Afterlife: Essays in Honor of John Freccero*, ed. Dana E. Stewart and Alison Cornish. Binghamton Medieval and Early Modern Studies, vol. 2. Turnhout, Belgium: Brepols].

Jakobson, Roman, and Krystyna Pomorska. 1982. *Poesie und Grammatik: Dialoge Roman Jakobson, Krystyna Pomorska; mit einem Verzeichnis der Veröffentlichungen Roman Jakobsons in deutscher Sprache 1921-1982*. trans. Horst Brühmann. Frankfurt am Main: Suhrkamp.

Jakobson, Roman. 1972. Die neueste russische Poesie. Erster Entwurf. Viktor Chlebnikov. In *Texte der russischen Formalisten*, vol. II, ed. Wolf-Dieter Stempel. Munich: Fink.

Jakobson, Roman. 1976. "Message sur Malévitch". In *La Peinture*, ed. Jean Paris, Collectif Change et al. vol. 26-27. Paris: Seghers/Laffont.

Jakobson, Roman. 1988. "Futurismus (1919)". In *Semiotik. Ausgewählte Texte 1919-1982*. Frankfurt am Main: Suhrkamp.

James, William. 1890. *The Principles of Psychology*. New York: H. Holt and company.

Jameson, Frederic. 1999. *Postmodernism or The Cultural Logic of Late Capitalism*. Durham, NC: Duke University Press.

Jensen, Amy Petersen. 2007. *Theatre in a Media Culture: Production, Performance and Perception since 1970*. Jefferson, NC: McFarland.

Kalb, Jonathan. 1998. *The Theater of Heiner Müller. Cambridge Studies in Modern Theatre*. Cambridge and New York: Cambridge University Press.

Kattenbelt, Chiel. 2006a. Theatre as the Art of the Performer and the Stage of Intermediality. In *Intermediality in Theatre and Performance*, ed. Freda Chapple and Chiel Kattenbelt, 29-39. Amsterdam and New York: Rodopi.

Kattenbelt, Chiel. 2006b. "De rol van technologie in de kunst van de performer". *Theater & Technologie*, ed. Henk Havens, Chiel Kattenbelt, Eric Ruijter and Kees Vuyk, 12-31. Amsterdam: Nederlands Theater Instituut.

Kattenbelt, Chiel. 2008. "Intermediality in Theatre and Performance: Definitions, Perceptions and Medial Relationships". In *Cultura, Lenguaje y Representación / Culture, Language & Representation* 6 (La Intermedialidad / Intermediality): 19-29.

Kawamura, Takeshi. 1999. *The Lost Babylon*, trans. Sarah Jansen. Tokyo: Daisan Erotica.

Kaye, Nick. 2007. *Multi-media: Video – Installation – Performance*. London: Routledge.

Kershaw, Baz. 1999. *The Radical in Performance: Between Brecht and Baudrillard*. London: Routledge.

Kershaw, Baz. 2003. "Curiosity or Contempt: On Spectacle, the Human, and Activism". *Theatre Journal* 55 (4): 591-611.

Kertscher, Jens, and Dieter Mersch. 2003. *Performativität und Praxis*. München: Fink.

Kittler, Friedrich A. 1986. *Grammophon, Film, Typewriter*. Berlin: Brinkmann & Bose. (English Translation. 1999. *Gramophone, Film, Typewriter*, trans. Geoffrey Winthrop-Young and Michael Wutz. Stanford: Stanford University Press).

Klein, Gabriele. 2005. *Performance Positionen zur zeitgenössischen szenischen Kunst*. TanzScripte, vol. 1. Bielefeld: transcript.

Klinenberg, Eric, and Claudio Benzecry. 2005. Introduction: Cultural Production in a Digital Age. In *Cultural Production in a Digital Age* (The Annals of the American Academy of Policital and Social Science, 597), ed. Eric Klinenberg. Thousand Oaks, London and New Delhi: Sage.

Klöck, Anja. 2005. Acting on the Media: The Actor's Modes of Being on Stage in an Age of Technological Mediation. *Performance Research* 10 (1): 114-126.

Knowbotic Research. 1998. "10_dencies." In *The Art of Accident*, ed. Andreas Broeckmann and Joke Brouwer, 186-191. Rotterdam: Nai Press.

Kowzan, Tadeusz. 2005. *Sémiologie du théâtre*. Paris: A. Colin.

Krämer, Sybille. 2002 [1998]. "Sprache – Stimme – Schrift: Sieben Gedanken über Performativität als Medialität". In *Performanz: Zwischen Sprachphilosophie und Kulturwissenschaften*, ed. Uwe Wirth, 323-346. Frankfurt am Main: Suhrkamp.

Krauss, Rosalind E. 2006 [1993]. 'Cindy Sherman: Untitled.' In *Cindy Sherman*, ed. Johanna Burton, 97-141. Cambridge: MIT Press.

Krauss, Rosalind E. 2000. *"A Voyage on the North Sea": Art in the Age of the Post-medium Condition*. London: Thames & Hudson.

Kristeva, Julia. 1967. "Pour une Sémiologie des Paragrammes" *Tel quel* 29 (Spring): 53-75.

Lakoff, George. 2006. Neuroscience of Form in Art. In *The Artful Mind: Cognitive Science and the Riddle of Human Creativity*, ed. M. Turner, 153-170. Oxford and New York: Oxford University Press.

Latham, Robert, and Saskia Sassen. 2005. Digital Formations: constructing and Object of Study. In *Digital Formations: IT and New Architectures in the Global Realm*, ed. Latham and Sassen, 1-33. Princeton and Oxford: Princeton University Press.

Latour, Bruno. 1996. *Der Berliner Schlüssel: Erkundungen eines Liebhabers der Wissenschaft*. Berlin: Akademie Verlag.

Latour, Bruno. 1997. "On Actor-Network Theory. A Few Clarifications". *Soziale Welt* 47 (4): 369-381.

Law, John, and John Hassard. 1999. *Actor Network Theory and After*. Sociological Review Monographs. Oxford: Blackwell Publishing.

Le Goff, Jacques. 1981. *La naissance du Purgatoire*. Collection folio/histoire. Paris: Gallimard.

Le Poidevin, Robin. 2000. The Experience and Perception of Time. In *The Stanford Encyclopedia of Philosophy*, ed. Edward N. Zalta. http://plato.stanford.edu/entries/time-experience/ (accessed March 22, 2010).

Lehmann, Hans-Thies. 1999. *Postdramatisches Theater*. Frankfurt am Main: Verlag der Autoren.

Lehmann, Hans-Thies. 2006. *Postdramatic Theatre*. London and New York: Routledge

Lepage, Robert. 1996. "Éloge de la technologie bancale". *Puck. La marionnette et les autres arts* 9 (Images virtuelles). 39-42.

Lepage, Robert. 2007. *Le projet Andersen*. Québec: L'Instant même.

Lilienthal, Matthias. 2000. *Schlingensiefs Ausländer raus: bitte liebt Österreich: Dokumentation*; [with Container-CD]. Frankfurt am Main: Suhrkamp.

Lindsmayer, Charles. 2005. Rückzug in die Miniaturwelten (Der Bund, May 26, 2005), reproduced at http://www.rimini-protokoll.de/website/de/article_1006.html (accessed April 15, 2010).

Liverpool Capital Of Culture 2008 Archive Website: http://www.liverpool08.com (accessed April 15, 2010).

Löw, Martina. 2001. *Raumsoziologie*. Frankfurt am Main: Suhrkamp.

Loxley, James. 2007. *Performativity*. The New Critical Idiom. London: Routledge.

Lukács, Georg. 1973 [1913]. Gedanken zu einer Ästhetik des Kino. In *Theorie des Kinos*, ed. Karsten Witte, 142-148. Frankfurt am Main: Suhrkamp.

Lunenfeld, Peter. 2000. Introduction: Screen Grabs: The Digital Dialectic and New Media Theory. In *The Digital Dialectic: New Essays on New Media*, ed. Peter Lunenfeld, 14-21. Cambridge, MA, and London: MIT Press.

Malbon, Ben. 1999. *Clubbing: Dancing, Ecstasy and Vitality*. London and New York: Routledge.

Malecki, Edward J., and Bruno Moriset. 2008. *The Digital Economy: Business Organization, Production Processes, and Regional Developments*. London: Routledge.

Malzacher, Florian. 2007. Dramaturgien der Fürsorge und der Verunsicherung. Die Geschichte von Rimini Protokoll. In *Experten des Alltags: Das Theater von Rimini Protokoll*, ed. Miriam Dreysse and Florian Malzacher, 14-43. Berlin: Alexander Verlag.

Manovich, Lev. 2001/2002. *The Language of New Media*. Cambridge, MA: MIT Press.

Maresch, Rudolf. 2003. "Empire Everywhere. On the Political Renaissance of Space". In: *Territories. Islands, Camps and Other States of Utopia*, ed. Kunstwerke Berlin: 15-18.

Mashek, Debra J., and Arthur Aron. 2004. *Handbook of Closeness and Intimacy*. Mahwah, NJ: Lawrence Erlbaum Associates.

Massumi, Brian. 2002. *Parables for the Virtual : Movement, Affect, Sensation*. Durham, NC: Duke University Press.

Matzke, Annemarie. 2007. Riminis Räume. In *Experten des Alltags: Das Theater von Rimini Protokoll*, ed. Miriam Dreysse and Florian Malzacher, 104-114. Berlin: Alexander Verlag.

Mauer, Barry J. 2005. "The Epistemology of Cindy Sherman: A Research Method for Media and Cultural Studies". *Mosaic : a Journal for the Comparative Study of Literature* 38 (1): 93.

McAuley, Gay. 1999. *Space in Performance. Making Meaning in the Theatre*. Ann Arbor: University of Michigan Press.

McCarthy, John, and Peter Wright. 2004. *Technology as Experience*. Cambridge, MA: MIT Press.

McGinley, Will. 2006. "Review of The Lost Babylon" (dir. Russell Fewster) in *dB Magazine* #379, 1-7 March. http://dbmagazine.com.au/379/fringerv-LostBabylon.shtml (accessed April 15, 2010).

McKenzie, Jon. 2001. *Perform or Else: From Discipline to Performance*. London: Routledge.

McLuhan, Marshall. 2003. *Understanding Media: The Extensions of Man*. Critical ed. Corte Madera CA: Gingko Press.

McLuhan, Marshall. 2004. *Understanding Media: The extensions of man*. London: Routledge.

Merleau-Ponty, Maurice. 1962. *Phenomenology of Perception*. London and New York: Routledge.

Mersch, Dieter. 2002. *Ereignis und Aura: Untersuchungen zu einer Ästhetik des Performativen*. Frankfurt am Main: Suhrkamp.

Mersch, Dieter. 2003. Ereignis und Respons. Elemente einer Theorie des Performativen. In *Performativität und Praxis*, ed. Jens Kertscher and Dieter Mersch, 69-94. Munich: Wilhelm Fink Verlag.

Merx, Sigrid. 2006a. Swann's Way: Video and Theatre as an Intermedial Stage. In *Intermediality in Theatre and Performance*, ed. Freda Chapple and Chiel Kattenbelt, 67-80. Amsterdam and New York: Rodopi.

Merx, Sigrid. 2006b. Verdubbeling en transformatie: De rol van video in de Proustcyclus van Guy Cassiers. In *Theater & Technologie*, ed. Henk Havens, Chiel Kattenbelt, Eric de Ruijter and Kees Vuyk, 48-61. Amsterdam: Nederlands Theater Instituut.

Merx, Sigrid. 2009. *Beelden van tijd. Op zoek naar de tijdsdramaturgie in de 'Proust-cyclus' van Guy Cassiers*. Ph.D. diss., Utrecht University.

Michelson, Annette. 1990. "The Kinetic Icon in the Work of Mourning: Prolegomena to the Analysis of a Textual System". *October* 52: 16-39.

Möbius, Hanno. 2000. *Montage und Collage: Literatur, bildende Künste, Film, Fotografie, Musik, Theater bis 1933*. Munich: Wilhelm Fink.

Moholy-Nagy, László, Renate Heyne, Floris Michael Neusüss, and Herbert Molderings. 1996. *Laszlo Moholy-Nagy: Fotogramme 1922-1943: aus den Sammlungen des Musée national d□art moderne, Centre de création industrielle, Centre Georges Pompidou, Paris und des Museum Folkwang, Essen*. Munich: Schirmer/Mosel.

Mosco, Vincent. 2005. *The Digital Sublime: Myth, Power, and Cyberspace*. Cambridge, MA: MIT.

Müller, Jürgen. 2010. Intermediality Revisited: Some Reflections About Basic Principles of the Axe de pertinence. In *Media Borders, Multimodality and Intermediality*, ed. Lars Elleström, 237-252. Houndmills, Basingstoke, Hampshire: Palgrave Macmillan.

Munk, Erika. 1987. Film is Ego: Radio is Good; Richard Foreman and the Arts of Control. *The Drama Review* 31, no. 4: 143-148.

Münker, Stefan and Alexander Roesler, ed. 2000: *Telefonbuch*. Frankfurt am Main: Suhrkamp.

Negroponte, Nicholas. 1995. *Being Digital*. New York: Knopf.

Noë, Alva. 2004. *Action in Perception. Representation and Mind.* Cambridge, MA: MIT Press.

Nora, Simon, and Alain Minc. 1978. *L'informatisation de la societe: rapport a M. le President de la Republique.* Paris: La Documentation francaise.

Ong, Walter J. 2002. *Orality and Literacy: The Technologizing of the Word.* London: Taylor & Francis Ltd.

Paris, Jean. 1976. *La Peinture.* Paris: Seghers/Laffont.

Parker-Starbuck, Jennifer. 2006. Lost in Space?: Global Placelessness and the Non-Places of Alladeen. In *Performance and Place*, ed. Leslie Hill and Helen Paris, 155-169. London: Palgrave Macmillan.

Parr, Mike. 2001. Interview with Edward Scheer on March 21.

Pavis, Patrice. 2002. *Dictionnaire du théâtre.* Paris: Armand Colin.

Pavis, Patrice. 2005. *L'analyse des spectacles.* Paris: Armand Colin.

Peirce, Charles Sanders. 1998 [1907]. On Phenomenology. In *The essential Peirce: Selected Philosophical Writings vol. 2 (1893-1913)*, ed. Peirce Edition Project, 145-159. Bloomington and Indianapolis: Indiana University Press.

Penny, Simon. 2000. *Intersecting Art, Technology, and the Body.* Presentation at Performative Sites Symposium, October 24-28, Penn State University.

Pepperell, Robert. 2000. The posthuman conception of consciousness: A 10-point guide. In *Art, Technology, Consciousness: Mind @ large*, ed. Roy Ascott, 13-16. Bristol, UK: Intellect.

Phelan, Peggy. 1993. *Unmarked: The politics of Performance.* London and New York: Routledge.

Picon-Vallin, Béatrice. 1998. *Les écrans sur la scène: tentations et résistances de la scène face aux images: études et témoignages. Théâtre XXe siècle.* Lausanne: Age d'Homme.

Pine, Joseph, and James Gilmore. 1999. *The Experience Economy: Work is Theatre & Every Business a Stage.* Boston: Harvard Business School Press.

Pluta, Izabella. 2006. "Alchemia spektaklu solowego. Rozmowa z Robertem Lepag'em". *Didaskalia* 72: 94-97.

Pontbriand, Chantal 1982, "The Eye Finds no Fixed Point on Which to Rest ...", trans. C.R. Parsons. *Modern Drama* 25 (1): 154-162.

Prager, Karen J. 1995. *The Psychology of Intimacy.* New York: Guildford Press.

Prager, Karen J. 2004. Deep Intimate Connection: Self and Intimacy in Couple Relationships. In *Handbook of Closeness and Intimacy*, ed. Debra J. Mashek and Arthur Aron, 43-60. MahWah, NJ: Lawrence Erlbaum Associates.

Raessens, Joost. 2001. "Cinema and beyond. Film en het proces van digitalisering". In: *E-view* 01-1. http://comcom.uvt.nl/e-view/01-1/raes.htm (accessed April 15, 2010).

Rajewsky, Irina O. 2002. *Intermedialität.* UTB für Wissenschaft, 2261. Medien- und Kommunikationswissenschaft. Tübingen: A. Francke.

Rajewsky, Irina O. 2005. "Intermediality, Intertextuality, and Remediation: A Literary Perspective on Intermediality". In *Intermédialités* 6: 43-64.

Rancière, Jacques. 2004. *The Politics of Aesthetics: The Distribution of the Sensible.* London: Continuum.

Rathmanner, Petra. 2005. Interview with Stefan Kaegi, *Wiener Zeitung* (October 6), reproduced at http://www.rimini-protokoll.de/website/de/article_1057.html (accessed April 15, 2010).

Rayner, Alice. 2002. E-scapes: Performance in the Time of Cyberspace. In *Land/Scape/Theater*, ed. Elinor Fuchs and Una Chaudhuri, 350-370. Ann Arbor, MI: University of Michigan Press.

Reinelt, Janelle G. 2007. Performance Analysis. In *Critical Theory and Performance*, ed. Janelle G. Reinelt and Joseph R. Roach. 7-12. Ann Arbor: University of Michigan Press.

Reynold, Nancy and Malcolm McCormick. 2003. *No Fixed Points – Dance in the Twentieth Century*. Yale: University Press.

Rimini Protokoll. http://www.rimini-protokoll.de/website/en/project_2484.html (accessed April 15, 2010).

Robertson, Roland. 1992. *Globalization: Social Theory and Global Culture*. London: Sage.

Roesner, David, Geesche Wartemann, and Volker Wortmann. 2005. *Szenische Orte – mediale Räume*. Medien und Theater, n.F. Bd. 1. Hildesheim: Olms.

Roselt, Jens. 2005. Die "Fünfte Wand": Medialität im Theater am Beispiel von Frank Castorfs Dostojewski-Inszenierungen. In *Szenische Orte, Mediale Räume*, ed. David Roesner, Geesche Wartemann, Volker Wortmann, 109-127. Hildesheim and New York: G. Olms.

Rotman, B. 2008. *Becoming Beside Ourselves: The Alphabet, Ghosts, and Distributed Human Being*. Durham, NC: Duke University Press.

Rush, Michael. 1999. *New Media in Late 20th-Century Art*. New York: Thames and Hudson.

Rush, Michael. 2005. *New Media in Art*. World of Art. London: Thames & Hudson.

Ryan, Christopher. 1993. The Theology of Dante. In *The Cambridge Companion to Dante*, ed. Rachel Jacoff, 136-152. Cambridge: Cambridge University Press.

Sassen, Saskia. 1997. Cyber-Segmentierungen. Elektronischer Raum und Macht". In *Mythos Internet*, ed. Stefan Münker and Alexander Roesler, 215-235. Frankfurt am Main: Suhrkamp.

Sassen, Saskia. 1999. Digital Networks and Power. In *Spaces of Culture. City, Nation, World*, ed. Mike Featherstone and Scott M. Lash, 48-63. London: Sage Publications.

Schade, Sigrid and Georg Christoph Tholen, ed. 1999. *Konfigurationen zwischen Kunst und Medien*. Munich: Wilhelm Fink.

Schechner, Richard, and Willa Appel, ed. 1990. *By Means of Performance. Intercultural Studies in Theatre and Ritual*. Cambridge: Cambridge University Press.

Schlingensief, Christoph, Paul Poet, Matthias Lilienthal, Elfriede Jelinek, and Burghart Schmidt. 2006. *Ausländer Raus! Schlingensiefs Container*. Österreichische Film, 32. Wien: Hoanzl.

Schnapp, Jeffrey T. 1993. Introduction to Purgatorio. In *The Cambridge Companion to Dante*, ed. Rachel Jacoff, 192-207. Cambridge: Cambridge University Press.

Schulte, Christian. 2006. "Alles, was Menschen in Bewegung setzt. Dialogische Autorschaft bei Alexander Kluge". In *Maske und Kothurn* 52: 105-114.

Seel, Martin. 1985. *Die Kunst der Entzweiung: zum Begriff der ästhetischen Rationalität*. Frankfurt am Main: Suhrkamp.

Seel, Martin. 2000. *Ästhetik des Erscheinens*. Munich: Hanser.

Seel, Martin. 2001. "Inszenieren als Erscheinenlassen. Thesen über die Reichweite eines Begriffs". In *Ästhetik der Inszenierung*, ed. Josef Früchtl and Jörg Zimmermann, 48-62. Frankfurt am Main: Suhrkamp.

Sellar, Tom. 2004. Foreman's Film Society. *Village Voice*, December 28.

Sels, Geert. 2004. "Crash, een overweldigende voorstelling van Eric Joris en Peter Verhelst." *De Standaard*, June 4. http://www.standaard.be/artikel/detail.aspx?artikelid= GC36L6CD (accessed April 15, 2010).

Sennett, Richard. 2008. *The Craftsman*. New Haven: Yale University Press.

Serres, Michel. 1985. *Les cinq sens*. Paris: Grasset.

Shepherd, Simon, and Mick Wallis. 2004. *Drama/ Theatre/ Performance*. London: Routledge.

Sherman, Cindy, Johanna Burton, and Craig Owens. 2006. *Cindy Sherman*. October files, 6. Cambridge, MA: MIT Press.

Shklovsky, Viktor. 1986. *Eisenstein: romanbiographie*. Berlin: Verlag Volk und Welt.

Siegmund, Gerald. 2002. Task Performance als Choreographie: Die Aufgabe des Schauspielers. In *Heiner Goebbels. Komposition als Inszenierung*, ed. Wolfgang Sandner, 127-131. Berlin: Henschel Verlag.

Sloterdijk, Peter. 2006. *Het Kristalpaleis. Een filosofie van de globalisering*. Trans. Hans Driessen. Amsterdam: Uitgeverij Boom/SUN. [In *Im Weltinnenraum des Kapitals. Für eine philosophische Theorie der Globalisierung*. 2004. Frankfurt am Main: Suhrkamp].

Speckenbach, Jan. 2002. Der Einbruch der Fernsehtechnologie. In *Politik und Verbrechen: Einbruch der Realität*, ed. Carl Hegemann, 80-84. Berlin: Alexander.

Spinrad, Paul. 2005. *The VJ book: Inspirations and Practical Advice for Live Visuals Performance*. Los Angeles: Feral House.

Steil, J.M. 1997. "Karen J. Prager: The Psychology of Intimacy". *Contemporary Psychology* 42 (4): 302.

Stein, Gertrude. 1935. *Lectures in America*. New York: Random House.

Stelarc. Authorized website. 2009. Available from http://www.stelarc.va.com.au/arcx.html (accessed August 31, 2009).

Stempel, Wolf-Dieter, and Inge Paulmann. 1972. *Texte der russischen Formalisten*. vol. 2, *Texte zur Theorie des Verses und der poetischen Sprache*. Munich: Wilhelm Fink Verlag.

Stigter, Bianca. 2009. "Surrealisme van de straat", *NRC Handelsblad*, March 20.

Stingelin, Martin. 2000. Metaphern des Netzes oder Wie deleuzianisch ist das Internet? In *Das Netzwerk von Gilles Deleuze: Immanenz im Internet und auf Video*. Internationaler Merve Diskurs, 223. Berlin: Merve. 15-31.

Terranova, Tiziana. 2004. *Network Culture: Politics for the Information Age*. London: Pluto Press.

Tsypin, George 2006 "Five Questions for George Tsypin Scenic Designer". *Live Design* March: 6-7.

Turner, Mark. 2006. *The Artful Mind: Cognitive Science and the Riddle of Human Creativity*. Oxford: Oxford University Press.

Turner, Victor. 1967. *The Forest of Symbols: Aspects of Ndembu Ritual*. Ithaca: Cornell University Press.

Ubersfeld, Anne. 1996. *Les termes clés de l'analyse du théâtre*. Paris: Seuil.

Van Dijk, Jan. 2006 (second edition). *The Network Society: Social Aspects of New Media*. London, Thousand Oaks and New Delhi: Sage Publications.

Van Gennep, Arnold. 2004. *The Rites of Passage*. London: Routledge.

Vargas, Jose Antonio. 2006. "Virtual Reality Prepares Soldiers for Real War". *Washington Post*, Tuesday, February 14.

Verschaffel, Bart. 1995. Over theatraliteit. In *Figuren: Essays*, by Bart Verschaffel, 17-31. Leuven: Van Halewyck, and Amsterdam: De Balie.

MAPPING INTERMEDIALITY IN PERFORMANCE

Virilio, Paul. 1995. *The Art of the Motor*. Minneapolis: University of Minnesota Press.

Wagner, Meike. 2006. "Of Other Bodies: The Intermedial Gaze in Theatre". In *Intermediality in Theatre and Performance*, ed. Freda Chapple and Chiel Kattenbelt, 125-136. Amsterdam and New York: Rodopi.

Volksbühne Berlin. 2001. *Erniedrigte und Beleidigte*. Programme Notes. Photocopied leaflet.

Wagner, Meike, and Wolf-Dieter Ernst. 2008. *Performing the Matrix: Mediating Cultural Performance*. Munich: ePodium Verlag.

Weber, Samuel. 1996. *Mass Mediauras: Form, Technics, Media*. Stanford: Stanford University Press.

Weems, Marianne. Interviewed by Rosemary Klich, Tape-recording, The Walker Arts Centre, Minneapolis, 16 October 2005.

Wetzel, Valentin. 2001. Spezialistentheater zwischen Labor und Ungunstraum, *spector cut & paste* (#2), reproduced at http://www.rimini-protokoll.de/website/de/article_2837.html (accessed April 15, 2010).

Wiegmink, Pia. 2008. Performing Resistance. Contemporary American Performance-Activism. In *Performing the Matrix – Mediating Cultural Performance*, ed. Meike Wagner and Wolf-Dieter Ernst, 307-320. München: ePodium Verlag.

Wiens, Birgit. 2010. "Modular Settings and 'Creative Light': The Legacy of Adolphe Appia in the Digital Age". *International Journal of Performance Arts and Digital Media* 6. 1, ed. by Nick Hunt and Dave Collins, 25-40.

Wirth, Uwe. 2003. *Performanz: zwischen Sprachphilosophie und Kulturwissenschaften*. Suhrkamp Taschenbuch Wissenschaft, 1575. Frankfurt am Main: Suhrkamp.

Witte, Karsten. 1973. *Theorie des Kinos*. Frankfurt am Main: Suhrkamp.

Youngblood, Gene. 1970. *Expanded Cinema*. London: Studio Vista and New York: E.P. Dutton & Company.

Zeki, Semir. 2006. The Neurology of Ambiguity. In *The Artful Mind: Cognitive Science and the Riddle of the Human Mind*, 243-270, ed. M. Turner. Oxford and New York: Oxford University Press.

Žižek, Slavoj. 2006. *The Parallax View*. Short circuits. Cambridge, MA: MIT Press.

Contributors

Dr. Katia Arfara received her PhD in Art History from Paris I in 2006 with a focus on the intermedial relations between visual and performing arts since the 1960s. Her essays and reviews on aspects of contemporary art, dance and theatre appear in journals such as *Performance Research, Alternatives Théâtrales, Ligéia, Perspective, 20/21. Siècles*. Her most recent publications discuss the work of Romeo Castellucci, The Wooster Group and Rimini Protokoll. Current research interests include new media practices, documentary devices and theatrical installations. Dr. Arfara has lectured in France (Paris I, Paris III, Université de Picardie) and currently teaches in Greece at the Aristotle University of Thessaloniki.

Dr. Bruce Barton is a creator/scholar at the University of Toronto where he teaches playmaking, dramaturgy, and intermedial performance. His book publications include *Developing Nation: New Play Creation in English-Speaking Canada* (2009), *Collective Creation, Collaboration and Devising* (2008), *Reluctant Texts from Exuberant Performance: Canadian Devised Theatre* (2008), *Imagination in Transition: Mamet Moves to Film* (2005) and *Marigraph* (2004). His essays and reviews have appeared in TDR, *Theatre Topics, Performance Research, Canadian Theatre Review, University of Toronto Quarterly*, and *Theatre Research in Canada*, as well as in several international essay collections. He is the co-editor of the forthcoming issue of *Theatre Research in Canada* on "Theatre and Intermediality". Current research interests include a SSHRC-funded study on dramaturgies of the body in physically-based devised theatre and intermedial performance. Barton's production work includes stage and radio plays produced across Canada, and his work as a dramaturge with physically-based, devising, and intermedial performance companies.

Dr. Sarah Bay-Cheng is Associate Professor and Director of Graduate Studies in Theatre at the University at Buffalo, where she teaches performance theory, avant-garde theatre and film, and intermedial performance. Her book publications include *Poets at Play: An Anthology of Modernist Drama* (2010) and *Mama Dada: Gertrude Stein's Avant-Garde Theater* (2005). Her essays have appeared in journals such as *Theatre Journal, Theatre Topics, The Journal of American Drama and Theatre*, and in several critical anthologies. Current research interests include the history of the body in intermedial performance and comparative studies in theories of performance and intermediality between Europe and the US. In 2005, Bay-Cheng co-founded the Intermedia Performance Studio, a research and performance collaborative working at the intersection of virtual reality, games, robotics, computer science, and theatre. She received her PhD in Theatre with a concentration in directing and film studies from the University of Michigan in 2001.

Prof. Dr. Maaike Bleeker is the Chair of Theatre Studies at Utrecht University. Previously, she lectured at the Department of Theatre Studies of the University of Amsterdam, The Piet Zwart Post-Graduate program in Fine Arts (Rotterdam), Media Gn: Centre for Emergent Media (Groningen), The School for New Dance Development (Amsterdam), the post graduate program Arts Performance Theatricality (Antwerp), and in the IPP Performance and Media Studies Summer School of the Johannes Gutenberg Universität, Mainz. She is currently Member of the Board of Performance Studies International, Member of the International Advisory Board of *Maska* (Ljubljana) and of *Inflexions: A Journal of Research-Creation* (Montreal), and Member of the Editorial Board (Humanities) of Amsterdam University Press. Since 1991, Prof. Bleeker has worked as a dramaturge for various theatre directors, choreographers and visual artists, created several lecture performances, run her own theatre company (Het Oranjehotel) and translated five plays performed by major Dutch theatre companies. She was an Artist in Residence at the Amsterdam School for the Arts (2006-2007) and member of the jury of the Dutch National Theatre Festival TF (2007-2008). She completed her PhD, *Visuality in Theatre* (2002) in Art History, Theatre Studies and Philosophy at the University of Amsterdam.

Dr. Peter M. Boenisch, originally from Munich, Germany, is a co-director, with Professors Patrice Pavis and Paul Allain, of the European Theatre Research Network (ETRN) at the University of Kent's School of Arts in Canterbury/UK. His most recent publications discuss the works of William Forsythe, Michael Thalheimer, Rimini Protokoll, and Thomas Ostermeier, and he is currently co-editing, with Lourdes Orozco, a forthcoming special issue of *Contemporary Theatre Review* on Flemish theatre and preparing a monograph on directing texts in contemporary European theatre. Prof. Boenisch's research interests focus on directing and dramaturgy in contemporary European theatre, dance and physical theatre, and intermediality and theatre.

Prof. Dr. Johan Callens teaches at the Vrije Universiteit Brussel. His book publications include *Double Binds: Existentialist Inspiration and Generic Experimentation in the Early Work of Jack Richardson* (1993), *Acte(s) de Présence* (1996), *From Middleton and Rowley's "Changeling" to Sam Shepard's "Bodyguard": A Contemporary Appropriation of a Renaissance Drama* (1997) and *Dis/Figuring Sam Shepard* (2007). For the Belgian Luxembourg American Studies Association he edited the volumes *American Literature and the Arts* (1991) and *Re-Discoveries of America: The Meeting of Cultures* (1993). Other edited collections include: *The Wooster Group and Its Traditions* (2004) and *Crossings:*

David Mamet's Work in Different Genres and Media (2009). Prof. Callens has also orga-nised several international conferences, resulting in a double issue of *Contemporary Theatre Review*, entitled *Sam Shepard: Between the Margin and the Centre* (1998), an in-termediality issue of *Degrés* (2000).

Dr. Michael Darroch is an Assistant Professor in the Department of Communica-tion, Media and Film at the University of Windsor, Canada. He is a Co-Investiga-tor for the Visible City Project + Archive (www.visiblecity.ca) and a member of the Centre de recherche sur l'intermédialité at the Université de Montréal. He is co-editing the anthology *Urban Mediations*, an interdisciplinary collection that situates different historical and methodological currents in urban media studies and has translated widely from German and French to English. Prof. Darroch's current research explores Canadian and German theories of media and materialities, with a focus on practices of media and art in a variety of urban contexts. He has published on aspects of media, technology, theatre, language, sound, and trans-lation. His PhD dissertation examined aspects of theatre and performance in light of contemporary theories of the materialities of communication.

Prof. Dr. Wolf-Dieter Ernst is Professor of Theatre. He has published widely on postdramatic theatre, performance and media art. He is review editor of the jour-nal *Forum Modernes Theater*, principle investigator of the DFG-funded project "Vors-chrift und Affekt" and his books include: *Performance der Schnittstelle* (Passagen Ver-lag, 2003); and *Performing the Matrix – Mediating Cultural Performance* (with Meike Wagner, 2007). Forthcoming book projects include the *Discourse of Actor Training 1870-1930* and *Image and Imagination: Critical Readings in Visual Studies and Acting Theory*. Wolf-Dieter has also contributed substantially to the development of the IFTR Intermediality, Theatre & Performance research group and he is convenor (with Prof. Anja Klöck) of the Gesellschaft für Theaterwissenschaft working group "Schauspieltheorie".

Russell Fewster is currently a Lecturer in Drama at the University of South Austra-lia, Magill Campus, and a PhD candidate in Theatre Studies at the University of Melbourne, where he examines the use of projection in performance. Fewster has worked as a theatre director for the past 25 years, including work with profes-sional actors, acting students and young people. He studied at Ecole Jacques Le-coq in Paris, and completed his Masters by Research at the Centre for Perfor-mance Studies at the University of Sydney (2000).

Drs. Liesbeth Groot Nibbelink is a teacher and researcher in Theatre Studies at Utrecht University. Research areas include the theory and analysis of theatre, dra-maturgy, and the use of technology in theatre and site-specific theatre. Prior to her work at Utrecht University, Drs. Groot Nibbelink studied at a visual arts academy, and has worked as a dramaturge and assistant-director. She is currently involved in a PhD research project on the mobility of the spectator in contemporary European theatre, developing the concept of nomadic theatre to explore transitions in performer/spectator positions and their impact on perception.

Prof. Dr. Klemens Gruber is Professor of Intermediality at the TFM (Institute for Theatre, Film and Media Studies), University of Vienna, Austria. His book publications include *Die zerstreute Avantgarde* (1989, 2010, Italian edition: *L'avanguardia inaudita*, 1997). His editorial projects include the journal *Maske & Kothurn: Internationale Beiträge zur Theater-, Film- und Medienwissenschaft, Digital Formalism* (2010), a two-volume anthology on Dziga Vertov, *Verschiedenes über denselben* (2006), and *Die Bauweise von Paradiesen: Für Alexander Kluge* (2007). He is currently preparing *Two or three things you should know about the avant-garde*.

Drs. Henk Havens is currently dramaturge at Maastricht Theatre Academy (MTA), where he has served as department head, and a member of the Arts Faculty of Zuyd University in Maastricht. In 2000 he was one of the initiators of a new study course at MTA, *Theatrical Performer*, and he led a working group on theatre and technology in the interdisciplinary research program, *New Theatricality*. His current research interests include the PhD research project, *Theatre in Transition*, as a co-production of Zuyd University and Maastricht University. He is a member of the international working group *Intermediality in Theatre and Performance* of the IFRT/FIRT (International Federation for Theatre Research/La Fédération Internationale pour la recherche théâtrale). He studied Theatre Studies in Utrecht and has worked for several years as a theatre critic.

Tim Hopkins is a director and theatre artist, currently working as the AHRC Research Fellow in the Creative and Performing Arts at the University of Sussex. As a director specializing in opera, he has been commissioned to direct new and existing repertoire for Welsh National Opera, ENO, The Royal Opera, Opera North, Glimmerglass, Teatro dell'Opera Roma, Bayerische Staatsoper Festspiel, Theatre Basel, Graz Oper, Staatsoper Hannover, Wexford Festival, ETO, Alternative Lyrique Paris, Almeida Opera, Aldeburgh Festival, Channel 4 TV, and others. His current research project is entitled "The potential of new technologies for transformations of lyric theatre" and in 2009 Hopkins developed work for his Les Noces project, a multi-media adaptation of Stravinsky's ballet-cantata of 1923, including work with the Russian vocal group The Prokovsky Ensemble and the composer Lena Langer in association with the Royal Opera Genesis project. A semi-public showcase of the work-in-progress, entitled "Give me your Blessing for I go to a Foreign Land", premiered at the Royal Opera Clore Studio in February 2009. He read English at Cambridge from 1983-86, and studied at the Sherman Theatre in Cardiff from 1986-87.

Falk Hübner is a composer, theatre maker and researcher. Besides composing and performing music and sound design for diverse theatre performances across Europe, he creates experimental music theatrical performances between concert, installation and performance as conceptualist, composer and director. His practice-based PhD research focuses on the musician as (theatrical) performer and the impact of experimental theatrical setups on the professional identity of the musician.

Dr. Chiel Kattenbelt is Associate Professor in Media Comparison and Intermediality at Utrecht University. He teaches in the BA program Theatre, Film and Television Studies, in the MA programs Theatre Studies and New Media and Digital Culture and in the Research MA program Media and Performance Studies. In teaching as well as research, his fields of interest are theatre and media theory, media comparison and intermediality, and aesthetics and semiotics. His publications include *Intermediality in Theatre and Performance* (2006). From 2002 to 2006 Dr. Kattenbelt was also associate professor at the Theatre Academy Maastricht (Zuyd University), where he led an interdisciplinary research program on new theatricality with particular emphasis on the public sphere, language and technology. In 2004 he was the visiting professor for intermediality and media theory at the Department for Theatre, Film and Media Studies, University of Vienna.

Dr. Rosemary Klich is currently Lecturer in Drama and Theatre at the University of Kent, where she specialises in multimedia performance. Her publications include *Multimedia Performance* (2010) as well as articles and chapters in the fields of contemporary narrative studies, postdramatic theatre and new media performance. Her research interests include the notion of 'interactivity' in media and performance, acting with new technologies, and contemporary performance art. Dr. Klich is currently researching the performativity of new media, narrativity in multimedia performance, and contemporary performance art. Dr. Klich completed her PhD at the University of New South Wales, Sydney, focusing on the Poetics of Multimedia Theatre in the Virtual Age.

Dr. Kaisu Koski is a Finnish media/performance artist and researcher, based in the Netherlands. She is currently a guest lecturer in Medical Humanities at Leiden University, where she conducts postdoctoral research with the Arts and Genomics Centre, and at Utrecht Medical Centre. Her publications include *Augmenting Theatre: Engaging with the Content of Performances and Installations on Intermedial Stages* (2007), which elaborates the ways screen- and phone-based technology are currently employed onstage. Kaisu's art practice is related to her scientific research focusing currently on the dialogue between art, medicine and life sciences. She specializes in so-called artistic research and thus employs art as an instrument to unravel the biomedical view on body. Dr. Kaisu graduated from the Faculty of Art and Design at the University of Lapland, and holds a PhD in Media Studies. In 2009 Kaisu also completed DasArts, a postgraduate program in Performing Arts at the Amsterdam School of the Arts.

Prof. Andy Lavender is Dean of Research and Professor of Contemporary Theatre at The Central School of Speech & Drama, University of London. He is the author of *Hamlet in Pieces: Shakespeare Reworked by Peter Brook, Robert Lepage and Robert Wilson* (2001) and co-editor (with Jen Harvie) of *Making Contemporary Theatre: International Rehearsal Processes* (2010). Other writing includes essays on multimedia performance in Mary Luckhurst (ed.), *A Companion to Modern British and Irish Drama* (2006) and Chapple and Kattenbelt (eds.), *Intermediality in Theatre and Performance* (2006). He is co-convener of the Intermediality in Theatre and Performance working group of the International Federation for Theatre Research, and was formerly co-convener of the New Technologies for Theatre working group of the Theatre and Performance Research Association. Prof. Lavender is the artistic director of the theatre/performance company Lightwork (www.lightwork.co.uk).

Dr. Kara McKechnie is a Lecturer in Dramaturgy and Literary Management at the University of Leeds. Her publications include a monograph on the British playwright Alan Bennett, published in the Television Series by Manchester University Press (2007). She has a professional background in German theatre and opera and is heavily involved in the partnership between the University and Opera North. Her recent productions have included the music theatre piece 'A Light in the Rhubarb Shed' for Leeds Light Night in 2008. Dr. McKechnie also works as a freelance dramaturge and translator.

Dr. Sigrid Merx is Assistant Professor of Theatre Studies at Utrecht University where she teaches in the BA programme Theater, Film and Television Studies and in the MA programme Theater Studies. She is also a lecturer at University College Utrecht in the BA programme Liberal Arts and Sciences. Her current teaching focuses on theatre and performance in the context of other media and performance and her research interests explore theatricality in politics and political art in order to outline what she calls "a dramaturgy of engagement". Dr. Merx is also a member of the board for the Domein voor Kunstkritiek (Institute for Art Criticism) and remains active as a freelance writer and dramaturge, especially in community art projects. In March 2009 she won the Prijs Jong Docenttalent 2009, for being the most inspiring and innovative young Utrecht University teacher of the year. As winner of this prize she was granted access to Nebula, a selective group of young ambitious teachers who strive to improve the quality of teaching at Utrecht University and to bridge the gap between research and teaching. She received her PhD in 2009, focusing on video and the (re)presentation of time in the Proust cycle, a series of four performances by Flemish director Guy Cassiers.

Prof. Dr. Robin Nelson is a professor at the University of London, Central School of Speech & Drama. His publications on theatre and media topics include essays in journals such as *Performance Research*, *Intermédialités*, *Media, Culture & Society*, *European Journal of Cultural Studies* and *Journal of British Cinema and Television*. He is a founding editor of the journal *Critical Studies in Television* and his books include: *State of Play: Contemporary "High End" TV Drama* (2007); *TV Drama in Transition* (1997); and (with Bob Millington) `Boys from the Blackstuff': The Making of TV Drama*, (1986). Forthcoming book chapters include essays on *The Sopranos* and *Life on Mars*. Prof. Robin Nelson has also contributed substantially to the development of `practice as research' in the UK and internationally (see *Performance Research*, Vol 11, No 4, Dec 2006) and to the IFTR Intermediality, Theatre & Performance research group.

Peter S. Petralia is a lecturer, producer, director, writer, curator and artistic director of Proto-type Theater, and a researcher and lecturer at Manchester Metropolitan University and Lancaster University. He has written fourteen full-length performance works that have premiered in the US, England, Romania and Amsterdam. He is the recipient of several awards, grants and residencies including the HERE Artist Residency Program (NYC), Lincoln Center Director's Lab (NYC), 2004 nytheatre.com Person of the Year (NYC), Artward Bound of the Field (NYC), Chashama Area Award (NYC), Mondo Cane Commission from Dixon Place (NYC), TCG/ITI Travel Grant (NYC/Russia), the Outside/Input Program of Richard Foreman's Ontological-Hysteric Theater (NYC), New Work Network Activator (UK), and a Jerome Foundation Commission from PS122 (NYC). Peter curated the 2002 Queer@HERE Festival, the 2003 Fuse Festival and Avant-Garde-Arama at PS122, and has been a guest artist in Busan (South Korea), Glasgow (Scotland) and Asheville (North Carolina). He collaborates with dance artist Tiffany Mills and will be participating in a residency at the Baryshnikov Arts Centre in New York in 2010. Peter has an MA (with Distinction) in Theatre Studies from Lancaster University and is currently completing his PhD publishing, new work and archival material is available at http://www.proto-type.org.

Dr. Izabella Pluta is an associated lecturer at the Haute école de théâtre de Suisse romande – la Manufacture in Lausanne. Her publications include her thesis on the relation between the actor and the new media on stage, of which a practical part was completed in Robert Lepage's *Caserne Dalhousie* in 2003. Her other publications include essays in theatrical journals such as *Didaskalia*, *Opcje*, *Teatr*, and *Ubu: Scènes d'Europe*, and in critical anthologies, such as *The Human Body – a Universal Sign: Bridging Art with Science* (2005) and *Teatr-przestrzen-cialo-dialog: Poszukiwania we wspolczesnym teatrze* (2006). Dr. Pluta has also collaborated with artists such as Krystian Lupa (including a workshop, conference, and courses) and more recently she coordinated the pedagogical project on experimental staging with the

Théâtre de l'Arsenic in Lausanne (*Ecole du spectateur: regarder et voir*). Dr. Pluta has also lectured in Poland (Universytet Opolski) and in France (Université de Tours), and currently works as a translator and a theater critic.

Dr. Ralf Remshardt is Associate Professor in the School of Theatre and Dance at the University of Florida, with degrees from the Freie Universität Berlin (MA) and the University of California, Santa Barbara (PhD). As well as directing productions, he teaches theatre history, dramaturgy, and contemporary European theatre. He has published widely in international journals and edited collections. His book *Staging the Savage God: The Grotesque in Performance* appeared in 2004. His current research focuses on the intermedial connections of theatre and early film.

Dr. Edward Scheer is Associate Professor in the School of English, Media and Performing Arts at UNSW in Sydney, Australia and President, PSi Performance Studies international. He is the founding editor of *Performance Paradigm*, an online journal of contemporary culture and performance (www.performanceparadigm. net/) and author of *The Infinity Machine. Mike Parr's Performance Art 1971-2005* (Schwartz City Press, 2009). Other publications include: editor, *Antonin Artaud. A Critical Reader* (2004); co-editor with Peter Eckersall, *The Ends of the 60s. Performance, Media and Contemporary Culture* (2006); and co-editor with John Potts, *Technologies of Magic: A Cultural Study of Ghosts, Machines and the Uncanny*, (Sydney : Power Publications 2006). His research areas include contemporary performance and multimedia arts and he has published on butoh, narrative theatre and performance art including the work of artists such as Stelarc, and Marina Abramović. Dr. Scheer is the former Chairman of the board of directors of the national centre for contemporary performance, Performance Space in Sydney.

Marina Turco is a curator, critic and researcher in the field of media art. Since 1999 she has collaborated with various new media institutes and art magazines in Italy and The Netherlands. In 2004, she curated the video art festival "Video Village" in Milan, Italy, and founded Art-U, an organisation for the promotion of the media arts. In the following years, she cultivated her interest in live video performance and pop culture, organizing workshops for VJs, VJ performances in clubs and publishing on 'television art' and on the construction of 'modular narratives' in live cinema performances. In January 2007 she began a PhD research project on VJing at Utrecht University, Department of Media and Culture Studies, focusing on the relations between video languages, technology and cultural context.

Prof. Dr. Kurt Vanhoutte is currently Professor of Performance Studies and Visual Arts Criticism at the University of Antwerp, where he helped to establish a Master Programme in Film and Theater Studies. He is member of the *Research Centre for Visual Poetics* (formerly *Aisthesis*) and participates in 20203D Media (http://

www.20203dmedia.eu), a large-scale European Research Consortium of 16 partners, including academic institutions and some of Europe's most prominent manufacturers of digital technologies. His current research is closely intertwined with the work of CREW (http://www.crewonline.org), a multi-disciplinary team of artists and researchers at the melting point of live arts and technology. Vanhoutte's current research focuses on the translation of cinematographic and performative codes in immersive environments and on changing notions of narrativity and spectatorship. He received his PhD from the University of Antwerp in 2001 for his research on the technological condition of contemporary live performance.

Dr. Meike Wagner is currently a lecturer and researcher in the Theatre Department at Munich University, where she teaches 19th-century theatre, theatre and performance, and theatre theory. From 2003-2006 she was coordinator of the PhD program in *Performance and Media Studies*. Her publications include *Performing the Matrix – Mediating Cultural Performance* (with Wolf-Dieter Ernst, 2007) and she is editor of "double: magazin für puppen-, figuren- und objektheater". Wagner's current areas of research include theatre and media, intermediality, internet communities and web-based animation film, theatre historiography, theatre and revolution. She received her PhD from Mainz University for her research on the subject of mediality and the staging of object bodies (e.g. the human body between perceiving subject and staged object in theatre) in 2002.

Dr. Birgit Wiens is currently researcher at the LMU Munich, working on the research project "Intermediale Szenographie" (funded by the German Research Foundation-DFG). She received her PhD in Theatre Studies at the University of Munich (1998). Since 1995, she has worked as dramaturge, curator and conference organizer for Bayerisches Staatsschauspiel Munich, for "China Fest" (Berlin 2001) and at the ZKM-Centre for Arts and Media Karlsruhe. 2004-09 she was Professor of Theatre Studies at the Hochschule für Bildende Künste (Academy of Fine Arts) Dresden. Since 2009/2010 she has been the Project Leader and Curator for the project "Towards an Alliance between Scenic Arts and Scientific Research", an initiative by École Polytechnique Fédérale de Lausanne (EPFL), La Manufacture – Haute École de Théâtre de Suisse-Romande, and other institutions. Her publications include numerous articles on scenography and stage design in contemporary theatre, art in public space, acting and performance theory. Her book project "Theater ohne Fluchtpunkt/Theatre without Vanishing Points. The Heritage of Adolphe Appia: Scenography and Choreography in Contemporary Theatre" (co-edited with G.Brandstetter, FU Berlin) is forthcoming in 2010.

Nele Wynants is a junior researcher at the Department of Theatre, Film and Literature Studies at the University of Antwerp. She studied History of Arts (performance and media arts) at the University of Ghent and the Université Paris X, and scenography at the Academy of Antwerp. She has worked as a dramaturge and designer and currently participates in the work and research of CREW, a performance group and multi-disciplinary team of artists and researchers. Since October 2008 she has been a fellow of the Research Foundation – Flanders (FWO), conducting her PhD research on new narratives in immersive environments.

Index